Kieler Studien · Kiel Studies 326
Horst Siebert (Editor)
Kiel Institute for World Economics

Springer
Berlin
Heidelberg
New York
Hong Kong
London
Milan
Paris
Singapore
Tokyo

Jörn Kleinert

The Role of Multinational Enterprises in Globalization

 Springer

Dr. Jörn Kleinert
Kiel Institute for World Economics
Structural Change and Growth Research Group
D-24100 Kiel
j.kleinert@ifw.uni-kiel.de

ISSN 0340-6989

ISBN 3-540-40636-0 Springer-Verlag Berlin Heidelberg New York

Cataloging-in-Publication Data applied for
A catalog record for this book is available from the Library of Congress.
Bibliographic information published by Die Deutsche Bibliothek
Die Deutsche Bibliothek lists this publication in the Deutsche Nationalbibliografie;
detailed bibliographic data is available in the Internet at <http://dnb.ddb.de>.

Springer-Verlag is a part of Springer Science+Business Media

springeronline.com

© Springer-Verlag Berlin Heidelberg 2004
Printed in Germany

Hardcover-Design: Erich Kirchner, Heidelberg

SPIN 10948163   42/2202-5 4 3 2 1 0 – Printed on acid-free paper

Preface

Globalization is a fascinating topic. Although globalization is often discredited in the public debate because of the adjustment pressure it causes, it creates benefits that we take too easily for granted. There are such benefits as easy travel all over the world, the opportunity to enjoy other countries beauty and historical and cultural achievements, easy and cheap communication with many people all over the world, which is due to the spread of English, the lower cost made possible by many technological improvements, and the deregulation of telecommunication sectors in many countries.

There is the plethora of information we can receive almost immediately about any event in almost any foreign country. There are the many goods, services, fashions, and habits which we import to make our life more convenient and more interesting. And there is the opportunity to find happiness in other places than the one we were born.

Two of the people I am deeply indebted to, Axel Schimmelpfennig and Hubert Strauss, have taken advantage of the opportunities of a global labor market to work for international organizations in Washington and Paris. I am very thankful for their guidance, the discussions and ideas developing from their guidance. I also wish to thank Andrea Schertler, Katja Gerling, Katrin and Daniel Piazolo, Karsten Junius, and Björn Christensen, who supported me from the beginning. Without you, the Kiel Institute for World Economics would not have been the wonderful research place that it was. Daniel Piazolo, Axel Schimmelpfennig, and Hubert Strauß also were the initiators of a jogging team, which regularly turned Thursdays' lunch break into an inspiring economic debate.

My thanks go to Henning Klodt and Jürgen Stehn, who provided guidance and freedom for my work, and constant encouragement. My thank go also to Horst Siebert for his efforts in creating a stimulating environment for research at the Kiel Institute for World Economics and to Horst Raff and his colleagues from the University of Kiel who always gave me a second home for my research.

I would like to thank all my coauthors in all my various projects which dealt with globalization. I have gained a lot from this joint work. I am particularly indebted to Claudia Buch and Farid Toubal in this respect. Thanks also to Carsten Eckel and the participants at the various Passau Workshops of International Economics whose comments and helpful suggestions improved this study a lot.

Further, I would like to thank the people who turned the manuscript into a book. Almut Hahn-Mieth edited various versions of the text with great expertise. Melanie Grosse, Dietmar Gebert, and Sylvia Künne carefully edited this study. Kerstin Stark did the final layout. I thank all these people and the many wonderful friends who are not listed here for their help.

Kiel, January 2004   Jörn Kleinert

Contents

List of Tables

List of Figures

List of Symbols

List of Variables and Indexes in the Theoretical Parts

Roman Variables

C	production costs
c	marginal production costs
cz	marginal production cost of an intermediate-goods producer
D	distance between two markets
Ex	export value
f	fixed costs at the plant level for a final-goods producer
fz	fixed costs of an individual intermediate-goods producer
I	amount spent on intermediate goods
L	labor endowment
m	number of multinational goods
n	number of national goods
P	price index of final goods
p	price of an individual final good
Pz	price index of intermediate goods
pz	price of an individual intermediate good
Q_A	output of the agricultural sector
Q_M	output of the manufacturing sector
q_i	output of an individual company in the manufacturing sector
qz	quantity of the intermediate-goods bundle used by a single final-goods producer
r	fixed costs at the company level for a final-goods producer
s	number of intermediate goods
t	share of final goods lost in export
tz	share of intermediate goods lost in export
U	utility
w	wage
Y	income
Z	aggregate output of the intermediate goods
z_i	output of an individual intermediate company

Greek Variables

Π	profits
Γ	degree of competition
Φ	difference in profits of a company operating as multinational company compared to the company operating as national company
μ	income share spent on manufacturing goods
ρ	degree of differentiation of final goods
γ	inverse measure of market power in manufacturing final-goods market $\gamma=\rho/1-\rho$
θ	share of labor used in production of the manufacturing good
ε	degree of differentiation of intermediate goods
ϕ	inverse measure of market power in the intermediate-goods market $\phi=\varepsilon/1-\varepsilon$
σ	elasticity of substitution of final goods
τ	distance costs
λ	total number of companies of final-goods producers

Subscripts

A	agricultural sector
F	foreign country
H	home country
i	individual company
In	inward FDI
j	country index, home or foreign
k	company index, national or international
κ	industry index
M	manufacturing sector
Out	outward FDI
P	plant level
Z	group of intermediate goods

Superscripts

A	agriculture
M	multinational company
MF	manufacturing
N	national company
S	services

List of Variables and Indexes in the Empirical Part

Roman Variables

A	technology parameter
$a_H(z)$	skilled labor intensity in the production of an intermediate good z
$a_L(z)$	unskilled labor intensity in the production of an intermediate good z
C	production costs
c	constant of a regression
D	domestic intermediate inputs
F_P	fixed costs at the plant level of a final-goods producer's foreign affiliate
H	skilled labor
L	unskilled labor
K	capital
p_D	price for domestic intermediate goods
p_I	price for imported intermediate goods
q	output of a foreign affiliate of a final-goods producer
r	interest rate
u	error term
w	wage
$x(z)$	output of the intermediate good z
Y	output
z	index of the intermediate good

Greek Variables

α	share of intermediate goods used in production
β	estimated parameter
ρ	degree of differentiation
θ	elasticity of factor substitution
λ	loading coefficient

Indexes and Others

Δ	first difference
i	individual cross-section index
t	time index

1 Motivation

In the mid-1980s, world economic integration reached a new era. Since then, international economic activities have increasingly affected economic conditions and national economic policies. The perceived economic distance between countries has fallen remarkably. Trade has continued to grow strongly. Capital movements have exploded. Knowledge and technology are being transferred to a much larger extent than ever before. Countries seem to be much more interrelated. Shocks transmit faster and more easily to other countries. Singular events in one country have significant effects on many other countries, too. People know much more about foreign countries through increased travel activities and through new sources of information. Some observers even claim "the death of distance" (Cairncross 1997), the end of the "nation state" (Panić 1997), and a "borderless world" (Ohmae 1990) with fading national differences.

Although these claims are certainly exaggerated, some important changes have occurred in international economic relationships since the mid-1980s. The new quality of world economic integration is distinct enough from those of preceding periods to coin a name for the new era: globalization. Globalization describes a process of increasing economic integration, or to follow the Siebert and Klodt's definition (1999: 116), globalization "can be defined as the process of converting separate national economies into an integrated world economy." The distinctive character of the globalization period which marks the difference to earlier periods of economic integration has two features: (i) a deepening of economic integration and (ii) an enlargement in the number of countries taking part in economic integration.

Economic integration can be achieved through three channels: (i) international trade, still the most important link between national economies, (ii) international capital movements and labor mobility, and (iii) international diffusion of information, knowledge, and technology. Although all three channels are used more intensively since the mid-1980s, the increase in international capital movements has been especially pronounced. International capital movements have replaced trade as the most dynamic channel of economic integration. In trade, important qualitative changes have occurred with intraindustry trade gaining further weight relative to interindustry trade. Finally, new communication technologies have allowed cheaper and faster cross-border transfer of information. The diffusion of the Internet will strengthen this tendency even more in the future.

Besides the deeper integration of the countries having taken part in this process already for a longer time, other countries entered the system of international division of labor. Strong long-run growth in East Asia has increased the share of this open region in world trade. Motivated by both the success of East and Southeast Asian countries' open-market development strategy and by their own failures, Latin American countries gave up their import substitution strategy and opened up to foreign competition. The most radical change, however, came at the beginning of the 1990s when the former socialist countries opened up politically and economically. The end of the cold war and the participation of former socialist countries in Europe and Asia in the international division of labor brought a large number of countries to the system of market-based economic relationships and created the chance to form real world markets. The effects of the enlargement in the number of countries taking part in economic integration has been analyzed in several papers (Freeman 1995; Siebert 1997; Eckel 2000b) and is not focus of this study. Instead, this work concentrates on the other feature of globalization: the deepening of economic integration.

This study offers a framework for analyzing the economic integration of countries. A theoretical model is proposed which rationalizes observed globalization patterns. The emergence and activities of multinational enterprises (MNEs) stand in the center of the theoretical explanation of the globalization process. In line with the globalization literature (Rodrik 1998; Baldwin and Martin 1999; Frankel 1997), changes in economic conditions in the model stem from a (exogenous) reduction in distance costs, i.e., a reduction in the degree of separation of countries. This affects, first of all, companies' international activities but also feeds back into competition within a country. Individuals and companies continuously adjust their consumption choices and competitive behavior to changing conditions.

In the first part of Chapter 2, I collect and describe the patterns of globalization that I want to explain. This part gives an empirical overview of globalization. Using different data sets at different levels of aggregation, basic patterns of globalization are presented. They can be summarized as follows: (i) the strong position and the impressive intensification of international economic activities is predominantly a developed-country phenomenon, (ii) all kind of international activities (trade, foreign direct investment, production abroad, and cross-border flows of knowledge and technology) increased over time, (iii) the extent of international activities shows large differences between sectors, (iv) international activities are to a large and increasing degree intraindustry activities, (v) international activities are strongly concentrated on a few large (multinational) companies.

The empirical analysis reveals a very important role of MNEs. They hold strong positions in all three channels of globalization: by definition, they account for all foreign direct investment (FDI), they are very active in trade, with one-third of world trade taking place within and not between companies, and they transfer the bulk of technology and knowledge across borders via intrafirm transactions. Because of this dominant position of MNEs, the explanation of the globalization process which is brought forward in this analysis builds on decisions made by (multinational) companies regarding their international activities under changing conditions of international competition.

In the second part of Chapter 2, I survey the literature on the emergence of MNEs, having recognized MNEs as the main vehicle for promoting the globalization process. Proximity-concentration general equilibrium models (Krugman 1983; Brainard 1993; Markusen and Venables 1998) which analyze trade and production abroad in one framework stand in the center of the literature survey, since these models seem to be best suited to explain the existence of MNEs and their importance for international economic activities between developed countries. In proximity-concentration models of MNEs, companies are assumed to have an ownership advantage and an internalization advantage. The ownership advantage implies that a company possesses an advantage in the production of a particular good relative to all other companies. Competition among companies is therefore imperfect. Each company produces a particular variety of a differentiated good. The observed high share of MNEs in industries which produce differentiated goods justifies this assumption. Furthermore, the large fraction of intrafirm transfer of knowledge and technology justifies the assumption that internalization is superior to other alternatives to exploit the ownership advantage. Knowledge about a product or a production process is not sold to an independent company abroad but is used within the company and exploited by production in a foreign affiliate. Imperfections in the market for information which cause the internalization advantage are not analyzed but are taken as given.

Economic theory has made great progress in explaining the regional pattern of trade and production abroad but did not focus on their development over time. Economic theory on trade and MNEs is mainly static. However, for an understanding of the process of globalization, an analytical framework is necessary which deals with trade and the internationalization of production in a world of falling distance costs. Therefore, the idea of evolution developed by the new economic geography literature (Krugman 1991; Fujita, Krugman, and Venables 1999) is harnessed. This allows for a "dynamic" interpretation of the static model and the analysis of a process like globalization.

In the third part of Chapter 2, I derive the requirements for and the ingredients of a model of globalization from the empirical overview and from the survey of the literature. I conclude that for a theory of globalization, companies should be modeled explicitly. Their strategic choices between the internationalization alternatives (exports or production abroad) should be at the center of the analysis. A proximity-concentration approach which allows for differentiated goods and heterogeneous consumers seems to be most suitable. As mentioned above, in a proximity-concentration approach, the ownership and the internalization advantages are assumed while the location advantage arises from better access to the foreign market if the firm produces abroad rather than serves the foreign market by exports. This kind of location advantage is sufficient to model the globalization process. Differences in locations that are driven by factor endowments do not seem to be the relevant explanation for the observed empirical pattern with the strong concentration of economic integration on developed countries and the large share of intraindustry trade and intraindustry affiliate production. Last but not least, the model should account for the role of trade in intermediate goods between the various units of an MNE.

In the first part of Chapter 3, I use the results of Chapter 2 to develop a two-country two-sector one-factor general equilibrium model which explains companies' internationalization strategies. The two countries are symmetric. There is only one factor of production, i.e., labor. Thus, all problems of within-country distribution of income are assumed away, since all individuals are identical in offering one unit of labor. Market structures differ in the two sectors that I model. The perfect competition sector producing a homogeneous good is called agriculture. The other sector, called manufacturing, produces many varieties of a differentiated final good. The knowledge of one particular variety gives each company the ownership advantage for this variety. The production process requires fixed costs at the company level (to create the ownership advantage) and at the plant level (to produce the good). Goods of different companies are imperfect substitutes for each other. Companies engage in monopolistic competition. Consumers are assumed to love variety. Aggregated, their decisions are reflected in those of the representative consumer who buys an average amount of each variety depending on its price.

Markets are segmented by distance costs. Imported goods sell for a higher price, because they incur these distance costs. Distance costs include costs of information, transport, communication, and doing business in a foreign environment. Distance costs in the model resemble closely McCallum's border effects (McCallum 1995), since they apply only to cross-border but not to within-country trade. These border effects have significantly fallen over time (Nitsch 2000). Border effects are reflected in the distance costs in the model which take Samuelson's "iceberg" form: a fraction of a good shipped smelts away in transit.

Production of each final-goods variety requires the use of a bundle of intermediate inputs, which includes all varieties of intermediate goods produced in one country. Intermediate goods are differentiated as well. Companies engage in monopolistic competition within the group of intermediate-goods producers. Intermediate goods are assumed to be specific to the product or the production process of the final-goods producers in the same country. Thus, final-goods producers and intermediate-goods producers form a national supplier-customer network. Final-goods producers use exclusively inputs from their home country. Now, in order to supply the foreign market, final-goods producers can choose between exporting and producing abroad whereas intermediate-goods producers are domestic companies by assumption. In choosing between these different strategies, final-goods producers face a tradeoff between higher variable distance costs when exporting and higher fixed costs when producing abroad and becoming an MNE. MNEs' distance costs are lower because only a fraction of the final goods sold by the MNEs, the intermediate goods, have to be shipped. The other input, labor, is drawn from the foreign country.

Relative profitability of the two alternative strategies changes with distance costs. For high distance costs, exporting is the optimal strategy, since sales of an affiliate in the foreign country are too small to generate enough variable profits to pay the additional fixed costs. Intermediate inputs which must be imported from the home country (since they are specific) are too expensive to allow larger sales. With falling distance costs, exports rise. However, at high and intermediate distance costs, the profitability of production abroad increases even more with falling distance costs than the profitability of exports. For intermediate distance cost levels, it might therefore pay for a company to produce abroad and to become an MNE. For very low distance costs, exporting is again the more profitable strategy to supply the foreign market. International activities of companies follow, therefore, a pattern in which exports increase over time (because of falling distance cost over time). A change of the internationalization strategy from exports to production abroad is possible when distance costs have fallen below a certain threshold. Finally, companies return to exports when distance costs have fallen even further.

The assumption of specific intermediate goods is important to derive these results. Therefore, I test this assumption empirically in the second part of Chapter 3. From the model introduced in the first part of Chapter 3, a testable equation for the relationship of a country's imports of intermediate inputs and foreign activities of companies in this country is derived and tested against alternative hypotheses of increased imports in intermediate goods. Input-output data of six OECD countries for three different points in time are employed in some cross-section estimations. Regression results support the hypothesis that imports of intermediate goods increase with the size of networks of foreign affiliates in a given country. A time-series analysis conducted with German data also supports this result. Affiliates of foreign MNEs make above-average use of imported inputs from their home country. These results substantiate the assumption of specific intermediate goods in the theoretical model.

The basic version of the model can describe the observed globalization patterns. International activities increase with falling distance costs with exports preceding production abroad. To a large extent, these international activities are intraindustry activities. However, relaxing some restrictions of the model gives additional insights. In Chapter 4, I give up the assumption of symmetry of both countries. Countries differ in size. Since there is only one production factor, countries differ only in absolute size; there is no relative factor-endowments difference as in a Heckscher–Ohlin framework, for instance. Country size differences yield differences in international activities which cause adjustments in the production structure in equilibrium. Smaller countries specialize partly in the production of agricultural goods, and larger countries in the production of manufacturing goods. Country size also affects the timing of the internationalization of production. Waves of internationalization of production arise at different points in time in countries which differ in size. One company's internationalization decision affects the profitability of its national competitors' internationalization of production positively. As a result, companies from the same country internationalize their production within a short time span. An internationalization wave arises which alters the market structure in manufacturing and the specialization pattern in production in both countries. The emergence of such internationalization waves is widely discussed in the theoretical and empirical literature (Graham 1996). Thereby, analyses often rely on the oligopolistic reaction hypothesis. Using the model with two countries which differ in size, I offer an alternative explanation.

In Chapter 5, I propose a multiindustry version of the model. Different groups of companies are introduced to study sectoral differences in international activities and in the relationship of exports and production abroad. Companies belonging to the same group are symmetric, but companies belonging to different groups are not. By assumption, there is no substitution between goods produced by companies from different groups. In the first three parts of Chapter 5, these groups are to be understood as industries. This model structure is employed in an analysis of the relationship of the two strategies to supply the foreign market, trade or production abroad. Results show that complementarity of exports and production abroad is more likely to occur on the aggregate level. Substitution of exports by production abroad can be found at the product level. This is in line with the findings of empirical studies concerning this relationship (Blonigen 2001; Markusen 2002).

In the fourth part of Chapter 5, I deal with the coexistence of national and multinational companies within one industry. In order to study the conditions of coexistence, the assumption of symmetry of companies within one industry must be relaxed. Introducing substitution (and therefore competition) between products from different groups of companies, alters the multiindustry version. Then, the model structure reflects an industry with heterogeneous companies grouped according to the different characteristics regarding technology and demand. The analysis reveals that national companies and MNEs coexist in an industry setting where the symmetry assumption between the companies in the industry is abandoned. However, the resulting market structure in equilibrium is sensitive to the grouping of the companies.

Globalization is a process of intensifying competition of companies from many countries. So far, for simplicity, only bilateral economic integration has been analyzed. In Chapter 6, I depart from this route by introducing a third country, thereby allowing the role of different distances of country pairs to be studied. Internationalization of activities between two countries has an effect on the market structure and the international activities of a third country. For instance, an internationalization wave of companies from one country into another country can yield a "contagion" effect in the sense that the internationalization of production of companies from the third country becomes profitable, too. The result is a "global internationalization wave" of companies from various home countries into one host country as seen in the late 1980s when companies from various countries set up affiliates in the United States.

In Chapter 7, I conclude that the theoretical framework can reflect the observed patterns of globalization. Globalization in this model is driven by a reduction of distance costs which forces individuals and companies to adjust to new conditions. The process is welfare improving, even without having recourse to a positive effect of openness on growth which is found by so many studies (Maurer 1998; World Bank 2002). Welfare improvements result only from the reduction of the segmentation of markets. Opportunities of globalization in form of a more efficient division of labor, better availability of varieties from companies from other countries, lower prices, and more intense competition outweigh the adjustment costs. The extensions of the basic model, which are proposed to introduce more heterogeneity among countries and companies, can be seen as robustness check and as the attempt to reflect observed globalization patterns as closely as possible. Furthermore, the model extensions allow for analyses of both political issues such as the relationship of exports and production abroad as well as topics mainly discussed in academia such as the co-existence of national companies and MNEs.

The message of this study is that globalization is not a zero-sum or even a negative-sum game. There are gains from globalization which are widely ignored in the public debate. Globalization raises the average welfare of all individuals even in a static framework such as the one proposed here. The globalization process leaves society as a whole better off. If there are groups of individuals who lose from globalization, they can be compensated. Negative welfare effects in this process result from too little, not from too much competition. Open markets and free market entry and exit are, therefore, preconditions for the welfare improvements made possible by globalization.

2   Globalization: Empirical Overview and Theoretical Explanations

2.1   Empirical Overview

The process of economic integration has accelerated remarkably in the last 15 years. The strong increase of foreign direct investment (FDI), and thus the internationalization of production, has attracted most of the attention. Also impressive is the increase in international transfer of knowledge and technology. International trade continues to grow stronger than world output. The degree of openness, i.e., the ratio of exports over GDP, surpassed the pre–World War I record levels in most countries. Separation of national markets has decreased. Competition from foreign companies has increased markedly in all developed countries. New products are introduced almost at the same time in Europe, North America, and Japan.

In this chapter, I show that multinational enterprises (MNEs) stand in the center of all these developments. In Section 2.1.1, I analyze FDI, which is by definition bound to MNEs. I discuss its long-term developments and sectoral and regional breakdowns. In the Section 2.1.2, I deal with the international transfer of knowledge and technology. MNEs are the main vehicle of this transfer as can be seen by the large share of the payments for royalties and license fees, which flew within, not between, companies in 1995 (UNCTAD 1997). In Section 2.1.3, I focus on international trade, especially MNE-related international trade. Two phenomena are of special interest: the large and increasing intrafirm trade and the role of MNEs in the trade of intermediate goods. In Section 2.1.4, I summarize the first part of Chapter 2 and draw some conclusions for the model I build in Chapter 3.

2.1.1   Foreign Direct Investment

The strong increase in worldwide economic integration can be attributed to a large degree to increasing FDI flows. This has especially been true since the mid-1980s. Up to then, foreign trade was the most dynamic channel of economic integration. Exports grew much stronger than FDI in the 1950s, 1960s, and 1970s. In the 1980s, this pattern changed. Annual FDI growth of 13.3 percent

Figure 1:
World Exports, World Industrial Production, and World Foreign Direct Investment, 1973–2000[a]

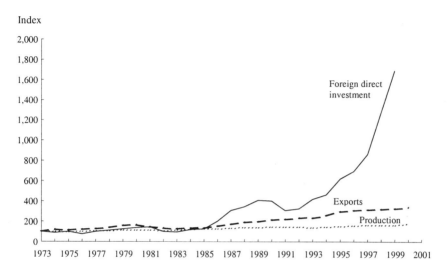

[a]Indexes; 1973=100. Exports without services. Foreign direct investment adjusted with the U.S. industrial goods price index.
Source: Siebert (2002).

vastly exceeded the 5.9 percent export growth per year (UNCTAD 2001). Figure 1 documents the increasing integration through stronger growth in trade relative to production and the impressive rise of FDI after 1985. It shows the trend of world real exports, world real industrial production, and world real FDI outflows from 1973 to 2000. Whereas a relatively parallel increase can be observed for the first 12 years, FDI began to increase much faster than exports and industrial production in 1985.

Real world industrial production increased by 66 percent over the whole 26-year period, which is equivalent to an annual growth rate of 2 percent. International trade, here shown by export figures, increased by 223 percent over the whole period, or 4.8 percent annually, more than twice as fast as industrial production. An even more dynamic contribution to economic integration came from FDI. From 1973 to 1999, FDI increased by 1,590 percent. That is an impressive annual growth rate of 11.5 percent, more than twice as large as the export growth rate. Over the shorter time span beginning in 1985—the period I refer to as the globalization period—the increase in FDI outflows was even stronger (19.1 percent annual growth), and its contribution to worldwide economic integration even more pronounced. There should be no doubt that the world entered a new phase of economic integration in the mid-1980s.

The sudden and strong increase of FDI in the second half of the 1980s has been widely discussed in recent years, but its explanation continues to be one of the challenges to economic research (Graham 1996). Worldwide FDI stocks increased from \$782 billion to \$1,768 billion in the second half of the 1980s. They more than doubled, therefore, in just six years (Table 1). This strong economic integration in this period was almost exclusively a developed-country phenomenon as shown in Table 2. Table 2 also reveals that the second boom of worldwide FDI outflows (Figure 1), which has started in 1993, included developing countries to a much larger extent.

Table 1:

Inward FDI Stocks, 1980–2000 (millions of dollars, current prices)

	World	OECD countries	United States	United Kingdom	Germany	Japan	Developing countries
1980	506,602	373,658	83,046	63,014	36,630	3,270	132,945
1985	782,298	545,060	184,615	64,028	36,926	4,740	237,239
1990	1,768,456	1,394,853	394,911	203,894	119,619	9,850	370,644
1995	2,937,539	2,051,739	535,553	199,760	192,898	33,508	849,376
2000	6,314,271	4,210,294	1,238,627	482,798	460,953	54,303	1,979,262

Source: UNCTAD (2001).

Table 2:

Accumulated Inward FDI Flows, 1971–2000

	World	OECD countries	United States	United Kingdom	Germany	Japan	Developing countries
	Absolute value (millions of dollars)						
1971–76	92,766	66,460	16,851	8,496	9,084	901	26,306
1985–90	790,572	672,535	283,680	105,151	24,823	2,220	118,037
1993–98	2,254,450	1,448,320	542,849	177,493	51,684	7,740	806,130
2000	1,301,200	1,052,540	287,680	119,930	189,180	8,230	248,660
	Ratio						
85–90 / 71–76	8.5	10.1	16.8	12.4	2.7	2.5	4.5
	Share in world total (percent)						
1971–76		71.6	18.2	9.2	9.8	1.0	28.4
1985–90		85.1	39.9	13.3	3.1	0.3	14.9
1993–98		64.2	24.1	7.9	2.3	0.3	35.8
2000		80.9	22.1	9.2	14.5	0.6	19.1

Source: IMF (various issues); own calculations.

In 2000, worldwide FDI stocks reached $6,314 billion. More than two-thirds of these stocks are invested in developed countries. The FDI boom in the second half of the 1980s was a phenomenon which was particularly engendered by OECD countries. Approximately 85 percent of the flows saw OECD countries as source and as host of FDI. Within the OECD, dynamics of in- and outflows have changed between the countries. The United States experienced the most impressive increase and became by far the largest host country. The share of FDI inflows in the United States increased from 18.2 percent in the early 1970s to 39.9 percent in the late 1980s.[1] The United States continued to be the most important host of FDI although its dominance faded a bit, mostly due to the emergence of China as a large recipient of FDI in the 1990s.

An interesting picture emerged in the second half of the 1980s with the United States as the dominant host country and many large source countries of FDI (Tables 2 and 3). That is the opposite of the situation in the 1960s and the early 1970s when U.S. companies dominated FDI outflows by investing heavily in other developed countries. The share of world FDI outflows coming from U.S. companies dropped from 56.7 percent in the early 1970s to 15.5 percent in the late 1980s. It recovered again in the 1990s to 26.1 percent, without regaining its dominant position of the 1960s.

Table 3:
Accumulated Outward FDI Flows, 1971–2000

	World	OECD countries	United States	United Kingdom	Germany	Japan	Developing countries
	Absolute value (millions of dollars)						
1971–76	126,179	123,613	71,573	17,721	10,726	8,610	2,566
1985–90	917,493	886,751	142,470	150,337	85,004	166,870	30,742
1993–98	2,242,993	2,107,937	585,284	309,856	251,029	128,551	135,056
2000	1,375,560	1,279,300	178,290	266,248	53,002	31,534	96,259
	Ratio						
85–90 / 71–76	7.3	7.2	2.0	8.5	7.9	19.4	12.0
93–98 / 85–90	2.4	2.4	4.1	2.1	3.0	0.8	4.4
	Share in world total (percent)						
1971–76		98.0	56.7	14.0	8.5	6.8	2.0
1985–90		96.7	15.5	16.4	9.3	18.2	3.3
1993–98		94.0	26.1	13.8	11.2	5.7	6.0
2000		93.0	13.0	19.4	3.9	2.3	7.0

Source: IMF (various issues); own calculations.

---

[1]   The differences in the growth rates of inward FDI reflected in Tables 1 and 2 result from the devaluation of the U.S. dollar after 1985. For problems regarding different FDI statistics, see Klodt (1999).

From the early 1990s up to the currency crises in Latin America and Asia, the share of FDI received by developing countries has been somewhat higher than in the decades before. It increased to about 35.8 percent of total FDI inflows in the period from 1993 to 1998 (Table 2). This higher share results from an FDI boom in China and Southeast Asia in the first half of the 1990s. China alone received 6 percent of all FDI inflows worldwide, or one-sixth of all inflows in developing countries over the FDI boom period in the 1990s. Southeast Asia (excluding China) received one-third.

After the Asian crisis, the strong increase of FDI was mainly driven by a cross-border mergers and acquisitions wave among developed countries. Developed countries increased their share of total FDI inflows to 80.9 percent in 2000 (IMF 2002). Germany's FDI inflows especially in 2000 reflect the large effect of mergers and acquisitions. The value was driven to a very large extent by just one transaction: the acquisition of Mannesmann by Vodaphone.

Developed countries as a group have been the dominant source of FDI throughout the time span analyzed. Developed countries' share in total outward FDI decreased slightly from 98.0 percent in the early 1970s to 94.0 percent in the 1993–1998 period (Table 3). This modest decrease results mainly from increasing FDI flows from newly industrializing economies (NIEs) into China. However, as already noticed, within the group of OECD countries the regional break-down changed strongly over time. Japan and the EU countries emerged as new sources of FDI, the U.S. dominance disappeared. Japanese outward FDI flows reached very high levels in the late 1980s. Although Japanese companies were relatively less active in the mid-1990s, the 1993–1998 period showed a much more even distribution of FDI outflows than the early 1970s.

It is important to note that the U.S. outward FDI flows experienced only a relative decrease in the 1980s, whereas in absolute numbers U.S. companies' outward FDI flows doubled in comparison with the early 1970s. However, the increase in other developed countries, most notably Japan and the United Kingdom, was much larger. The relative decrease of U.S. outward FDI becomes even larger if an adjustment for the higher rate of reinvested earnings in U.S. outflows in the 1980s is made (Table 4). The high share of reinvested earnings in FDI outflows of the United States and the United Kingdom points to the longer history of internationalization of production of companies in these countries compared to those in Japan and Germany. Germany's drop in the reinvested-earnings ratio can be explained by the strong increase in outflows which could not have been financed by reinvested earnings alone. The reinvested-earnings ratio of developing countries is slowly increasing. However, reinvested earnings play no important role in financing developing countries' outward FDI flows. Their share in total reinvested earnings is very low (0.8 percent).

Table 4:
Reinvested-Earnings Ratio[a], 1971–2000

	World	Developed countries	United States	United Kingdom	Germany	Japan	Developing countries
1971–1976	n.a.	37.0	55.9	60.2	21.5	n.a.	0.6
1985–1990	22.7	23.4	82.2	48.8	9.3	n.a.	2.6
1993–1998	25.2	26.6	54.9	46.0	6.1	14.0	3.4
2000	16.4	16.7	65.4	15.7	9.8	−5.8	12.7

[a]Reinvested earnings relative to FDI outflows.

Source: IMF (various issues); own calculations.

Table 5:
Correlation Coefficients of Current Account Balance and Net FDI Flows, 1960–1997

United States	Canada	United Kingdom	France	Germany	Japan
0.197	−0.183	0.0	0.16	−0.055	0.659

Number of observations: 38
Critical value: 0.324

Source: IMF (various issues); own calculations.

The reason for the change in relative positions in FDI among developed countries is still not well understood. The drastic change in the U.S. current account does not seem to be the cause, since net FDI flows and the balance of the current account are not correlated for the United States and other developed countries with the exception of Japan. Table 5 shows the correlation coefficients for the six largest source countries of FDI. For Germany and Canada the correlation is negative, for the United Kingdom the correlation is zero, and for the United States and France the correlation is positive. None of them is statistically significant. Only for Japan the data shows a significant correlation of current account balance and net FDI flows. It seems fair to conclude that changes in current account are not the main drivers behind the change in the relative position in inward and outward FDI.

Related to the large share of intra–OECD FDI stocks and flows is another phenomenon which is also striking: the large share of intraindustry FDI. This can be seen in Table 6 for U.S. and German sectoral data. The Grubel–Lloyd IIT indexes, which are also given there, show the fraction of balanced FDI stocks in total FDI stocks (Grubel and Lloyd 1971). The index varies between 0 and 1. If FDI is mainly one-way, the Grubel–Lloyd index is low. For most industries shown in Table 6, the indexes are surprisingly high. Since Grubel–Lloyd indexes

Table 6:

Sectoral Breakdown of German and U.S. Inward and Outward FDI Stocks in 1999 (percent)

	Germany			United States		
	Share		GL index[a]	Share		GL index[a]
	inward	outward		inward	outward	
Petroleum	0.23	0.62	0.29	9.62	8.48	0.94
Manufacturing	45.62	40.14	0.68	41.37	27.64	0.93
Food	3.03	0.90	0.79	2.03	2.96	0.69
Chemicals	11.13	11.75	0.60	10.08	6.92	0.94
Machinery	4.63	3.11	0.81	8.69	3.43	0.67
Electronics	7.61	5.50	0.77	5.38	3.49	0.91
Transport equipment	3.99	10.19	0.30	5.18	3.30	0.90
Services	53.66	58.73	0.59	46.94	62.92	0.73
Trade related	18.58	14.57	0.73	9.80	7.08	0.96
Financial institutions	22.23	35.93	0.44	15.30	39.95	0.46
Michaely index[b]	0.58			0.63		

[a]The Grubel–Lloyd index is: $GL_\kappa = (FDI_{Out,\kappa} + FDI_{In,\kappa} - |FDI_{Out,\kappa} - FDI_{In,\kappa}|)/(FDI_{Out,\kappa}$

$+FDI_{In,\kappa})$ for all industries κ. — [b]Michaely index: $M = 1 - \sum_\kappa \left| \dfrac{FDI_{Out,\kappa}}{FDI_{Out}} - \dfrac{FDI_{In,\kappa}}{FDI_{In}} \right|$

for all industries κ.

Source: U.S. Department of Commerce (2001a); Deutsche Bundesbank (2001); own calculations.

are sensitive to imbalances in total outward and inward FDI stocks, Table 6 also presents the Michaely index, which measures the structure of the sectoral breakdown of outward and inward FDI. For mainly one-way FDI stocks, the Michaely index is low. This measure is robust against imbalances in outward and inward FDI stocks. The large Michaely indexes point to a remarkably similar structure of outward and inward FDI.

The Grubel–Lloyd indexes of U.S. industries are especially high. With 0.46, financial institutions show the lowest value of all industries reported here. Thus, U.S. financial institutions possess a competitive advantage in this sector relative to institutions in other countries, which allows them to be "twice as active" in foreign markets than foreigners in the U.S. market. In the manufacturing sector, e.g., FDI positions are more balanced. For German industries, about the same pattern emerges, with the exceptions of the transport equipment industry (GL_{TE}=0.30), which results from the dominant position of German companies in this industry and the low value of petroleum (GL_P=0.29), which results from the lack of this natural resource in Germany and consequently low inward FDI stocks.

Table 7:
Share of Top MNEs in Outward FDI Stocks, Latest Available Year (percent)

	Year	Top 5	Top 10	Top 15	Top 25	Top 50
Australia	1996	45.0	57.0	66.0	80.0	96.0
Austria	1998	25.0	35.0	41.0	50.0	63.0
Canada	1995	22.6	33.5	40.1	50.1	64.4
Finland	1995	33.0	47.0	56.0	69.0	84.0
France	1995	14.0	23.0	31.0	42.0	59.0
Germany	1999	20.1	29.6	36.2	44.0	55.5
Norway	1997	61.7	74.5	80.5	86.1	92.6
Sweden	1999	25.2	41.2	51.2	64.6	80.7
Switzerland	1999	32.0	47.0	56.0	67.0	81.0
United Kingdom	1999	36.0	48.7	55.8	65.3	79.0
United States	1999	13.9	22.6	28.7	37.9	52.1

Source: UNCTAD (2001: 52, Table II.3).

The industries which hold the highest shares of inward and outward FDI stocks in the manufacturing sector are industries in which product differentiation prevails. This is in line with the findings of Cantwell and Sanna Randaccio (1992), who present large and increasing shares of intraindustry direct investment in the EU. Furthermore, they show that FDI often takes place in technology-intensive industries. This can also be seen from Table 6 in the high shares of chemicals, machinery, electronics, and transport equipment.

The dominance of large companies in outward FDI stocks can be seen in Table 7, which presents the share of top MNEs in outward FDI stocks for various countries. The top 50 companies account for more than half of outward FDI stocks in all economies. Note that the strong concentration in FDI stocks on that few companies is calculated at aggregate country level. Concentration in individual sectors is even more pronounced. Given the strong position of a few dominant companies in outward FDI stocks of all countries, the balanced pattern of inward and outward FDI stocks is especially surprising. Daimler Benz' acquisition of Chrysler in 1998 alone increased the sectoral share of transport equipment in total outward FDI stocks by 3.9 percentage points. This is a rather drastic change given that Germany as a relatively large economy is much less dominated by some big players than other (smaller) countries.

FDI stocks are just one indicator of the progress in the internationalization of production in the last two decades. The high and increasing share of employees who work for an affiliate of a foreign MNE is also striking. In Germany, 4.9 percent of the labor force was employed by a foreign MNE in 1999, while German companies employed 11.2 percent of their labor force in foreign countries, up from 5.2 percent in 1976. The U.S. shares are at about the same level. In the manufacturing sector, however, these shares are much larger. In U.S. manufacturing, for instance, 13.6 percent of the labor force in 1999 was employed by foreign affiliates, while U.S. companies employed 22.3 percent of their labor force in foreign countries (U.S. Department of Commerce 2001b).

2.1.2   International Transfer of Knowledge and Technology

The international transfer of knowledge and technology, here measured as cross-border payments for royalties and licensing fees (short: technology payments), have increased at about the same rate as FDI flows. Technology payments have increased from $12 billion in 1983 to $65 billion in 1999 (UNCTAD 1997, 2000). The annual growth rate of 11.1 percent in the 1990s even slightly exceeded FDI-outflow growth. The parallel increase in FDI stocks and knowledge transfer could be an indication of a common driving force for both phenomena. Increasing activities of MNEs are a very likely candidate, since MNEs hold a strong position in FDI as well as in international transfer of knowledge and technology. MNEs are often seen as a vehicle to transfer knowledge and technology (Krugman 1983). Increasing knowledge transfer is, therefore, very likely related to increasing FDI stocks.

The regional distribution of royalties and license fee payments (Table 8) is even more dominated by developed countries than the regional structure of inward FDI stocks (Table 1). This is not surprising, given developed countries' advantage in the production of technology-intensive goods and their larger capacity to use and absorb new technologies. IMF data on royalties and license fees has only been available since 1990. For comparison with earlier periods, national U.S. and German data sources have to be employed. Over the 1990s, Japan paid the largest amount of cross-border royalties and license fees. Japanese companies held a share of 18.6 percent of all royalties and license fees paid worldwide. U.S. and German companies followed with 15.4 percent and 12.3 percent, respectively. Companies from developing countries as a group held a small share of 11.7 percent.

The same few countries held strong positions in payments as well as in receipts of royalties and license fees. 88.3 percent of all payments and 98.3 percent of all receipts of royalties and license fees were due to developed countries. The United States alone received about 58 percent of all royalties and license fees in the 1990s. This demonstrates the dominant position of U.S. companies in the development of new products and production processes. Japan, the United Kingdom, Germany, and France received a share of 10 percent, 9 percent, 6 percent, and 4 percent, respectively (IMF various issues). According to this data,

Table 8:
Accumulated Cross-Border Payments of Royalties and License Fees

	World	OECD countries	United States[a]	United Kingdom	Germany	Japan[b]	Developing countries
	Absolute value (millions of dollars)						
1980–89	n.a.	n.a.	12,470	n.a.	17,358	n.a.	n.a
1990–97	308,756	272,696	47,400	22,530	37,970	57,610	36,060
	Ratio						
90–97 / 80–89	n.a.	n.a.	3.80	n.a.	2.19	n.a.	n.a.
	Share in world total (percent)						
1990–98	100	88.3	15.4	7.3	12.3	18.6	11.7

[a]1982–89: U.S. Department of Commerce (1999). — [b]1991–1997.

Source: IMF (various issues); U.S. Department of Commerce (1999); Deutsche Bundesbank (2000); own calculations.

international transfer of technology takes place almost without developing countries. Among the developing countries, South Korea pays and receives the highest shares, with one-third of the payments and one-fifth of the receipts of all developing countries.

Intrafirm flows of technology account for a very high share of total technology flows (Table 9). By using data from the United States, Japan, and Germany, UNCTAD (1997) calculated this share to be about 80 percent of all flows. This highlights the important role of MNEs to overcome market imperfections on markets for information goods. The high share also documents the internalization advantage, which is, according to the ownership, location, and internalization (OLI) paradigm (Dunning 1980), a necessary condition for the superiority of production abroad within an MNE compared to a licensing agreement with an independent foreign company. Such licensing agreements with independent companies account for only a small fraction of business-to-business flows of royalties and licensing fees.

The intrafirm share in Table 9 is biased downwards. The numbers on cross-border royalties and license fees include payments for copyrights of software, books, film, live entertainment, and other consumer-to-business fees, which cannot be internalized within a firm. The intrafirm share in business-to-business knowledge transfers is larger than 80 percent and did not fall in the 1990s. The falling intrafirm share in the last decade, which is shown in Table 9, results exclusively from increasing technology payments in the consumer-to-business relationship.

Table 9:

Cross-Border Royalties and License Fees Receipts, 1982–1998

	United States			Germany		
	Total receipts	Intrafirm receipts		Total receipts	Intrafirm receipts	
		$ mil.	percent		$ mil.	percent
1982	5,603	3,377	60.3	n.a.	n.a.	n.a.
1990	16,634	13,251	79.7	1,990	n.a.	n.a.
1998	36,808	26,761	72.7	3,250	2,454	75.5

Source: U.S. Department of Commerce (various issues); Deutsche Bundesbank (2000); IMF (various issues); own calculations.

Table 10:

Patent Applications in Germany, Japan, and the United States, 1980–1997

	1980	1985	1990	1995	1997
Germany					
Resident application (absolute)	30,582	32,708	30,928	38,675	45,105
Foreign share[a] (percent)	54.2	56.8	67.5	67.7	66.5
External ratio[b]	2.70	2.87	5.08	6.00	9.61
Japan					
Resident application (absolute)	165,730	274,348	332,952	333,770	349,211
Foreign share[a] (percent)	14.5	10.2	11.5	13.9	16.0
External ratio[b]	0.27	0.27	0.39	0.46	1.09
United States					
Resident application (absolute)	62,098	63,673	90,643	124,210	119,452
Foreign share[a] (percent)	41.5	47.2	48.3	46.5	48.1
External ratio[b]	1.87	2.35	3.26	6.86	13.26

[a](Patent applications by nonresidents / total national patent applications) x 100; total national patent applications = patent applications by nonresidents + patent applications by residents. — [b]External patent applications by residents / patent applications by residents.

Source: OECD (2000); own calculations.

Table 8 above shows the rise of international technology flows in the globalization era. New knowledge and technology is spread at much higher speed to other developed countries than in former times. This phenomenon can also be observed from the patent applications given in Table 10. Increasingly, companies apply for patents not only to the authorities of the home country, but to foreign authorities as well. This may point to a faster penetration of foreign markets not only by exports, but also by production in foreign countries. The importance of knowledge production, approximated by the number of resident patent applications, has increased over the last two decades in all of the three economies shown here. This fact and the internationalization of the use of this knowledge have led to a rising internationalization of knowledge protection, shown by the external ratio and the foreign share in Table 10. In 1997, a U.S. company applied (on average) for one patent in the United States and for 13 in other countries, compared to two in other countries in 1980. Similarly, the foreign share of national applications has grown in all three countries. Increasing international technology flows are protected by a rising number of patents granted by foreign-countries authorities.

Table 10 gives information about the internationalization of the knowledge use, but not about the internationalization of knowledge production. The internationalization of knowledge production has not kept pace with the globalization of trade and production. Even large companies, in most cases, perform most of their research and development (R&D) at home (Pavitt and Patel 1999). On the aggregate level, only U.S. data are available. These are shown in Table 11, which points to growing R&D expenditures of foreign affiliates of U.S. MNEs in absolute numbers. Although growing in absolute numbers, R&D expenditures of foreign affiliates of U.S. MNEs account for a rather constant share of these expenditures in the whole expenditure for R&D of U.S. MNEs. This share stands at about 10 percent. Globalization thus includes increasing international flows of knowledge and technology, but not the internationalization of knowledge production on a large scale. Knowledge production remains a task predominantly performed in the home country. The large and rising flows of knowledge from the home country to the host countries (Table 8) reflect the dependence of the internationalized production on R&D and other information goods which are supplied by the parent company. U.S. parent companies received royalties and license fees of $23.3 billion in 1999 but bought technology for only $2.0 billion. U.S. affiliates of foreign MNEs received $7.7 billion and paid $1.6 billion (U.S. Department of Commerce 2000b, 2000a). The reluctance of U.S. companies to conduct R&D in foreign countries can probably not be explained with comparative advantages of the United States in R&D. If this were the reason, R&D expenditures of affiliates of non-U.S. MNEs in the United States would be higher. With $19.6 billion in 1998, they have been only slightly higher than expenditures of foreign affiliates of U.S. MNEs. Foreign R&D activities often focus on the application of production processes and goods to the conditions in the foreign market.

To sum up, one phenomenon of globalization is the rising speed of the international spread of new know-how and technology, especially among developed countries. MNEs are the most important vehicle of international knowledge transfer. These intrafirm transfers of technology, which account for a very large share of technology flows, keep knowledge as a very important source of competitive advantages within the boundaries of the firm. To ensure the exclusive

Table 11:
R&D Expenditure of U.S. MNEs and U.S. Affiliates of Foreign MNEs, 1982–
1998

	U.S. parents ($ mil.)	Foreign affiliates of U.S. MNEs ($ mil.)	Foreign affiliates share[a] (percent)	U.S. affiliates of foreign MNEs ($ mil.)
1982	38,157	3,647	8.72	3,744
1989	59,925	7,048	10.52	9,465
1991	67,457	9,358	12.18	11,772
1995	96,500	14,075	12.02	17,500
1998	114,201	14,986	11.60	19,690[b]

[a]R&D expenditure of foreign affiliates of U.S. MNEs / (R&D expenditure of U.S. parent + foreign affiliates of U.S. MNEs) x 100. — [b]1997.

Source: U.S. Department of Commerce (various issues); own calculations.

but global use of this knowledge, internationalization of knowledge protection is extended. However, the internationalization of knowledge production has not increased significantly over the last two decades. Knowledge is produced at home and exported to the foreign affiliates of an MNE. Thereby, growing trade in headquarter services contributes to the rise in trade in services.

2.1.3   International Trade

Traditionally, trade has been the most important channel of the integration of the world economy. It is a very recent phenomenon that the internationalization of production challenges the role of trade in goods and services as the most important aspect of economic integration. Since the end of World War II, international trade has pushed worldwide economic integration. Its growth rates exceeded production growth rates by far. Figure 1 documents this process for the last 25 years.

Merchandise exports have almost tripled in nominal terms since 1980. Like FDI flows and the transfer of knowledge and technology, trade takes place mostly between developed countries (Table 12). The merchandise export share of developed countries in total merchandise exports has remained relatively stable at about two-thirds throughout the last two decades. The emergence of the Asian exporting countries has not changed this dominance of developed countries. Trade in merchandise goods has been the largest component in world trade in the analyzed period. The other component, trade in services, has grown a bit faster than trade in goods. Its share in total trade has increased marginally to about 20 percent in 1999 (WTO various issues).

Table 12:
Nominal World Merchandise Exports and Regional Export Shares, 1980–2000

	World exports	OECD countries	USA	UK	Germany	Japan	Developing countries
	$ bil.			percent			
1980	1,932	65.5	11.7	5.7	9.9	6.7	34.5
1985	1,875	68.4	11.7	5.4	9.7	9.4	31.6
1990	3,423	71.7	11.5	5.4	11.9	8.4	28.3
1995	5,104	68.0	11.5	4.7	10.2	8.7	32.0
2000	6,360	62.8	12.6	4.4	8.6	7.5	37.2

Source: IMF (2000); own calculations.

What cannot be seen in Figure 1 is that the structure of trade has changed within this 26-year time span. Intraindustry trade first accompanied and then exceeded traditional interindustry trade. Countries, especially developed countries, now trade increasingly different varieties of similar products. As early as 1971, Grubel and Lloyd (1971) pointed to the fact that a large and increasing share of trade especially between developed countries takes place within the same industry. The development of a new group of international trade models, the new trade theory, was motivated by the empirical findings of the composition of trade, especially the high intraindustry trade (IIT) shares (Greenaway and Torstensson 1997). These high IIT shares are mainly explained by imperfect competition on world markets. Comparative advantages are not seen as the driving force behind IIT, although advantages which result from technological differences can also explain intraindustry trade. Table 13 shows IIT shares for Germany and its most important trading partners on basis of bilateral trade volumes. German companies increased their trade with all three trading partners shown in Table 13. The IIT share of German trade within the group of European countries is highest for France, Germany's largest trading partner. It even exceeded 80 percent in 1996 (Heitger et al. 1999). High trade volumes seem to be related to high IIT shares. The rank correlation coefficient between the IIT share and the volume of bilateral German trade with its 14 European trading partners is 0.94, which exceeds the critical value of 0.55.

The high IIT shares shown in Table 13 might result partly from trade in intermediate goods. The largest share of inputs in the production of a good usually comes from the same industry. Imports of intermediate goods and raw materials make up for approximately one-half of all imports of developed economies. Trade in intermediate goods is partly caused by differences in the endowments with natural resources between the countries. For example, the share of imported intermediate goods and raw materials in the wood products & furniture sector in Canada with 46.0 percent of all imports in this sector in 1990 is much lower than

Table 13:
Inter- and Intraindustry Trade Shares of Germany and Its Most Important Trading Partners (percent)

	European Union		United States		Japan	
	1988	1996	1988	1996	1988	1996
Interindustry Trade	36.7	32.9	55.8	35.7	64.8	57.6
Intraindustry Trade	63.3	67.1	44.2	64.3	35.3	42.4

Source: Heitger et al. (1999: 107).

in Japan with 90.7 percent in 1990, because Canada is better endowed with wood. But for manufacturing sectors such as nonelectrical machinery, professional goods, or motor vehicles, where the production process is likely to be less raw-material dependent, the share of imported input in total input is also very high. It stays at approximately 50 percent (Table 14).

The most interesting group for this analysis is the one which I called here technology-intensive industries. The industries belonging to this group are listed in Table 14. Their production processes involve many different stages, with different requirements. The reasons for importing intermediate goods can be very different. Availability is, of course, one reason. Different factor contents are another reason to import inputs from countries with comparative advantages in the production of these inputs. Technological leadership of a company in a foreign country is another reason to import intermediate inputs from a technically superior country. Finally, established networks are another reason for increasing intermediate imports when companies internationalize their production.

Table 15 shows the change in the imported-input share in total imports of the more technology-intensive sectors from 1970 to 1990. More recent data are not available from the OECD input-output data set. Shares and changes are rather similar across the OECD countries shown here. Interestingly, smaller countries do not have larger shares of imported inputs in general, as might be expected given the impossibility to support all stages of production in all industries in smaller countries. Remoteness does not seem to be an obstacle to high imports in intermediate goods (at least relative to total imports) as the high shares of Australia point out. European countries do also not seem to have higher imported-input shares than non-European countries.

The share of imported inputs in total imports of technology-intensive sectors remained stable at about 50 percent over the 1970s and 1980s. The share increased noticeable only in the United Kingdom starting from the lowest level of all countries. Thereby, the share of imported inputs in total imports of the United Kingdom converged to levels of other OECD countries. Given the mostly

Table 14:
Share of Imported Inputs to Total Imports, 1990 (percent)

	Agriculture, mining, and manufacturing	Raw-material-intensive industries[a]	Technology-intensive industries[b]
Australia	52.4	80.5	45.5
Canada	55.4	72.4	53.5
Denmark	57.6	86.6	46.5
France	56.5	84.4	47.7
Germany	53.0	77.4	44.8
Japan	70.8	91.7	48.0
Netherlands	63.5	88.5	52.8
United Kingdom	58.2	86.1	53.4
United States	48.4	71.4	40.5

[a]Wood products and furniture, paper, paper products and printing, petroleum and coal products, nonmetallic mineral products, iron and steel, nonferrous metals. — [b]Industrial chemicals, drugs and medicine, rubber and plastic products, metal products, nonelectrical machinery, office and computing machinery, electrical apparatus, radio, TV and communication equipment, shipbuilding and repairing, motor vehicles, aircraft, other transport, professional goods.

Source: OECD (1997); own calculations.

Table 15:
Imported-Inputs Share in Total Imports of the Technology-Intensive Sectors, 1970–1990 (percent)

	1970	1975	1980	1985	1990
Australia	50.7[a]	50.2[b]	n.a.	51.7[c]	45.5[d]
Canada	53.1[e]	49.9[f]	47.7[g]	51.0[c]	53.5
Denmark	45.7[h]	45.9[i]	47.5	47.4	44.3
France	51.6[h]	51.6[i]	52.6	52.3	47.7
Germany	n.a.	n.a.	52.1[j]	50.6[c]	44.8
Japan	43.3	53.7	60.0	60.1	48.0
Netherlands	54.3	52.3	58.8[g]	52.8[c]	n.a.
United Kingdom	35.0[a]	n.a.	48.7	41.3	53.4
United States	40.5[h]	41.1[i]	40.9[k]	44.2	40.5

[a]1968. — [b]1974. — [c]1986. — [d]1989. — [e]1971. — [f]1976. — [g]1981. — [h]1972. — [i]1977. — [j]1978. — [k]1982.

Source: OECD (1997); own calculations.

stable shares, trade in intermediate goods in technology-intensive sectors increased, therefore, as fast as total trade. Since total trade experienced a strong increase in the last three decades and grew faster than production, imported inputs used in production increased relative to total inputs. This can be seen in Table 16 where imported intermediate inputs are shown relative to total inputs used in production.

Table 16:
Import Shares of Intermediate Inputs in Total Intermediate Inputs in Technology-Intensive Sectors, 1970–1990 (percent)

	1970	1975	1980	1985	1990
Australia	17.8[a]	20.3[b]	n.a.	24.1[c]	23.7[d]
Canada	31.5[e]	33.9[f]	34.6[g]	40.8[c]	40.0
Denmark	45.7[h]	45.9[i]	47.5	47.4	44.3
France	18.3[h]	20.0[i]	21.1	24.4	24.6
Germany	n.a.	n.a.	15.2[j]	16.9[c]	16.8
Japan	3.4	3.8	5.0	4.9	5.2
Netherlands	47.4	47.1	52.4[g]	49.9[c]	n.a.
United Kingdom	12.6[a]	n.a.	22.8	28.0	30.7
United States	5.1[h]	6.3[i]	7.5[k]	9.3	11.0
Weighted average	14.2	15.8	17.3	20.0	19.3

[a]1968. — [b]1974. — [c]1986. — [d]1989. — [e]1971. — [f]1976. — [g]1981. — [h]1972. — [i]1977. — [j]1978. — [k]1982.

Source: OECD (1997); own calculations.

Table 16 shows large differences in the use of imported intermediate inputs in technology-intensive sectors between the countries. Small countries tend to rely much more on imported inputs than large countries. For economies-of-scale reasons, large countries can more easily support every stage of production in many differentiated goods than small countries (Hummels et al. 1998). This could explain the low import shares of intermediate goods used in production in the United States, Japan, and Germany. However, in particular Germany's low share is surprising, since it is situated in an integrating area with generally high trade volumes and a distinct division of labor. Australia suffers from its geographical "isolation", which lowers the degree of openness.

The average import share of intermediate goods used by companies in the nine countries increased from 14.2 percent in 1970 to 19.3 percent in 1990. This is an increase of 36 percent in 20 years, which indicates a higher integration of these countries in the world economy. Larger imports of intermediate goods could be the link between larger foreign production and larger international trade (Kleinert 2003). With increasing FDI stocks, the share of production which takes place in foreign affiliates of MNE increases, too. Affiliates' sales in foreign countries overtook exports in the late 1970s and have continued to grow at higher rates than exports (Figure 2). Sales by foreign affiliates give the upper bound of "foreign production" since they include sales of "pure" sales units, which import finished goods and sell them to local consumers. Sales minus intrafirm exports from the parent company to the affiliates give the lower bound of foreign production since they exclude not only finished-goods sales abroad but intrafirm exports of intermediate goods as well.

Figure 2:
Exports and Sales by Foreign Affiliates Worldwide, 1980–1998

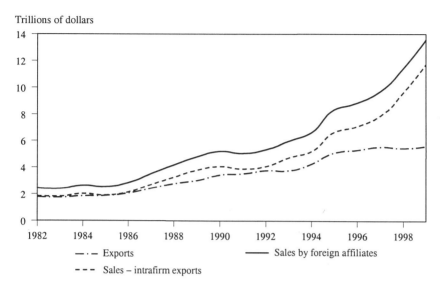

Trillions of dollars

— · — Exports ——— Sales by foreign affiliates

— — — Sales – intrafirm exports

Source: UNCTAD (1998, 1999).

Expanding MNE networks, which are connected by intense trade relations between parent companies and affiliates and between the affiliates, could be the explanation for growing trade and growing production abroad. Of course, substitution of exports by foreign production may occur for some products, but new trade opportunities, especially in intermediate and capital goods, are also opened up with the internationalization of production. Both effects, the substitution effect and the trade creation effect, are found in MITI (2000), which studied the consequences of the increased foreign activities of Japanese companies. Figure 3 shows, in addition to the amount of foreign affiliates' sales by Japanese MNEs, only the trade creation effects of the internationalization of production. Japanese companies increased their exports of intermediate goods to foreign affiliates. Japanese (re)imports increased with the imports from their foreign affiliates, but to a much lower degree. The trade-reducing substitution effect is not shown in Figure 3. The size of the substitution effect on exports through foreign production could not be found for the whole period in MITI (2000). A rough estimation for the early 1990s can be found in MITI (1998). Throughout the analyzed period, the substitution effect is significantly smaller than the trade creation through additional intermediate-goods exports.

Figure 3:

Sales by Japanese Affiliates, Japanese Exports of Intermediate Goods to Foreign Affiliates, and Japanese Reverse Imports from Foreign Affiliates, 1987–1998

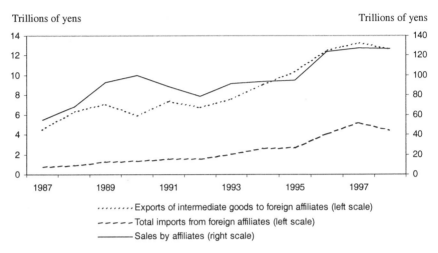

Source: MITI (2000).

Exports of intermediate goods to foreign affiliates of Japanese MNEs have increased remarkably in this rather short period. A large fraction of these exports takes place within companies. Japanese intrafirm export levels rose from 12.8 percent of Japan's total exports in 1986 to 26.6 percent in 1998 (MITI 2000). High intermediate-goods shares in intrafirm trade are not specific to Japanese companies. In 1994, more than half of all U.S. MNEs' intrafirm exports have been exports in intermediate goods (U.S. Department of Commerce 1998). The intermediate-goods share of Swedish MNEs' exports in 1990 was even higher, with about two-thirds of MNEs' total exports (Andersson and Fredriksson 2000).

The increase in intrafirm trade volume is an often-noticed fact. UNCTAD (1998) estimated the intrafirm trade share in total trade to be about one-third. Table 17 shows the rising share of U.S. MNE intrafirm trade in the last 20 years. The same holds for trade of U.S. affiliates of foreign MNEs with their parent companies. Intrafirm exports of U.S. affiliates of foreign MNEs decreased in its share in the total U.S. exports from 11.6 percent in 1982 to 8.4 percent in 1998. This slowed the increase in the total intrafirm export share. In 1998, 35.6 percent of U.S. exports were intrafirm exports, compared with 33.5 percent in 1982 (U.S. Department of Commerce various issues). However, the role of MNEs in trade is larger than the 35 percent intrafirm trade. About 65 percent of total U.S. exports

Table 17:
U.S. MNE-Related U.S. Exports, 1982–1998

	Total exports	U.S. MNE-related exports	Intra-U.S. firm exports	Share (intra firm/ total exports)
	$ mil.			percent
1982	212,275	163,383	46,559	21.9
1985	218,815	171,904	57,567	26.3
1989	363,836	236,371	86,050	23.7
1991	421,763	262,005	115,258	27.3
1993	465,090	274,666	113,762	24.5
1995	584,742	362,610	149,740	25.6
1997	689,182	441,272	183,062	26.6
1998	682,138	438,292	185,372	27.2

Source: U.S. Department of Commerce (various issues); own calculations.

in 1998 have been related to U.S. MNEs, i.e., at least one of the trading partners belonged to an U.S. MNE. However, in addition to U.S. MNEs, MNEs which have their headquarters in other countries are also active in the U.S. market. To account for their activities but avoid double counting, only the 8 percent U.S. exports which result from foreign MNEs' intrafirm trade are added. This gives the lower bound of the role of MNEs in U.S. exports. In U.S. imports, the role of MNEs is almost as important (with at least 61 percent in 1998).

To sum up, foreign trade has kept its position as the most important channel of economic integration also in the era of globalization, although the internationalization of production has risen even more dynamically in recent years. Foreign trade has continued to increase more strongly than world industrial production since the mid-1980s. This development is mainly driven by MNEs which hold an important position in international trade. Approximately one-third of worldwide trade takes place within MNEs, and about 80 percent involve at least one MNE at one side of the transaction. This trade is increasingly intraindustry trade and consists to one-half of intermediate-goods trade. International trade is concentrated on developed countries, which have remarkably intensified their trade relations.

2.1.4   Conclusions

Globalization is a process which moves separated national economies towards an integrated world economy. This includes a widening and a deepening of economic integration. The widening results from including new countries like the developing countries of Latin America or the former socialist countries in Central and Eastern Europe in the global economic system. The deepening, which is the focus of this analysis, mainly takes place among developed countries. The intensive use of three channels—international trade, FDI, and international technology flows—gives economic integration a new quality in the era of globalization.

The internationalization of economic activity is driven to a large extent by MNEs. At least 80 percent of international trade is related to MNEs. One-third takes place within MNEs. A large share of international trade is intraindustry trade between developed countries. This holds also for the large share of trade in intermediate goods. The same holds for FDI, which is strongly concentrated on developed countries. Intraindustry FDI shares in total FDI are also remarkably high. Furthermore, FDI and trade are concentrated on a few industries. Concentration in developed countries is most pronounced in technology flows. Their increase, driven by intra-MNE knowledge flows which account for 80 percent of all flows of technology, points to the internationalization of knowledge and technology use. However, the internationalization of knowledge production remains rather modest. Research and development is still largely a headquarter service supplied by the parent company and applied by foreign affiliates.

Given this strong position of MNEs in globalization, an analysis of the globalization process must take the activities of MNEs explicitly into account. In the next section, I survey the theoretical literature on emergence and activities of MNEs. The survey is focused on general equilibrium approaches, mostly developed from trade models, because they seem most suitable to study the globalization process. In particular, I present models which are based on the proximity-concentration approach because this approach allows one to explain intensified international activities between developed countries. By using this approach, the rise of foreign trade, production abroad, and international technology transfer can be analyzed in one framework.

2.2   Approaches to the Multinational Company: A Selective Review of the Literature

The first studies of the determinants and decisive characteristics of MNE activities were motivated by the increasing importance of foreign affiliates of U.S. companies in Europe and Latin America in the 1950s and 1960s. Company-specific and country-specific approaches were brought forward to explain this development. Surveys of this work can be found in Dunning (1973), Hufbauer (1975), Agarwal (1980), and Stehn (1992). In my short review of the literature, only Mundel's approach to capital movement, Vernon's product cycle approach, and Kojima's extension of Akamatsu's flying wild geese pattern are shortly discussed. These approaches explain FDI of advanced countries in developing countries on the basis of comparative advantage.

However, since the early 1980s at the latest, a new bi-directional pattern of activities of MNEs from developed countries has become dominant. For an explanation of this pattern, new approaches were needed. The management literature initiated a conceptual change. Not FDI or capital flows, but the MNE itself became the object of analysis. Two major approaches to MNEs have been developed: the eclectic approach and the transaction cost approach to MNEs. I discuss them in Section 2.2.2. The eclectic approach, also known as OLI framework, points to three requirements necessary for an MNE to exist: the company must possess ownership advantages, the location where an activity is carried out must have advantages over alternative locations, and it must be advantageous to internalize the activity into the company. If these three conditions are met, an MNE arises. The other approach applies Coase's and Williamson's transaction cost approach to multinational firms. Thus, the internalization decision is in the center of interest.

Since the early 1980s, new approaches have inspired theoretical analyses. They have incorporated MNEs into the microeconomic, general equilibrium theory of international trade. I discuss these approaches in subsequent sections. In Section 2.2.3, I discuss a factor proportion approach developed from the Heckscher–Ohlin framework. MNEs allow for an extension of the factor-price-equalization set. MNEs emerge when countries are very different. Thereby, MNEs are based in one country, thus bi-directional activities cannot be explained. The approach might be suitable to analyze the activities of MNEs from developed countries in developing countries. The strength of the approaches in Section 2.2.4 is their ability to explain bi-directional activities of MNEs. Companies can choose how to serve the foreign market: through exports or production abroad. These approaches take market imperfections into account. Production takes place in a multistage process which relies on fixed production factors. Markets are separated by distance costs. Theories along this line are able to explain much of the observed pattern of MNE activities.

2.2.1 Earlier Explanations of the Existence of Multinational Enterprises

Earlier works that introduced capital movements in international economics do not distinguish FDI from other kinds of cross-border capital flows. Capital flows are seen as motivated by differences in interest rates between countries which result from differences in relative factor endowments and time preferences between the countries (Mundell 1957). Factor price equalization can be achieved by international trade or by factor movements depending on the cost of the different strategies. Given identical technology and consumer preferences, perfect competition on the product markets, and the absence of distortions on the factor markets, only the international factor movement is important. In the model, bank credits, portfolio investment, and FDI are not distinguishable from each other. Above that, the mode of capital transfer is irrelevant, since the factor price equalization can be achieved by any of these. Given the structure of the model there is no room for a particular role of MNEs.

Vernon (1966) takes a microeconomic look at MNEs and FDI. The position of a company's product in the product cycle is decisive for its strategy. New products are developed by the technological leader and sold only at home in their early phase. That is because the high price of modern, fashionable, high-quality products can only be afforded by consumers in a country with high per capita income, i.e., the technological leader. The price drops in the second phase of the life cycle because of learning curve effects and economies of scale in larger markets. The product becomes affordable for consumers in foreign countries with lower per capita income as well. The technological leader starts to export the good. The former innovative product becomes a standardized mass product. Comparative advantages become more important in production; innovation rents decrease. Markets grow in the foreign countries and start to mature at home. Companies from other countries enter the market and compete with the leading company, first in their home market in the foreign country, later via exports in the innovating company's market. To keep a competitive edge the innovator may choose to relocate production to a cheaper foreign location. FDI takes place which includes the transfer of capital, skilled labor, know-how, an organizational form, and a supplier network.

Kojima (1973) extended Vernon's approach and integrated it into Akamatsu's (1961) flying wild geese model to explain the development of production, investment, and trade pattern in Asia. He combines firm-specific and country-specific explanations for the emergence of MNEs. In this model, the production of goods within industries is handed over from the technological leader to the follower countries according to comparative advantages. Comparative advantages result from differences in technologies used in different countries and from differences in factor endowments. Factor endowments are seen as endogenous over time. Capital and human capital are accumulated over time, a process which is fostered by structural changes. The structural change results in a succession of countries producing a good. The pattern does not apply only to goods within one industry which differ in quality but also between industries that differ in capital and/or human capital intensities.

These early approaches can explain comparative-advantage-driven FDI of advanced countries in developing countries. Until the 1970s, this seemed to be the dominant pattern, since U.S. companies' FDI in Western Europe could be interpreted as investment in catching-up countries. But when Western Europe and Japan had caught up, two-way investment, even two-way cross investment within an industry, emerged and gained importance. Parallel to factor proportion theories of international trade, factor proportion theories of FDI increasingly missed parts of the story. Other, complementary explanations were looked for and found in the OLI paradigm and the transaction cost approach. Not the FDI pattern, but the MNE itself became the focus of analysis.

2.2.2   The OLI Paradigm and the Transaction Cost Approach

Because of the increasing importance of MNEs, research on their activities has increasingly received attention within the field of economics. First studies came from the management literature (Hymer 1960; Dunning 1977; Buckley and Casson 1976) which structured the knowledge on MNEs and explained the existence of MNEs with market imperfections. The eclectic paradigm (Dunning 1980) and the transaction cost approach were brought forward (Buckley and Casson 1985). Both stressed the importance of intangible assets for understanding the existence of MNEs. In particular, a firm's technological skills and marketing abilities were seen as important determinants for FDI. Research and development expenditures (as proxy variable for technological skills) were harnessed in many empirical analyses of MNEs and FDI.

The eclectic approach became known as OLI paradigm because, according to this theory, there are three conditions that must be satisfied for an MNE to emerge: *Ownership* advantage, *location* advantage and *internalization* advantage. FDI can only be profitable if the investing company has some kind of ownership advantage: knowledge of a product or a production process which gives the company an advantage over domestic companies to make up for the disadvantages the company has by producing in a foreign country. The emergence of MNEs is, therefore, bound to market imperfections. Perfect competition and MNEs cannot go together in this approach. The location an MNE chooses to invest in must have a location advantage, not only compared to the home country of the MNE, but also to all other possible locations. And it must be profitable to internalize the ownership advantage in the company. Licensing of the product or process to foreign companies, for instance, as an alternative to internalization must be inferior.

The transaction cost approach gives internalization more weight than the ownership and the location advantage, the other two characteristics which a company has to possess in order to become an MNE. According to the theory of the firm, developed by Coase (1937) and Williamson (1973), MNEs have the choice of market transaction or intrafirm transaction for production and complementary activities (marketing). The decision is made on basis of relative costs of both transaction modes. An MNE emerges if it is cheaper for a company to internalize a transaction which is carried out across national borders. Ownership advantages are important in the transaction cost approach, too, since they constitute the firm. The ownership advantage generates market power, which enables the firm to escape from perfect competition, where strategic decisions of companies, such as the one to become an MNE, have no room. But the focus of the transaction cost approach is different. Buckley and Casson (1985: 18) state that "the existence of separate (and separable) ownership advantages is doubtful and logically redundant because internalization explains why firms exist in the absence of such advantages."

Since the mid-1980s, various efforts have been made to formulize the different explanations of FDI in order to give them a rigorous theoretical formulation. Building on the transaction cost approach, Ethier (1986) endogenized the internalization decision in a two-by-two-by-two general equilibrium model. Ethier assumes a production process which involves an upstream activity, located in the home country, and a downstream activity which must locate in both countries. Companies must decide whether licensing or supply through a foreign affiliate is the more profitable strategy in serving the foreign market. The basic problem is to distinguish those cases in which upstream and downstream units can deal with each other at arm's length from those in which internalization of the transaction is more profitable. Simple (state-invariant) contracts can be agreed on ex ante, but an agreement on more complex ones cannot be reached. When the partners agree on a contract ex ante, licensing is possible. The incompleteness of more complex contracting causes a problem. Given the uncertainty about the future, there might still be too many unknown states the contract partners cannot agree on. In Ethier (1986), optimal contracts vary across ex ante unknown states (they are therefore not state-invariant) if the endowment differences of the two countries are modest and the ownership advantage of a company is large. Then, no licensing contracts can be closed. Affiliate production steps in. In this setting, activities of MNEs are more pronounced between similar countries. Bi-directional activities within the same industry can be explained. Other papers which aim at endogenization of the internalization decision include Horstmann and Markusen (1987), Ethier and Markusen (1996), Saggi (1999), Grossman and Helpman (2002), and Antràs (2003).

Another direction that built more on the OLI paradigm included MNEs into microeconomic general equilibrium trade models, the traditional workhorse of international economics. I survey this line of research, which takes internalization as given, in the next two subsections. The work of Helpman (1984) on the one hand, and Krugman (1983) and Markusen (1984) on the other introduced two explanations of MNEs' activities. The explanations differ in scope and technique and were the origin of two lines of research, i.e., the factor proportion theory and the proximity-concentration approach.

2.2.3 Factor Proportion Theory

Helpman (1984, 1985), Helpman and Krugman (1985), and Krugman (1995b) explain the emergence of MNEs within the perfect competition framework used in trade theory. In its simplest version by Krugman (1995b), the two countries, capital-rich Home and labor-rich Foreign, are endowed only with these two production factors: capital K and labor L. There are two industries, X and Y, with X producing many differentiated products. In the X industry, a two-stage production process with different factor intensities in each stage is assumed. The production output of the first stage, called headquarter service H, can be traded within the company but not on an arm's length basis. If the factor endowment distribution is too uneven and factor price equalization is, therefore, not possible, i.e., the endowment point lies outside the factor-price-equalization set (like E^* in Figure 4), trade alone cannot equalize factor costs even with full specialization. A trade equilibrium is, therefore, not first best. Because of the factor cost differences, FDI is profitable, since wages w are lower in the capital-scarce foreign country. Capital-rich home country's endowment will be employed by a combination of stand-alone headquarters ($O_H R$ in Figure 4) and integrated X industry operations (RE^* in Figure 4).[2] The foreign country produces the Y good ($O_F S$ in Figure 4), the production stage of the X industry products, which is supplied with headquarter services from the stand-alone headquarters in the home country (SE^* in Figure 4) and (depending on endowment) the remainder of the X products.

Inside the trade factor equalization set $O_H Q_F O_F Q_H$ there is no reason for FDI and multinational production. Outside this set, however, FDI is welfare-increasing because it widens the (trade) factor-price-equalization set. First-best allocations can be achieved even between countries which are too different in factor endowment to achieve factor price equalization through trade. An equilibrium with MNEs is in general not balanced in trade in physical goods. The trade balance deficit is offset by a surplus in trade in (headquarter) service of the same size. Approaches in this tradition give good reasoning for vertical integration and outsourcing (Venables 1999; Eckel 2000a), but since this theory depends on factor price differences, it fails to explain the large investment in

---

[2] One more assumption is needed: the equilibrium should include as little direct investment as possible.

Figure 4:
Equilibrium with MNEs in the Home Country

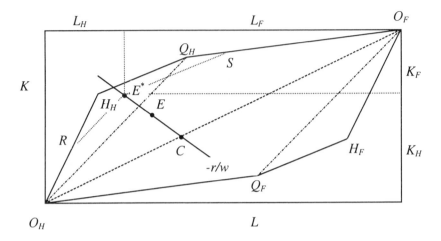

industrialized countries in general and bi-directional intraindustry cross-invest-ment in particular. The main problem, however, is that "multinationals fit awk-wardly into perfect-competition trade theory. After all, the whole subject is con-cerned with the way that the boundaries of firms may cut across the boundaries of nations; yet in a perfectly competitive, constant-returns model firms are essentially invisible" (Krugman 1995b: 1257).

2.2.4   Proximity-Concentration Models

Beginning with Krugman (1983), trade theorists included MNEs in imperfect competition models because MNEs generally work in oligopolistic markets. Krugman (1983) started from a monopolistic competition trade model with two countries, Home and Foreign. Each country uses only labor as single factor of production. Labor force is equal in both countries. Within each country, any of a large number of differentiated goods can be produced. Because of fixed costs in production, there is an optimal output level of each of the differentiated goods which are produced in equilibrium. Hence, given the factor constraints not all goods can be produced. Although consumers love variety, the number of goods produced in equilibrium is smaller than the number of potential goods. It is assumed that it is not profitable for a company to produce more than one good. Companies producing the different varieties engage in monopolistic competition.

The different but symmetric varieties are sold at the same price and produced at the same output level. Although technology is assumed to be the same in both countries and the two countries start out identical, they end by specializing in the production of a different bundle of a few differentiated goods.

Markets in the two countries are segmented by transport cost of the iceberg type: a part $1-g$ (with $g < 1$) of a shipped good smelts away, only the fraction g arrives. Since there are identical consumer preferences, technologies, and factor endowments in both countries, the only reason for trade is to enlarge the consumption bundle by importing other varieties of the differentiated good from the foreign country. Even with transport costs there are gains from trade which stem from the exchange of varieties from different bundles of the horizontally differentiated goods in which the two countries have specialized their production. Trade leads to an enlargement of the numbers of the differentiated goods available for the consumer.

Krugman reinterpreted the model in a way that it can be used as a theory of MNEs. The fixed costs were thought of as occurring not in the production but in the development of a product. This implies that fixed costs incur only once even if the production takes place in more than one location. This results from the nonrivalry in the intrafirm use of the headquarter service, i.e. the product development. Production in the foreign country becomes an alternative to trade in goods. Production could be done by a local producer who required the "blueprint" of the product by licensing or in an affiliate of an MNE. Krugman rules out licensing by assumption. If production abroad is as easy as production at home, overseas production dominates exports, since no transport costs incur when producing abroad. But it is an often-noted fact that production abroad is more costly than at home. Krugman (1983) assumes a productivity of k (with $k < 1$) of foreign relative to home production. Companies choose exports to serve the foreign market if $g > k$, and production abroad otherwise. They trade off higher productivity against transport costs.

If $k > g$, overseas production is welfare-increasing for both countries. The budget line shifts outward. The reason is that while trade in goods incurs transport costs, trade in headquarter services does not. In the MNE equilibrium, the headquarter service is traded between the two countries and replaces goods trade. Countries acquire different technologies and develop different goods. They can trade this knowledge directly through a transfer within the MNE or they can trade it embodied in physical goods. The choice depends on the productivity-transportation cost tradeoff. Multinationals are a vehicle for trade in knowledge.

Multinationals as the vehicle of trade in knowledge is also the rationale behind Markusen's (1984) approach to MNEs. Markusen develops a theory of MNEs driven by economies of multiplant operation which satisfies five conditions. (i) The theory gives a reason why a firm wants to engage in FDI rather than portfolio investment. (ii) The emergence of MNEs is independent of factor movements or factor price differences. (iii) The model explains why multiplant operation is superior to price collusion among independent suppliers. (iv) It gives an explanation why companies choose not to export instead, and (v) the analysis allows for positive economic profits of companies in the imperfect competitive sector, since different allocation of profits have important implications for welfare.

Markusen's multiplant firms approach is motivated by the fact that firm-specific activities such as R&D, marketing, or management often show a public good character within the company. They can be used jointly by additional plants, without reducing the marginal productivity of any existing plant of the firm. These activities are centralized in the headquarters (headquarter services). Fixed costs in Markusen's approach are split into a company and a plant fixed costs bloc. The ownership advantage a company possesses over its rivals stems often from firm-specific, not plant-specific activities. The efficiency advantage of multiplant firms lies, therefore, in its ability to avoid duplication in the supply of headquarter services.

In contrast to Krugman (1983), Markusen models the imperfect competition sector X as duopolistic and not as a sector of monopolistic competition. This allows for economic profits, which are competed away by free entry in the Krugman model. The X good is the result of two activities: company level output C and plant level output F. C and F can be geographically separated. The C activity, which is located at a single location, has public good characteristics in the sense that an additional F may be added to the firm without reducing the marginal product of C in the existing F activities. The other assumptions, two goods (X and Y), two countries (home m and host h), identical taste, endowment, and technology in both countries, fixed total endowment, perfect competition in the Y sector, and no cross-border factor mobility apply as well for Markusen (1984) as for Krugman (1983). A further difference is the absence of trade barriers in the Markusen model. Markusen (1984) has one additional assumption concerning the imperfect competition sector X: it is thought of being very small, too small to support more than one company.

Again, Heckscher–Ohlin, Ricardian, and demand-based trade are excluded by assumption. Only the multiplant operation economies affect the pattern of trade and production. Markusen compares an equilibrium with two national monopolies to an equilibrium which include an MNE with headquarter in the m country to show that, first, the efficient production frontier in the MNE equilibrium always lies outside the efficient production frontier in equilibria with national companies in both countries because of the avoidance of duplication in the supply of the C activity. Second, if the MNE increases the output of the X good, this is a sufficient condition for the MNE to increase real world income.

Third, whereas the home country always gains, host countries' gains depend on the pricing of the MNE and the ability of the host country's government to retain a share of the MNE profits via a tax. Fourth, countries in the MNE equilibrium have different factor prices, with higher factor prices for the factor used intensively in its dominant activity. Fifth, MNE activities are trade-creating.

Horstmann and Markusen (1992) proceed on the line of Markusen (1984) by endogenizing the market structure. Whereas in Markusen (1984) market structure with or without MNE in one country is exogenously given, in Horstmann and Markusen (1992) companies in the two countries decide about their plant configuration. The structure of the model is set up as in Markusen's earlier work: two sectors, one of them too small to support more than one company in each country. Technology in the industry requires fixed costs at the plant and the company level. In both of the two (symmetric) countries, such an industry exists. Companies in the imperfect-competition sector play a two-stage simultaneous game. At the first stage, they decide about entry and plant configuration, i.e., they choose to build a plant in both countries and become an MNE or to produce only at home and serve the foreign market by exports. At the second stage, companies engage in Cournot competition in quantities.

The plant configuration choice of companies is made by comparing profits under different configurations. Such profits are dependent on exogenous technology parameters such as fixed costs at plant and company level and on transport costs separating the two countries. A structure with two national exporting companies arises in equilibrium, when fixed costs at plant level are large relative to company level fixed costs and transport costs. Two possible equilibria with MNE can arise. One, as in Markusen (1984), with one MNE existing in equilibrium and a second with two MNEs in equilibrium, one from each country. These situations come up when plant-specific costs are relatively low compared to company-specific costs. If the sum of fixed costs at plant and company level is low enough to support two MNEs, the second equilibrium arises.

The Krugman (1983) and the Markusen (1984) approach have been further developed since then. Brainard (1993) introduced a general equilibrium model that integrates central features of the former two in a more general model. By choosing between different strategies of overseas expansion (exports or production abroad), a company faces the tradeoff between proximity and concentration. Proximity describes the advantage of being close to customers; concentration describes the advantage of using economies of scale by production at only one location. Brainard goes beyond Krugman in modeling the concentration advantage by assuming fixed costs at the company and the plant level in the production of the differentiated good sector. Furthermore, Brainard's monopolistic competition market structure includes the duopolistic structure of Markusen as a special case.

To allow for an analytical solution, the model assumes two identical countries. With identical absolute and relative factor endowments, there is no room for factor-based multinational activities. As in the Krugman (1983) model, differentiated goods and love of variety of consumers motivate international activities of companies in manufacturing. The differentiated goods bundle consumed by each individual is enlarged by international activities. Companies can serve the foreign market by exports or by production abroad. Markets in the two countries are separated by transport costs. This gives domestic companies an advantage over foreign competitors, since foreign goods are more expensive for consumers in the home market. Hence, there is a home market bias in consumption.

Additionally, there are imperfections in production in manufacturing. It is assumed that production in the manufacturing sector requires fixed inputs. Companies in this sector produce in two stages: a headquarter and a production stage. In the first stage, headquarter services are produced such as R&D, marketing, management, or a brand name using only fixed inputs. The headquarter service can be used on a nonrival basis in more than one plant of the company. In the second stage, the actual good is produced in the plant using fixed and variable inputs. The fixed inputs are buildings, facilities, and equipment. They cannot be used on a nonrival basis but must be supplied for each plant. Hence, there are economies of scale in production, resulting from the need to use fixed inputs.

Companies can serve the foreign market by exports or by production abroad. Exports save on additional fixed costs at the plant level; production abroad saves on (variable) transport costs. A company's decision whether to set up a foreign affiliate or to export its differentiated good depends on the conditions of competition, technology, and consumption parameters. The attractiveness of multi-plant production (and, therefore, FDI) is due to the use of economies of scope which result from the nonrivalry in the use of the headquarter service.

Brainard models a two-stage game for the companies in the differentiated-goods sector. First, companies in both countries decide simultaneously about market entrance and choose their plant configuration (national or multinational companies), including the level of headquarter services provided. In the second stage, companies compete in prices, yielding a Bertrand equilibrium. There is a Nash equilibrium in each stage. In equilibrium, the number of companies is endogenous. Free entry and exit assure that profits are competed away and losses are avoided. For equilibrium it must hold that no company can increase profits by changing its plant configuration from single to double plant or vice versa (nondefection condition from the existing equilibrium). Further, in equilibrium, consumers cannot improve utility, and the current account between the two countries is balanced.

The outcome of this model can be a pure national company equilibrium with intraindustry trade in differentiated goods, a pure multinational equilibrium, where two-way intraindustry investment completely replaces trade in goods, or a mixed equilibrium with intraindustry trade and two-way investment depending on the exogenous parameters. The multinational equilibrium is the more likely the higher transport costs are relative to plant-level fixed costs and the higher scale economies on the company level are, i.e., the costs of R&D. The mixed equilibria are knife-edge solutions which depend on special parameter constellations and symmetry of the two countries.

As an extension, a three-stage production process is modeled in the second part of Brainard (1993). The third stage is thought of as distribution activities. It has its own proximity-concentration tradeoff, since there are fixed costs of establishing distribution and sales facilities and distance costs of exporting the distribution service. Again, companies in the differentiated-goods sector compete in two stages: a Nash equilibrium in production configuration is followed by a Nash equilibrium in prices. There are three possible configurations in the differentiated-goods sector: (i) national companies with production and distribution facilities at home, exporting the good and the distribution service, (ii) companies which produce at home but have invested in distribution facilities at home and abroad and, (iii) multinational companies, which run production and distribution facilities at home and abroad. Headquarter services are always exclusively provided by the headquarters at home.

Equilibria with fully diversified companies, which carry out both activities in both countries, are more likely with smaller fixed costs on the production plant level, with higher company fixed costs, with higher transport and distance costs (incur when distribution services are exported), and with a higher elasticity of substitution between the varieties of the differentiated good. A downstream-diversified equilibrium with companies which invest in distribution facilities abroad but produce in a single plant at home is more likely to emerge, the smaller fixed costs in the distribution unit are, the higher fixed costs in production are, and the smaller the transport costs relative to the distance costs are. Both diversified equilibria are more likely, the higher the fixed costs at the company level are.

The three-stage production process modeled by Brainard can explain complementary trade and production abroad relationships as well as substitution of trade by production abroad. In diversified distribution equilibria, there are balanced two-way flows of intraindustry, intrafirm trade, and two-way internationalization of production. The relationship of trade in differentiated goods and setting up distribution units is complementary and substitutionary. On the one hand, foreign affiliates activities enhance trade (in goods). On the other hand, however, activities of distribution units crowd out exports in distribution services. Which effect prevails depends on the parameters, i.e., the conditions of competition.

Markusen and Venables (1998), Markusen et al. (1996), and Koop (1997) followed the line of Markusen (1984) and Horstmann and Markusen (1992) in modeling the internationalization of production in an oligopolistic framework. Markusen and Venables (1998) introduce long-run equilibria by assuming free entry and exit of companies in the markets and, therefore, endogenize the number of companies. They analyze two countries which differ in absolute and relative factor endowments. The model structure is similar to Markusen (1984), but the endogenous market structure does not allow for a closed-form solution. Instead, Markusen and Venables use numerical simulations to examine the emergences of MNEs.

Markusen and Venables (1998) use an Edgeworth box as tool of analysis. The vertical dimension gives the total world endowment with R, (resources), i.e., the factor land, which is only used in the perfect competitive Y sector, the horizontal dimension gives the total world endowment with L (labor). Any endowment point within the box gives a division of the world endowment between the two countries. The endowment of h (home) is measured from the southwest (SW) corner of the Edgeworth box. The endowment of f (foreign) is measured from the northeast (NE) corner. Along the SW-NE diagonal, both countries have the same relative but different absolute endowments.

The model predicts the emergence of MNE between similar countries for moderate to high trade costs and plant-level as well as company-level scale economies. MNEs become more important relative to trade as the countries become more similar in size and in relative factor endowments (convergence hypothesis). Furthermore, growing world income enhances production in MNEs. The approach explains why the bulk of FDI takes place among OECD countries. However, in a model of horizontally integrated MNEs like this, which assumes that fixed and variable costs have the same factor intensities, incentives to vertical integration by a single-plant company are largely ruled out (Markusen and Maskus 2002). That is why Markusen (1997) integrates the proximity-concentration (horizontal) approach and the factor proportion (vertical) approach into the knowledge-capital model.

Markusen (1999) presents a general equilibrium model with two factors (skilled labor S and unskilled labor L), two sectors (perfectly competitive Y and oligopolistic X), and two countries (home h and foreign f) in the tradition of his earlier work but with a second production factor in the X industry. Some additional assumptions about the factor intensities are made: headquarter services are the most skilled-labor-intensive activity, followed by the activities of an integrated plant and headquarters unit and by solely plant activities, respectively. The Y sector is the least skilled-labor-intensive. After the inclusion of differences in the factor intensities in the different production stages of a former horizontal model, Markusen (1999) has provided everything necessary to analyze factor-proportion-driven and proximity-concentration-driven multinational activities within one framework.

Horizontal MNEs (two-plant companies) emerge if the two countries are similar in size and in factor endowment, and trade costs are moderate to high. National companies of the larger country dominate if the difference in size is very large. Vertical MNEs (headquarter at home, plant in foreign country) emerge if the countries differ strongly in relative factor endowments, especially if the skilled-labor-rich home country is small. In this case, the headquarters would be located in the skilled-labor-rich country, the plant in the unskilled-labor-rich country. If the skilled-labor-rich country is large, it is not clear what configuration emerges, since it is optimal to locate the only plant or (at least) one of the two plants in the larger country given the costly transport of X goods. A configuration with horizontal MNEs is possible if the country size effect dominates the factor costs effect, and a configuration with vertical MNEs if the factor costs effect dominates. It is also possible that national companies from the larger country prevail in an equilibrium without MNEs. Countries with similar relative factor endowments support equilibria with horizontal MNEs. Affiliates' output is higher, the more similar absolute endowments of the two countries are. With identical countries, affiliate production is maximized at exactly half of the world production of the X industry as companies symmetrically invade each other's market.

2.3 Building Blocs for a Model of Globalization

The empirical overview shows the general pattern of increasing international integration. In all three activities (exports, internationalization of production, and international knowledge and technology transfer), which are found to be decisive characteristics of the globalization process, the empirical overview demonstrates the concentration on developed countries. Within the group of developing countries taking part in globalization, a strong concentration on a few countries can also be observed (Katseli 1992; UNCTAD 2001). Within countries, a strong concentration on a few large players is documented. The largest 50 companies hold more than half of total outward FDI stocks in every country, including the huge foreign FDI stocks of the United States which have been accumulated over almost five decades. Few large MNEs have a dominant role in the globalization process. A model of globalization must account for these facts and explicitly model companies and their internationalization decisions. Perfect competition models might, therefore, not be the right tools to study globalization (Krugman 1995a). An imperfect competition framework is needed.

High intraindustry shares in trade, FDI, and affiliate sales are further arguments for imperfect competition models. Such bi-directional intraindustry activities of companies can be explained in oligopolistic settings (Brander and Krugman 1983; Markusen and Venables 1998) or in monopolistic competition models (Krugman 1979, 1980; Brainard 1993). Perfect competition approaches, in contrast, fail to explain the high and increasing intraindustry shares.

For three reasons, exploitation of factor cost differentials might not be the central explanation of the activities of MNEs in globalization. First, the regional structure of activities with its dominance of developed countries at both sides of the transactions points to other causes than relative factor endowment. Second, the sectoral structure is fairly similar on the inward and on the outward side for most countries. Third, there is the missing correlation between FDI flows and capital account balances of a country. MNEs seem to be no means of real capital movement (Ethier 1986), but vehicles for trade in knowledge (Krugman 1983). The high share of intrafirm flows of royalties and license fees strengthens this view.

Proximity-concentration approaches are better suited to explain the observed pattern of international activity. This is true not only for the presented descriptive statistics but holds also in multivariate regression analyses. Brainard (1997) tested the proximity-concentration hypothesis and the factor proportion hypothesis for activities of U.S. MNEs. Whereas she concluded that the proximity-concentration hypothesis appears to be fairly robust in explaining the regional concentration of international activities, her findings were inconsistent with the factor proportion hypothesis. Using German data, Kleinert (1999) comes up with the same result.

Carr et al. (2001) estimate the knowledge-capital model by Markusen (1997). They find the results of a panel estimation for 36 partner countries of the United States between 1986 and 1994 very supportive for Markusen (1997). Since the knowledge-capital model includes the horizontal proximity-concentration hypothesis as well as the vertical factor proportion hypothesis, in Markusen and Maskus (1999) a nested version of these two models is estimated. The statistical test could not discriminate between the (pure horizontal) proximity-concentration model and the knowledge-capital model, but rejected the vertical (factor proportion) model at the 99 percent level of confidence. According to these results, there is no substantial loss in refraining from modeling differences in relative factor endowments between two countries. A one-factor model would serve the purpose of explaining internationalization patterns as well.

It is often noted and supported by the sectoral breakdown in the descriptive overview that MNEs are particularly dominant especially in differentiated-goods industries. Competition in these industries is different from competition in homogeneous-goods industries because companies can act as monopolist for their variety with its unique characteristics. The price is not the only means of competition; there is scope for a range of prices from which companies can choose the profit-maximizing price. Heterogeneous consumers make mutually exclusive choices among alternatives according to their individual preferences for certain characteristics of the goods. They are prepared to pay more for their most preferred variety. This premium is where the market power of the companies comes from.

There are two approaches to deal with discrete choices of heterogeneous consumers in product differentiation models: the representative consumer approach (love of variety) and the address approach (ideal variety). Both lead to a utility function with a constant elasticity of substitution (CES). The CES function is often used in product differentiation models because it combines a relatively simple functional form with a convenient parameterization of aggregate preferences for variety. The representative consumer is assumed to posit such a utility function that represents the aggregate preference of the whole population. From this utility function, the demand for the different variants is derived. Furthermore, the utility function acts as welfare index (Anderson et al. 1992). The CES preference model pioneered by Spence (1976) and Dixit and Stiglitz (1977) is characterized by a constant elasticity of substitution among the variants.

In address models, products can be described as points in a characteristic space. Consumer preferences are defined over all potential products. Each consumer has a most preferred product defined by her ideal point (address) in the characteristic space. For different consumers, these addresses differ. The dispersed ideal points aggregate to a preference for diversity. If the number of characteristics is large enough compared to the number of variants, the CES representative consumer represents the aggregate preferences of consumers distributed in a certain manner over a characteristics space (Anderson et al. 1992). All variants must be symmetric substitutes à la Chamberlin (1933), in address models as well as in representative consumer models.

Despite a wide diversity in tastes, markets support only some products. Technology requires the use of fixed input factors in research and development, production, marketing, and distribution to ensure an efficient production process. This yields internal increasing returns over a certain range of output which are necessary for a company to exist. Since companies must capture a sufficiently large fraction of demand to cover their fixed costs, only some survive. Consumer's preference for one particular variety gives the surviving companies scope for strategic decisions. The decision to produce a particular product, the use of a particular production process, a capacity investment decision, or an internationalization decision are examples for strategic decisions made by companies. The internationalization decision is of special interest in this analysis. A model of MNE-driven globalization should incorporate heterogeneous consumers' choices for differentiated goods and a production process which includes the use of fixed costs. Monopolistic competition models à la Krugman (1983) and Brainard (1993) are the ideal starting point.

A framework which models all channels of globalization should include intermediate goods. Modern production takes place in various stages using many intermediate goods at every stage. About half of total world trade is trade in intermediates. Dependence on imported intermediate goods has increased strongly in developed countries (Hummels et al. 1998; Campa and Goldberg 1997). The large fraction alone would be a reason to explicitly model intermediate goods if trade in these goods possess characteristics which are decisively different from trade in final goods. With regard to the role of MNEs in globalization, there might be a special feature of trade in intermediate goods: these goods are inputs in the production process of foreign affiliates of MNEs. Whereas trade and production abroad can be seen as different strategies to serve the foreign market, intermediate goods and foreign production show a more complementary relationship. An analysis of Japanese FDI flows since the mid-1980s, for instance, reveals a strong positive effect on trade in intermediates and capital goods, which balanced the falling exports in final goods and the rising imports from the host countries (MITI 2000). Figure 3 shows the positive relationship of foreign affiliates' sales and trade in intermediate goods.

Intermediate goods are often specific to a product or a production process. Not all of them are substitutable in the short run. An MNE starting production in a foreign country relies, therefore, on intermediate goods which must be imported from its home country, at least in the beginning. Trade in differentiated goods takes place predominantly in networks, since "connection between sellers and buyers are made through a search process that because of its costliness does not proceed until the best match is achieved" (Rauch 1999: 7–8). Gould (1994) and Dunlevy and Hutchinson (1999) support this presumption in studies on trade networks. These studies find a broad trade-enhancing effect of networks.

Head and Ries (2001) provide empirical evidence for the important role of intermediate goods in a study on the FDI-export relationship using a panel of 932 Japanese manufacturing exporters. A 25-year period from 1966 to 1990 is examined. They find that companies which increase their manufacturing investments overseas also tend to increase exports. Head and Ries present evidence that sales of intermediate goods are the source of this complementarity. Trade in intermediate goods links affiliates with each other and with the parent company. It is an important part in the internationalization of production.

The requirements on a model of MNEs in globalization discussed so far can be summarized as follows. Companies should be modeled explicitly; their strategic choice between different internationalization strategies should be in the center of the analysis. A proximity-concentration model which allows for differentiated goods and heterogeneous consumers seems to be most suitable. Ownership and internalization advantages are assumed in this model, localization advantages result from differences in foreign market access. The model should account for the role of intermediate goods, i.e., link the various units of an MNE.

Globalization is a process. The theories presented so far are stationary. This is also true for the proximity-concentration approach, which is shown to be a good starting point of analysis. To address questions of globalization, another idea has to be added to these models: the evolutionary approach applied in new economic geography. In the new economic geography, which made impressive progress in explaining the emergences of the regional distribution of activities over time, models are not based on any explicit dynamic decision making over time, but on static optimization for each period to which ad hoc dynamics are imposed. These ad hoc dynamics are used to categorize some of the possible multiple equilibria as stable, some as unstable (Fujita, Krugman, and Venables 1999). In Fujita and Mori (1997) and in Fujita, Krugman, and Mori (1999), an exogenously growing population alters the existing equilibrium at any time. Individuals and companies adjust to a new equilibrium which is altered again by population growth. The economy "moves" from equilibrium to equilibrium.

In an application of this evolutionary approach to globalization models, falling distance costs are imposed as ad hoc dynamics to the static (proximity-concentration) model. Falling distance costs are regarded as the major reason of globalization in academic literature and public debate. Hence, a model of globalization must include falling distance costs as driving force. Individuals and companies optimize consumption and production given the conditions at a particular time. These conditions depend on exogenous (to the model) parameters; with one of them being the distance cost level. Certainly, distance costs are not exogenous in reality but endogenously determined. They can be and have been altered by innovations, reorganizations of the production process, and changes in competition. The change in distance costs is as much a cause of globalization as its result. However, to keep the model as simple as possible, they are taken as exogenous in the model of globalization proposed in this study. Neither a transportation nor a communication service sector is modeled. Distance costs, which include in addition to transport and communication costs all costs which incur for doing business in a foreign environment, are assumed to fall exogenously throughout the time.

Applying this evolutionary approach à la economic geographers to the proposed model of international activities of companies, phenomena which result from the dynamics of the process of globalization can be modeled within proximity-concentration models. The explanation of the wave behavior of FDI, for instance, relies so far on the very different approach of oligopolistic reaction (Knickerbocker 1973; Graham 1996). Using an evolutionary version of a proximity-concentration model, wave behavior of FDI can be analyzed in a proximity-concentration framework which generates new insights in this process. In Chapter 4, I discuss the wave character of the internationalization process.

To summarize, the model I introduce in Chapter 3 employs the proximity-concentration approach for explaining international activities of companies. It takes differentiated goods into account, which allow for market power of companies. I explicitly model the strategic decision of companies about their internationalization strategy. The model pays attention to the role of intermediate goods as one important link between the different units of a company. I apply the evolutionary framework to the (static) model in order to allow for an analysis of globalization as a process.

3 Multinational Enterprises in Globalization: Model and Test of the Main Assumptions

3.1 A Model of Multinational Enterprises in Globalization

3.1.1 Introduction

Economic theory has made great progress in explaining the regional pattern of trade and foreign production (Markusen and Venables 1998), but it has not focused much on their development over time. However, for an understanding of the progress of globalization, an analytical framework is needed that deals with trade and internationalization of production and accounts for the role of falling distance costs in globalization. Therefore, I introduce a general equilibrium model in this part of Chapter 3 which is suited to analyze the endogenous emergences of MNEs. Exogenously changing conditions of competition which are due to falling distance costs induce changing incentives of companies to internationalize production. Falling distance costs are the only source of change in this model. I do not consider capital accumulation or endogenous technical change. In the initial (preglobalization) situation, distance costs are assumed to be high. Distance costs can be thought of as border effects (McCallum 1995). They separate the two markets in this two-country model but do not apply to domestic transactions. According to empirical studies, these border effects have fallen over the last two decades (Nitsch 2000). By assumption, distance costs only occur in the imperfectly competitive manufacturing sector but not in the perfectly competitive agricultural sector.

The model stands in the tradition of Brainard (1993). I model a perfectly competitive agricultural sector producing a homogeneous good and an imperfectly competitive manufacturing sector. In the manufacturing sector, there are two groups of companies: final-goods producers and intermediate-goods producers. Both groups produce a bundle of differentiated goods, which consists of many varieties. The manufacturing sector is characterized by monopolistic competition among the many producers within their groups. I assume fixed input factors in production which leads to decreasing average costs. It is, therefore, profitable to produce a single variety of the bundle of differentiated goods in only one company. The final-goods producers in the manufacturing sector produce in a multistage process, which include fixed inputs at the corporate level (R&D, marketing, financing) and at the plant level (equipment). They choose between exports and production abroad to serve the foreign market. Exporting saves on additional fixed costs at the plant level, while production abroad saves on distance costs. All goods in both economies are produced by using labor, the only production factor.

The model goes beyond Brainard (1993) in modeling the usage of intermediate goods in the production process of the final good. Recent work (Feenstra 1998; Campa and Goldberg 1997) has called attention to the increasing use of imported intermediate goods in various developed economies and has related this to rising activities of MNEs (Hummels et al. 1998). Intermediate-goods companies in the model presented here are assumed to produce in a single stage using fixed input factors like plant equipment. Intermediate goods are considered to be specific either to the final good or to the production process, or to both. Final-goods producers use, therefore, intermediate goods exclusively from their home country, even if they produce abroad. Intermediate-goods producers and final-goods producers of the same country compose a network. That is, of course, a simplification which does not hold for all intermediates. However, it is an important aspect in the internationalization of production, as empirical studies on an aggregated level (Figure 3; METI 2001) and on micro level (Head and Ries 2001) show. Nonspecific intermediate goods could be modeled as an additional production factor similar to labor, which is taken from the host country. For simplicity, nonspecific intermediate goods are excluded. Table 18 gives a short summary of the model structure.

This specific modeling of the production process with intermediate goods alters the results regarding the effect of changing distance cost in this model compared to other models of endogenous emergences of MNEs (Brainard 1993; Markusen and Venables 1998). Whereas in models without intermediate goods falling distance costs always reduce the profitability of foreign production relative to exports, this is not true in the model proposed here. Because intermediate goods used in the foreign affiliate incur distance costs as well, prices and quantities of foreign affiliates' goods are also affected by falling distance costs. Although the one-unit profit increase induced by a distance costs reduction is larger for exports than for affiliates' goods, the total effect of distance costs reductions on relative profits of foreign production and exports is ambiguous a priori, because export markets are smaller than foreign affiliates' markets. Thus, the larger per unit decrease of costs of exports applies to less sales.

The analysis reveals that the change in relative profits depends on the level of distance costs. For high distance costs, exports and foreign production are low. Profits of the foreign affiliate are not high enough to cover the additional fixed costs at the plant level. The company serves the foreign market through exports,

Table 18:
Model Structure

	Agricultural goods	Intermediate goods	Final manufacturing goods
Product characteristic	Homogeneous	Many differentiated varieties	Many differentiated varieties
Competition	Perfect competition	Monopolistic competition	Monopolistic competition
Input factors	Labor	Labor	Labor, intermediate goods
Production stages	One stage	One stage; fixed costs at plant level	Headquarter service and production stage using fixed costs at plant level
Foreign market service	Trade without incurring distance costs	Exports to foreign affil. of home-based MNE, incurring distance costs	Exports with incurring distance costs or foreign production
Number of companies	–	Endogenous	Endogenous

because exports do not require fixed costs and are therefore also profitable with low sales. But a small reduction in distance costs increases profits of production abroad more than profits of exports. For intermediate distance cost levels, profits of foreign affiliates might be or might not be sufficient to cover the additional fixed costs at the plant level. Hence, MNEs may arise depending on industry characteristics (fixed costs levels, degree of product differentiation, share of intermediate goods in production). For small distance cost levels, savings of distance cost are not large enough to make up for the additional fixed cost at the plant level. Companies always prefer exports to production abroad.

In Section 3.1.2, I describe the two-country, two-sector, one-factor general equilibrium model. I assume the two countries are symmetric to make an analytic solution possible. This static model can be solved for given conditions. For any state of conditions, there might be equilibria of national companies, of MNEs, or of a mix of both kinds of companies. In Section 3.1.3, I introduce the trigger curve which I use to analyze whether a deviation from the equilibrium is profitable. Deviation involves a change in the mode of serving the foreign market. The initial equilibrium assumed in this section is one of only national companies. This could be thought of as the situation prior to globalization. I then check how falling distance costs alter the incentives of a company to become an MNE (deviate from the pure national company equilibrium). In Section 3.1.4, I analyze the change from an equilibrium with only national companies to an equilibrium which consists of national and multinational companies or only MNEs. In Section 3.1.5, I derive some welfare implications of this globalization process. Whereas prices tend to fall with falling distance costs, which leads to an increase in utility, the number of variants in equilibrium falls too, which decreases utility. In total, the effect could go either way. To assess the effects, I run numerical simulations for a particular example in Section 3.1.6. In Section 3.1.7, I conclude.

3.1.2   The Basic Model

There are two symmetric countries, home H and foreign F, each with two sectors of production. One sector, agriculture, produces a homogeneous product Q_A with constant returns to scale under perfect competition. The other sector, manufacturing, produces a variety of final goods and a variety of intermediate goods under imperfect competition. The aggregate output of the final goods in the manufacturing sector is Q_M. An individual final-goods producer's output is denoted q_i. The final-goods producer, which can serve the foreign market through exports or production abroad, uses intermediate goods. These are produced by intermediate-goods producers also in the manufacturing sector. The aggregate output of the intermediate goods Z is used as input exclusively by the final-goods producer headquartered in the same country. This does not assume nontradable intermediates, since foreign affiliates of the MNEs import their intermediate goods from the home country, but intermediates which are specific and which can therefore not be used by foreign companies. An individual intermediate firm's output is denoted z_i. Because of the symmetry of the two countries, it is sufficient to describe the economy of the home country H. All definitions, conditions and derivations apply to the foreign country F in the same way.

It is assumed that every individual in H is endowed with one unit of labor, L. The individual is free to choose any job in his country. There is no cross-border mobility of labor. The labor market equilibrium gives wage level w_H in country H. Full employment is assumed.

3.1.2.1 Consumption

L_H inhabitants live in H. They have identical preferences. Their utility function is increasing in the agricultural product and the aggregate manufacturing product:

(1) $U_H = Q_{A,H}{}^{1-\mu} Q_{M,H}{}^{\mu}, \quad \mu \in (0,1),$

where μ gives the income share spent on manufacturing goods. The aggregate Q_M is a CES function with λ different products:

$$(2) \qquad Q_{M,H} = \left[\sum_{i=1}^{\lambda} q_{i,H}{}^{\rho} \right]^{1/\rho}, \qquad \rho \in (0,1),$$

where ρ defines the degree of differentiation among the manufacturing goods. The products are poor substitutes for each other if ρ is small, leaving the companies with more market power. If ρ increases, it becomes easier for consumers to substitute one good for the other. Therefore, companies' market power decreases. Equation (2) implies that consumers love variety. If they are indifferent between two products, they prefer a mix of half a unit of each good. The CES function (2) implies a constant elasticity of substitution σ, with $\sigma = 1/(1-\rho)$, between any two varieties of the final goods in the manufacturing sector.

Individuals maximize their utility (1) subject to budget constraints

$$(3) \qquad Y_H = P_{A,H} Q_{A,H} + \sum_{i=1}^{\lambda} q_{i,H} p_{i,H} \,,$$

to obtain the optimum quantities of agricultural and manufacturing goods

$$(4) \qquad Q_{A,H} = (1-\mu) Y_H / P_{A,H} \text{ and}$$

$$(5) \qquad Q_{M,H} = \mu Y_H / P_{M,H} \,,$$

where $P_{A,H}$ is the price of agricultural goods, $P_{M,H}$ is the price index of the varieties of manufacturing goods. The price index, $P_{M,H}$, depends on the price, $p_{i,H}$, of each individual product.

Since agriculture is the perfectly competitive sector of the economy and since the agricultural good can be traded without incurring costs, the price of the agricultural good will be the same in the two economies. It will be set equal to one ($p_A=1$). The agricultural good Q_A will, therefore, be used as a numeraire throughout the remaining sections.

3.1.2.2 Production

Agricultural-Goods Producers

The agricultural good is assumed to be produced under constant returns to scale. Since agriculture is a perfectly competitive sector, the wage, w_H, is paid according to the marginal product of the production factor labor:

$$(6) \qquad \frac{\partial Q_{A,H}}{\partial L_{A,H}} = w_H \,.$$

Perfect mobility of workers across sectors ensures that the wage is identical in every sector of the economy.

Production costs in agriculture are given by

(7) $C_{A,H} = w_H Q_{A,H}$.

Manufacturing-Goods Producers

In the manufacturing sector, companies engage in monopolistic competition. Consumers view the differentiated products as imperfect substitutes for each other. Each company produces a single variety. Hence, the number of differentiated goods equals the number of firms in the two countries.

There are two groups of companies in the manufacturing sector, intermediate-goods producers and final-goods producers. Each final-goods producer uses a bundle of intermediate goods as input in the final-goods production. Since intermediate goods are often very specific to a production process or a final good, the production of this final good in a foreign country depends on the supply of intermediate goods from the home country. For the sake of simplicity, it is assumed that MNEs exclusively use intermediate goods produced in their home country, irrespective of whether production of the final good occurs in the home or in the foreign country.

Intermediate-Goods Producers

Intermediate goods are not perfect substitutes for each other. The bundle of intermediate goods used by any final-goods producing company in the manufacturing sector contains all varieties of intermediate goods:

(8) $Z_H = \left[\sum_{i=1}^{s_H} z_i^{\varepsilon} \right]^{\frac{1}{\varepsilon}}$, $\varepsilon \in (0,1)$.

Aggregate output is also assumed to follow a CES function. The intermediates' degree of differentiation is given by ε. s_H is the number of intermediate goods produced in country H. The price index, Pz_H, for intermediate goods can be calculated from (8):

(9) $Pz_H = \left[s_H \, pz_{i,H}^{-\phi} \right]^{-\frac{1}{\phi}}$,

where $\phi = \varepsilon/(1-\varepsilon)$. s_H is the number of varieties of intermediate goods in the bundle Z_H. $pz_{i,H}$ is the price of any of these varieties. Pz_H increases in the prices of a single variety of the intermediate, $pz_{i,H}$, i.e. $\delta Pz_H/\delta pz_{i,H}=Pz_H/pz_{i,H}>0$, and decreases in the number of varieties, s_H, i.e. $\delta Pz_H/\delta s_H= -Pz_H/\phi s_H <0$.

The costs of production of an intermediate-goods variety are given by

$$(10) \quad C_{i,H}^Z = fz_H w_H + z_{i,H} w_H .$$

The first term on the right-hand side shows the fixed costs. fz_H is the amount of fixed input which is determined by the production technology. The second term describes the marginal costs cz_H, given by w_H multiplied by the output $z_{i,H}$. Because all producers of intermediate goods face the same factor costs and use the same technology, their marginal costs and their fixed costs are identical.

Final-goods producers of country H spent an amount of I_H on intermediate goods. From the composition of the aggregate intermediate good in (8), the demand for any of the varieties can be derived (Appendix A):

$$(11) \quad z_{i,H} = \cdot \frac{pz_{i,H}^{-(1+\phi)}}{Pz_H^{-\phi}} I_H .$$

In equilibrium, the demand for each intermediate good equals its production. Therefore, the output of an intermediate-goods producer decreases in its own price $pz_{i,H}$, and increases in the price index of intermediate goods Pz_H as well as in the amount spent on intermediate goods by the final-goods producers, I_H. Maximizing the profit function of an intermediate-goods producer yields the optimal price for his intermediate good

$$(12) \quad pz_{i,H} = cz_H /\varepsilon .$$

The producers of intermediate goods set their prices equal to a fixed markup of $1/\varepsilon$ over their marginal costs cz_H. The prices are identical among all intermediate goods, because their marginal costs are identical, as are their output levels, z_H. Variable profits in the market for intermediate goods are proportional to sales. They add up to $(1-\varepsilon)I_H$. These variable profits, however, are (at least partly) necessary to cover the fixed costs of the indermediate-goods producers, $s_H fz_H w_H$.

The number of companies producing the intermediate goods, s_H, in country H is determined by the zero-profit condition:

$$(13) \quad \Pi_j^Z = (1-\varepsilon)pz_H z_H - fz_H w_H = 0 .$$

Since there is free market entry and exit in both countries of this model, new companies will enter profitable markets until profits fall to zero. New entrants influence the profit of existing firms by increasing competition: the price index decreases $(\delta Pz_H/\delta s_H < 0)$ as a result. Sales and profits of the incumbent companies fall, the average size of the companies falls, and the sum of fixed costs used in the production of the intermediate good increases. In equilibrium, the zero-profit condition holds. The sum of the fixed costs must equal the sum of variable profits. The number of intermediate-goods producers is therefore given by

$$(14) \quad s_H = \frac{(1-\varepsilon)I_H}{w_H f_H} \ .$$

Equation (9) gives the price index of the intermediate goods without distance costs. The price index perceived by affiliates in the foreign country Pz_H^M, however, must take distance costs $(\tau_M D)$ into account. Foreign affiliates of H-based MNEs have to pay c.i.f. prices (which include distance costs) for the intermediate goods they use. The price index of an affiliate's intermediate inputs is given by

$$(15) \quad Pz_H^M = \left[s_H \left(pz_H e^{\tau_M D} \right)^{-\phi} \right]^{-\frac{1}{\phi}} \ .$$

Distance costs are modeled in Samuelson's iceberg form: a part of the value of every product must be paid for "transportation." This fraction increases with the distance D between the two markets (D is set equal to one for the remainder of this chapter). To buy one unit of an imported intermediate good, e^{τ_M} (with $e^{\tau_M} > 1$) units have to be paid by the producer of the final good in the foreign country, $(e^{\tau_M} - 1)$ units being distance costs. For very high distance costs, τ_M, the price index for intermediate goods used as inputs in the foreign country, Pz_H^M, goes to infinity, for very small distance costs, it approaches Pz_H.

Final-goods Producers

There are two possible types of final-goods producers in every country: (i) national firms producing in their home market and serving the foreign country through exports and (ii) MNEs producing domestically and abroad. Given the symmetry of both countries in this model, exports of the multinational companies' affiliates to the home country cannot be profitable.

Final-goods producers manufacture their products in a multistage process. In the first stage, headquarter services are produced in each company. Headquarter services, like R&D or marketing, can be used in a nonrival way within the company. In the second stage, production takes place at the plant level. Headquarter services and intermediates are used as inputs. The cost function of any national final-goods producer is given by

(16) $\quad C_{i,H}^{N} = w_H r_H + w_H f_H + \left(\dfrac{w_H}{\theta}\right)^{\theta}\left(\dfrac{Pz_H}{1-\theta}\right)^{1-\theta} q_{i,H}^{N}, \quad \theta \in (0,1).$

The first term represents fixed costs at the company level, the second term fixed costs at the plant level. Fixed costs increase in wages, w_H, and in r_H and f_H. r_H is the level of headquarter services produced by the companies in the home country. f_H is the amount of fixed input necessary for the production of the final good. r_H and f_H are given by the production technology and, therefore, exogenous to the company.

Variable costs, the third term in (16), increase in the factor price of labor at home, w_H, the price index of the intermediates, Pz_H, and the output level, $q_{i,H}^{N}$. Marginal costs $(w_H/\theta)^{\theta}(Pz_H/(1-\theta))^{1-\theta}$ are denoted by c_H^{N}.

A multinational company's production costs in its home country, $C_{i,H,H}^{M}$, are

(17) $\quad C_{i,H,H}^{M} = w_H r_H + w_H f_H + \left(\dfrac{w_H}{\theta}\right)^{\theta}\left(\dfrac{Pz_H}{1-\theta}\right)^{1-\theta} q_{i,H,H}^{M}, \quad \theta \in (0,1).$

MNEs' production costs differ from costs of a national producer only in the third term, the variable costs. Factor prices and technologies used are the same, but MNEs produce at their home country plant only for the home market and not for export. The quantities produced by a H-based national and a multinational company in country H differ $\left(q_{i,H}^{N} \neq q_{i,H,H}^{M}\right)$. Marginal costs are the same $\left(c_H^{N} = c_H^{M}\right)$, but variable costs differ because quantities differ.

Different plants of an MNE have different variable costs in each country because of differences in the prices of the intermediates $\left(Pz_H^{M} \neq Pz_H\right)$ they use in both countries. In the foreign country affiliates pay c.i.f. prices. An affiliate's costs in the foreign country F, $C_{P,i,H,F}^{M}$, are

(18) $\quad C_{P,i,H,F}^{M} = w_F f_F + \left(\dfrac{w_F}{\theta}\right)^{\theta}\left(\dfrac{Pz_H^{M}}{1-\theta}\right)^{1-\theta} q_{i,H,F}^{M}, \quad \theta \in (0,1).$

Costs of production in the foreign country do not include costs at the corporate level due to the public goods character of the headquarter service. Headquarter services are produced at home. They are used on a nonrivalry basis in both plants, at home in H and in the foreign country F. MNE's production costs abroad depend on the wage rate in F, w_F, the amount of fixed inputs used in production, f_F, the elasticity of production, θ, which are technology parameters and the costs of the intermediate goods, Pz_H^{M}, which include their distance costs from the home country. Production costs of the MNE in the affiliate abroad increase in distance costs, because the price index of intermediate goods increases in distance costs. For very high distance costs, MNE's production costs in the foreign country approach infinity.

The output, $q_{i,H}^k$ with $k=N$, M, differs between domestic suppliers and MNEs in the same country, as well as between the MNE's home country plant and the affiliate in the foreign country. In equilibrium, companies produce the amount of goods they can sell at an optimal price. Given the utility function (1) and the composition of the aggregated manufacturing good (2), equation (19) gives the demand for a single product of a national firm, $q_{i,H}^N$, which serves the foreign country through exports:

$$(19) \quad q_{i,H} = \frac{p_{i,H}^{-(1+\gamma)}}{P_{M,H}^{-\gamma}} \mu Y_H + \frac{p_{i,H}^{-(1+\gamma)} e^{-(1+\gamma)\tau_M}}{P_{M,F}^{-\gamma}} \mu Y_F, \quad \gamma = \rho/(1-\rho).$$

The optimal quantity of good i produced in H depends on: its price, $p_{i,H}$, the price indexes in both final-goods markets, $P_{M,H}$, $P_{M,F}$, the size of the markets, μY, and distance costs, τ_M. The lower the price of good i relative to the price index in both countries, the higher the optimal output of this good. High distance costs decrease the optimal output by increasing the good's price in the foreign market. Consumers in the importing country F must pay the distance costs and, therefore, react by partially substituting imported goods by goods produced in their country F. For very high distance costs, exports approach zero. Given the symmetry between both countries, exported quantities equal home-sold quantities for distance costs of zero.

A multinational company headquartered in H produces in both countries. It supplies goods which are produced in both countries. The optimal output from the domestic plant

$$(20) \quad q_{i,H,H}^M = \frac{p_{i,H,H}^{M}{}^{-(1+\gamma)}}{P_{M,H}^{-\gamma}} \mu Y_H$$

equals the demand in the home country, since re-export is excluded. The price of a good of an MNE from country H in the foreign market F is lower than the price for an imported good, since consumers do not have to pay distance costs. Hence, the output is higher:

$$(21) \quad q_{i,H,F}^M = \frac{p_{i,H,F}^{M}{}^{-(1+\gamma)}}{P_{M,F}^{-\gamma}} \mu Y_F,$$

where $q_{i,H,F}^M$ is the output in F of MNE i with headquarters in H. It is positively related to the price index, $P_{M,F}$, and the market size in country F, μY_F, and negatively related to its own price, $p_{i,H,F}^M$.

The quantity of the intermediate-goods bundle used by a single final-goods producer can be calculated from the cost functions (16)–(18) by taking the partial derivatives with respect to the price index Pz_H (Shephard's Lemma):

$$(22) \qquad qz_{i,H}^N = \frac{\partial C_{i,H}}{\partial Pz_H} = \left(\frac{w_H}{\theta}\right)^\theta \left(\frac{1-\theta}{Pz_H}\right)^\theta q_{i,H}^N \ ,$$

$$(23) \qquad qz_{i,H}^M = \frac{\partial C_{i,H,H}^M}{\partial Pz_H} + \frac{\partial C_{P,i,H,F}^M}{\partial Pz_H^M} = qz_{i,H,H}^M + qz_{i,H,F}^M$$

$$= \left(\frac{w_H}{\theta}\right)^\theta \left(\frac{1-\theta}{Pz_H}\right)^\theta q_{i,H,H}^M + \left(\frac{w_F}{\theta}\right)^\theta \left(\frac{1-\theta}{Pz_H^M}\right)^\theta q_{i,H,F}^M \ .$$

In equilibrium, the aggregate demand for intermediate goods, given by $\sum_{i=1}^{m_H} qz_{i,H}^M + \sum_{i=1}^{n_H} qz_{i,H}$, equals aggregate supply, Z_H. The amount spent on intermediate goods, $\sum_{i=1}^{m_H} (pz_{i,H} e^{\tau_M}) qz_{i,H}^M + \sum_{i=1}^{n_H} pz_{i,H} qz_{i,H}$, equals the total costs of the intermediate-goods producers.

Every final-goods producer sets her price to maximize profits. The solution to this maximization problem is a fixed markup factor over marginal costs, $c_{PV,i,H}^k$:

$$(24) \qquad p_{i,H}^k = c_H^k / \rho \ , \qquad k = N, M \ .$$

The price of a single final good depends only on the good's marginal costs, c_H^k, and on ρ, the parameters of differentiation. Marginal costs can be obtained from variable costs (16)–(18). Since all companies use the same technology, the marginal costs differ only if the factor prices differ. But factor prices cannot differ within one country because of inter-sectoral mobility of labor.

In each country j, there are four different potential suppliers of final manufacturing goods: (i) country j's national firms producing for their home market, (ii) foreign national firms serving country H through exports, (iii) MNEs, with their headquarters in country H, producing at their plant in H, and (iv) MNEs, based in country F, producing at their affiliate in country H.

F.o.b. prices (net of distance costs) set by companies located in H and F do not differ. By assumption, the economies are symmetric. Thus, companies do not differ in their ability to use economies of scale. All operate at the same scale in their home market. However, prices set by national and multinational enterprises differ in their foreign market but not at home. There are, therefore, up to three different prices $p^k_{j,H}$ (with $j=H,F$ and $k=N,M$) for different varieties of the manufacturing good in each market H depending on the strategy by which the market is served: the price of goods produced by H-based firms (nationals and multinationals), the price of imported goods, and the price of goods produced by an F-headquartered multinational affiliate's plant in H. The price of a national firm's good in the foreign market, $p^N_{H,F}$, equals the home-market price multiplied by distance costs, $p^N_{H,F} = p^N_{H,H}e^{\tau M}$.

From the utility function (1) and equation (2), the price index, $P_{M,H}$, for each market H can be calculated:

$$(25) \qquad P_{M,H} = \frac{\mu Y_H}{Q_{M,H}} = \left[\sum_{i=1}^{\lambda} p_i^{-\gamma} \right]^{-\frac{1}{\gamma}}.$$

Using the different product prices of the different companies, (25) changes to

$$(26) \qquad P_{M,H} = \frac{\mu Y_H}{Q_{M,H}}$$
$$= \left[\sum_{i=1}^{n_H} \left(p^N_{H,H} \right)^{-\gamma} + \sum_{i=1}^{n_F} \left(p^N_{F,H} \right)^{-\gamma} + \sum_{i=1}^{m_H} \left(p^M_{H,H} \right)^{-\gamma} + \sum_{i=1}^{m_F} \left(p^M_{F,H} \right)^{-\gamma} \right]^{-\frac{1}{\gamma}},$$

where n_H is the number of national companies located in H, n_F the number of nationals located in F, and m_H and m_F are the numbers of MNEs headquartered in H and F, respectively. n_H, n_F, m_H, and m_F, added together equal λ. The price index, $P_{M,H}$, increases in the prices of each kind of company and therefore in distance costs, since distance costs increase the prices of national, exporting companies, and MNEs producing in the foreign country.

Since there is free market entry and exit, the zero-profit condition holds in equilibrium for both national and multinational companies:

$$(27) \qquad \Pi^N_H = (1-\rho)p^N_H q^N_H - w_H(r_H + f_H) = 0,$$

$$(28) \qquad \Pi^M_H = (1-\rho)\left(p^M_{H,H} q^M_{H,H} + p^M_{H,F} q^M_{H,F} \right) - w_H(r_H + f_H) + w_F f_F = 0.$$

The zero-profit conditions (27) and (28) are sufficient to determine the number of national companies, n_H, and the number of multinational companies, m_H, in country H in equilibrium. The numbers depend on the market share of the total market $\mu(Y_H+Y_F)$ each group holds, which is endogenous. For the special cases of only national companies or only MNEs in equilibrium and zero distance costs, the number of companies is given by

$$(29) \quad n_H = \frac{(1-\rho)\mu Y_H}{r_H w_H + f_H w_H},$$

$$(30) \quad m_H = \frac{(1-\rho)\mu Y_H}{r_H w_H + f_H w_H + f_F w_F}.$$

It is easy to see that the number of companies in an equilibrium with only national companies is larger than in an MNE equilibrium. For positive distance cost levels, the sum of the distance costs has to be subtracted from the gross variable profits, $(1-\rho)\mu Y_H$, of all companies in country H. As discussed above, these distance costs are larger for national (exporting) companies than for MNEs' foreign affiliates which import only a fraction, the intermediate goods.

3.1.2.3 Distance Costs and Factor Demand

Because of the iceberg form of distance costs, a share t_H of final goods is lost in the case of export. The loss of intermediate goods which results from distance costs is represented by tz_H. Distance costs incur when the intermediate goods are shipped because the final-goods producer decided to produce abroad:

$$(31) \quad t_H = (e^{\tau_M} - 1)\frac{(p_H e^{\tau_M})^{-(1+\gamma)}}{P_{M,F}^{-\gamma}}\mu Y_F,$$

$$(32) \quad tz_H = (e^{\tau_M} - 1)\frac{(pz_H e^{\tau_M})^{-(1+\gamma)}}{Pz_H^{M-\gamma}}m_H qz_{H,F}^M pz_H^M.$$

Labor demand is derived by using Shephard's Lemma. The cost functions (7), (10), (16) through (18) are differentiated with respect to the factor price w. The derivatives are given in Appendix A. The labor demand for the good that smelt when exported (given in the distance costs equations (31) and (32)) is also derived in Appendix A.

3.1.2.4 Market Equilibrium

Full employment of all resources is assumed in both economies. For a given endowment of labor in H, L_H, the labor market condition is given by

$$(33) \quad \begin{aligned} L_H = &L_{A,H} + n_H \left(r_H + f_H + L_H^N + L_{t,H}^N \right) + s_H \left(fz_H + z_H + L_{tz,H} \right) \\ &+ m_H \left(r_H + f_H + L_{H,H}^M \right) + m_F \left(f_H + L_{F,H}^M \right) \end{aligned}$$

with

$$L_H^N = (\theta/(1-\theta))^{1-\theta}(Pz_H/w_H)^{1-\theta} q_H^N, \quad L_{t,H}^N = (\theta/(1-\theta))^{1-\theta}(Pz_H/w_H)^{1-\theta} t_H,$$

$$L_{tz,H} = (\theta/(1-\theta))^{1-\theta}(Pz_H/w_H)^{1-\theta} tz_H, \quad L_{H,H}^M = (\theta/(1-\theta))^{1-\theta}(Pz_H/w_H)^{1-\theta} q_{H,H}^M,$$

and $L_{F,H}^M = (\theta/(1-\theta))^{1-\theta}(Pz_F^M/w_H)^{1-\theta} q_{F,H}^M$.

The labor market clears if the fixed labor supply L_H in country H equals the sum of the labor demand of the agricultural sector, of all stages of production of H's national and multinational companies producing final goods, of the inter-mediate-goods producers in H, of the affiliates in H of MNE's headquartered in F, and of the transport of final and intermediate goods.

Wages are set in order to clear factor markets in each country. The wage level determines the size of the agricultural sector because this is a perfectly com-petitive sector. In both countries, the price of agricultural goods equals marginal costs:

(34) $P_{A,H} = c_{A,H} = w_H$.

The income Y_H in each country is given by the sum of the incomes of all individuals:

(35) $Y_H = w_H L_H$.

The demand functions (4) and (5), the income equation (35), and the budget constraint (3) ensure that goods markets clear. The factor market clearance is given by (33). The value of the marginal product of labor (6) determines the wage in each economy. The pricing rule (24) and the equations (19) to (21), (27), and (28) determine the prices and output of the national and multinational com-panies and their number in each country. The number of intermediate-goods pro-ducers and their production levels and prices are given by (13), (11), and (12). The pricing rule (34) determines the agricultural goods output in each economy and, therefore, with demand equation (4), the level of interindustry trade. The free-of-cost one-way trade of the homogeneous good, Ex_H^A, leads to price equality of this good in both economies. Since symmetry between the two countries is assumed, there is only intraindustry trade; Ex_H^A is zero in any equilibrium. If the countries are symmetric, there is no trade in the agricultural good, since each country satisfies its own demand for this good.

There is always intraindustry trade of final manufacturing products, Ex_H^{MF}, in this model, because final goods are not perfect substitutes for each other:

(36) $Ex_H^{MF} = n_H p_{H,F}^N q_{H,F}^N$.

The final-goods export sales, Ex_H^{MF}, rise with the number of exporting companies, the price of the exported good, and its quantity. The exported quantity, $q_{H,F}^N = p_H^{-(1+\gamma)} e^{-(1+\gamma)\tau} / P_{M,F}^{-\gamma} \mu Y_F$ falls with rising distance costs and rises with the price index in the foreign market and the market size. If distance costs are almost prohibitive, exported quantities are very small.

Trade in services depends on the existence of MNEs, since trade in services in this model is trade in headquarter services. It rises with the number of MNEs, the level of headquarter services which is necessary for production, and with the quantities produced by the MNE abroad. Trade in services from the home country to the foreign country equals the amount of headquarter service, $w_H r_H$, used by each affiliate multiplied by the number of foreign affiliates, m_H:

$$(37) \quad Ex_H^S = m_H w_H r_H \frac{q_{H,F}^M}{q_{H,H}^M + q_{H,F}^M}.$$

Since this is a static model, trade must be balanced, otherwise one country would be giving away goods for free:

$$(38) \quad Ex_H^A + Ex_H^{MF} + Ex_H^S = Ex_F^M + Ex_F^S.$$

Ex_H^S can be positive or negative, depending on whether H is an exporter or an importer of the agricultural good. For the symmetric case, Ex_H^A equals zero. Ex^{MF} must be positive for both economies except in the case of prohibitively high distance costs ($\tau_M \rightarrow \infty$). Ex_H^S can be zero or positive for both countries depending on the existence of MNEs.

3.1.3   The Strategic Decision: Trade or Production Abroad

All final-goods producers can decide whether to serve the foreign market through exports or to become an MNE and produce abroad. If there are no restrictions to FDI, a company will invest in the foreign market if it is profitable to do so. Profitability of internationalization of production depends on technical parameters which enter the production function (fixed costs on plant and company level, f and r, and the share of intermediate goods used in production, $1-\theta$), on the degree of differentiation, ρ, on the degree of competition, Γ (defined below), which is affected by the type of companies in equilibrium, and on the exogenously given distance cost level, τ_M, which separates the two markets. In the following analysis, I examine the effect of exogenously falling distance costs on the internationalization strategies of the companies.

In the initial situation, I assume that all companies in equilibrium are national companies which serve the foreign market through exports. Whether the equilibrium is stable, is determined by using a function which gives the relative profitability of exports and production abroad. If, at the given structure, foreign production is not profitable relative to exports, the equilibrium with national companies is stable. However, for changing conditions of competition because of exogenously falling distance costs, it must be analyzed at every distance cost level whether deviating from the pure national company equilibrium is a profitable strategy for any company. If one company deviates, the price index and the market structure change.

The price of a good in the foreign market drops when an exporting company becomes an MNE, since consumers in the foreign market do not have to pay distance costs on the final good anymore. There are only distance costs on intermediate goods, which increase the price of a foreign affiliate's final good, relative to foreign companies (in their home market), because of more expensive intermediate inputs. However, this increase is smaller than the price increase of an exporting company resulting from incurring distance costs. The quantity of the final goods, which is sold in the foreign market, rises with the establishment of an affiliate in the foreign country, and so do variable profits. A national final-goods producer decides to produce abroad if the gains in variable profits are at least as high as the additional fixed costs at the plant level:

$$(39) \qquad w_F f_F \leq (1-\rho)\left(p^M_{H,H} q^M_{H,H} + p^M_{H,F} q^M_{H,F} - p^N_H q^N_H\right).$$

Condition (39) is essential for the resulting equilibrium. The effect of distance cost changes on relative profits of production abroad and exports clarifies the mechanism which drives this model of globalization. Assuming symmetry is necessary in order to continue with an analytical solution, because price indexes are then identical in both countries and companies are symmetric. Only for this special case, the effect of distance cost changes on the investment decision can be analyzed without recourse to numerical simulations.

In (39), it is easy to see that the lower the fixed costs at the plant level, $w_F f_F$, are, the more likely it is that a national company will decide to build a plant abroad. Furthermore, the internationalization decision depends only on the profits earned in the foreign market since prices, quantities, and markups, and therefore profits, of national and multinational companies at home are the same. But foreign profits differ. Rewriting (39) yields

$$\Phi = \left(p^M - c^M\right)D\left(p^M\right) - \left(p^N - c^N\right)D\left(p^N e^{\tau_M}\right) - w_F f_F \quad \text{or}$$

$$(40) \quad \Phi = \left[\frac{1-\rho}{\rho} c^M \frac{\left(c^M/\rho\right)^{-\frac{1}{1-\rho}}}{\Gamma} - \frac{1-\rho}{\rho} c^N \frac{\left(c^N e^{\tau_M}/\rho\right)^{-\frac{1}{1-\rho}}}{\Gamma} \right] \mu Y_F - w_F f_F \, ,$$

where $\Gamma = n\left(c^N/\rho\right)^{-\frac{\rho}{1-\rho}} + n\left(e^{\tau_M} c^N/\rho\right)^{-\frac{\rho}{1-\rho}}$.

For convenience, p^N, p^M, c^N, and c^M stand for $p^N_{H,F}, p^M_{H,F}, c^N_{H,F}$, and $c^M_{H,F}$, respectively. Companies refrain from establishing a foreign affiliate if distance costs are very high, since the term in square brackets becomes very small. However, it remains positive in any case, because $c^M > c^N$ and $(c^M/\rho)^\wedge(-1/(1-\rho)) > (c^N e^{\tau}/\rho)^\wedge$ $(-1/(1-\rho))$ for any $\tau_M > 0$. For very high distance costs, demand for home country's goods in the foreign market is too small to generate enough variable profits to make up for the additional fixed costs at the plant level, $w_F f_F$. For very low distance costs, foreign production is not a profitable alternative either, since the term in square brackets approaches zero. In this case, Φ is negative. Equation (41) shows the derivative of Φ with respect to distance costs, τ_M:

$$(41) \quad \frac{\partial \Phi}{\partial \tau_M} = \underbrace{\begin{aligned} &\frac{c^M \left(\frac{c^M}{\rho}\right)^{-\frac{1}{1-\rho}} n \left(\frac{c^N}{\rho}\right)^{-\frac{\rho}{1-\rho}} \left[e^{\tau_M\left(-\frac{\rho}{1-\rho}\right)} - (1-\theta)\left(1 + e^{\tau_M\left(-\frac{\rho}{1-\rho}\right)}\right) \right]}{\Gamma^2} \mu Y \\ &- \frac{c^N \left(\frac{c^N e^{\tau_M}}{\rho}\right)^{-\frac{1}{1-\rho}} n \left(\frac{c^N}{\rho}\right)^{-\frac{\rho}{1-\rho}} \left[e^{\tau_M\left(-\frac{\rho}{1-\rho}\right)} - \frac{1}{\rho}\left(1 + e^{\tau_M\left(-\frac{\rho}{1-\rho}\right)}\right) \right]}{\Gamma^2} \mu Y. \end{aligned}}_{>0}$$

The first line of (41) gives the effect of changes in distance costs on the (variable) profits of production in the foreign country, the second line the effect on exports. For convenience, the first line is denoted Φ'_M (for multinational production), the second Φ'_N (for national production). Φ'_N is negative for not too low distance costs levels, τ_M, and a share of intermediate goods, $1-\theta$, which is not too low. Then, falling distance costs allow for larger profits through foreign production. For very high distance costs, the term in brackets approaches $-(1-\theta)$. For a production function which does not require intermediate goods, $(1-\theta=0)$, the first line turns positive. For all distance cost levels, higher distance costs are then related to higher profits of production abroad.

The second line of (41) is always positive, since the minus sign in front of the term changes the negative sign of Φ'_N. The term in square brackets in the second line is always negative because ρ is defined as $0 < \rho < 1$. Hence, exports increase with falling distance costs for all distance costs levels. The total effect is determined by the difference of the two effects ($\Phi_M' - \Phi_N'$). For most parameter constellations (distance cost levels not too low, intermediate-goods share not too low) they have the same sign. Hence, the sign of the difference depends on the size of the two effects. For very low distance cost levels and very low intermediate-goods shares, however, the total effect must be positive. Φ increases with rising distance costs and decreases with falling. For an intermediate-goods share of zero, this applies for all distance cost levels. The model converges to the Brainard (1993) model.

For intermediate-goods shares which are higher than zero, the total effect is not easily calculated since it depends on various exogenous parameters in a non-linear manner. The absolute size of the terms in square brackets is always larger in the second line than in the first one, since $1-\theta < 1/\rho$. This term expresses the effect of distance cost changes on the variable profits of one unit of the final good. The per unit effect is always higher for exported goods because distance costs raise the price for exports more than for goods produced abroad. Foreign affiliate products are only partly affected, through the imported intermediate goods, by distance costs.

For any $\tau_M > 0$ holds that $c^M > c^N$ and $(c^M/\rho)^\wedge(-1/(1-\rho)) > (c^N e^\tau/\rho)^\wedge(-1/(1-\rho))$. Higher marginal costs of c^M relative to c^N increase the variable profits of production abroad relative to exports, because higher costs translate into higher unit variable profits with a constant and equal-size markup ρ. In addition, demand for goods produced in affiliates of foreign MNEs is larger than for imported final goods, because their c.i.f. prices are lower, as can be seen from $(c^M/\rho)^\wedge(-1/(1-\rho)) > (c^N e^\tau/\rho)^\wedge(-1/(1-\rho))$. These terms give the own-price effects on demand. With the price index being equal in both cases, the own-price effect is sufficient for comparison of demand. Demand is always higher for affiliates' goods. With falling distance costs, higher increases in one-unit variable profits of exports than for goods produced abroad apply to lower sales in the foreign market. The total effect is parameter-dependent, and in particular dependent on the distance cost level, τ_M.

The second derivatives help to determine the curvature of Φ_M' and Φ_N' and therefore of Φ' and Φ. The second derivative of the variable profits of affiliates' products with respect to distance costs, Φ_M'', is negative for low distance cost levels and positive for high distance costs. The second derivative of variable export profits with respect to distance costs, Φ_N'', is always positive (see Appendix A for derivation). Hence, the negative slope becomes steeper for foreign production and less steep for exports with rising distance costs. Table 19 summarizes the derivatives for both functions.

Figure 5 sketches the curvature of the two effects. On the left-hand side, the functions are shown in a graph with increasing distance costs (τ_M increasing from

Table 19:
Level and Curvature of the Profitability Functions

Distance cost level	Foreign production Φ_M (net of fixed costs)	Exports Φ_N	Total Φ (including fixed costs)
$\tau_M = 0$	$\Phi_M = \Phi_N$, $\Phi'_M > 0$, $\Phi''_M < 0$	$\Phi_N = \Phi_M$, $\Phi'_N < 0$, $\Phi''_N > 0$	$\Phi = -w_F f_F$, $\Phi' > 0$, $\Phi'' < 0$
$0 < \tau_M < ((1-\theta)/\theta > e^{\tau_M\left(-\frac{\rho}{1-\rho}\right)}$	Φ_M high, $\Phi'_M > 0$, $\Phi''_M < 0$	Φ_N medium, $\Phi'_N < 0$, $\Phi''_N > 0$	$\Phi' > 0$, $\Phi'' < 0$
$(1-\theta)/\theta > e^{\tau_M\left(-\frac{\rho}{1-\rho}\right)} < \tau_M < \tau_M^*$	Φ_M medium, $\Phi'_M < 0$, $\Phi''_M < 0$	Φ_N low, $\Phi'_N < 0$, $\Phi''_N > 0$	$\Phi' < 0$, $\Phi'' < 0$
$\tau_M^* < \tau_M$	Φ_M low, $\Phi'_M < 0$, $\Phi''_M > 0$	Φ_N very low, $\Phi'_N < 0$, $\Phi''_N > 0$	
$\tau_M \to \infty$	$\Phi_M \to 0$, positive, $\Phi'_M < 0$, $\Phi''_M > 0$	$\Phi_N \to 0$, positive, $\Phi'_N < 0$, $\Phi''_N > 0$	$\Phi \to -w_F f_F$,

Figure 5:
Variable Profits of Production Abroad Φ_M and Exports Φ_N for Changing Distance Cost Levels τ_M

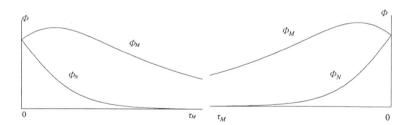

zero to higher values). The graph on the right-hand side gives the same functions on an x-axis which shows τ_M decreasing from higher values to zero.

The difference of both functions gives one part of trigger curve, Φ, which is relevant for the decision of a company to internationalize production. Additionally, fixed costs must be added at the intercept. This trigger curve Φ, which describes the profitability of production abroad relative to exports, is given in Figure 6. A trigger curve, Φ, exceeding zero indicates a higher profitability of production abroad, an Φ below zero a higher profitability of exports.

Figure 6:
Relative Profitability of Production Abroad and Exports

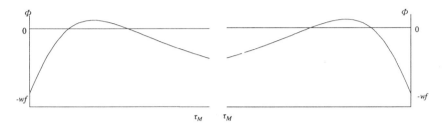

The analysis reveals that the shape of the trigger curve, Φ, depends on four exogenous parameters. Easiest to see is the effect of the fixed costs at the plant level, wf, that marks the intercept on the y-axis in the left graph. At $\tau_M=0$ variable profits for exports and affiliate production are equal, only fixed costs determine the level of the trigger curve. Higher fixed costs at the plant level shift the trigger curve downwards. In addition, the share of intermediate goods, $1-\theta$, affects level and slope of Φ_M. The level of Φ_M decreases with rising $1-\theta$ for all $\tau_M>0$ if $1-\theta$ is not too small. With increasing $1-\theta$, the curvature of Φ is less pronounced. The maximum of Φ is reached at a lower distance cost level. The range of low distance costs for which the first derivative of Φ_M with respect to τ_M is positive shrinks. The influence of ρ is not easily described either. The degree of differentiation, ρ, shapes the trigger curve. For homogeneous goods $(\rho\rightarrow 1)$, the trigger curve is a straight line parallel to the x-axis at minus fixed costs $(-wf)$. With no product differentiation, there is no room for MNEs. Exports in the foreign market would neither be possible with perfect price competition. The fourth exogenous parameter affecting Φ is r, the fixed costs at company level. It enters the decision via Γ. Γ is the price index from (26) weighted by $(\cdot)^{-y}$ and represents the degree of competition. Γ increases in the number of companies n in equilibrium, which depend negatively on r (see 29). Since Γ is negatively related to Φ, Φ increases in r. The trigger curve shifts up with increasing fixed costs at the company level.

The emergence of MNEs is parameter-dependent. For a range of realistic parameter constellations, MNEs may emerge in a process of globalization which is characterized by falling distance costs. In this process, companies rely on exports to serve the foreign market until the distance costs have fallen below a certain threshold. Then, internationalization of production is possible. However, the parameters are industry-specific or even company-specific. This may explain the observed pattern of internationalization of production with strong concentration on some industries and some industries preceding others. The internationalization of production in the discussion above is brought about by falling distance costs only, but other factors, such as falling required minimum size of a plant or increasing importance of headquarter services, may also contribute.

3.1.4 From a National Company Equilibrium to a Multinational Enterprise Equilibrium

The trigger curve compares the profits of a company under different conditions. Every point on the trigger curve represents a relative profitability at a particular point in time which is characterized by a certain level of distance costs. Distance costs fall over time. Falling distance costs alter the equilibrium prices, output quantities, the number of companies in equilibrium, and export and utility levels. Adjustment occurs in reaction to every change in distance costs. The trigger curve compares profits of a deviation from the equilibrium with the equilibrium profits at every point in time. For the outcome of the comparison, the structure of the equilibrium is essential. This structure is represented in Γ in (40). Competition would yield different equilibrium outcomes for a Γ which includes MNEs than for a Γ which does not.[3] As long deviating is not profitable, the composition of Γ does not change (although prices and numbers of companies change). However, with the emergence of the first MNE, composition and level of Γ change. Then, two effects, one from the exogenous fall of distance costs, and one from changes in Γ, alter the economy. To separate these two effects, I assume adjustments to changes in Γ to materialize immediately (at the same distance cost level).

The trigger curves used above are valid only until the first company has decided to deviate from the pure national company equilibrium by setting up a foreign affiliate. Then, the weighted price index, Γ, which includes only national companies, changes. With a company deciding to become an MNE, the number of national companies in the economy decreases by one and the number of MNEs increases by one. Since prices of national companies and MNEs differ in the foreign market, the price index changes. Although companies do not take the effect into account (the change of Γ is small for a large number of companies), the change in the price index affects the trigger curve Φ of a company. From (40) it can be seen that $\partial\Phi/\partial\Gamma < 0$, because $(c^M/\rho)^{\wedge}(-1/(1-\rho)) > (c^N e^{\tau}/\rho)^{\wedge}(-1/(1-\rho))$ and $c^M > c^N$.

In order to analyze the effect on the weighted price index, Γ, which stems from the change in the strategy of serving the foreign market, one additional

---

[3]   Thus, the economies and their economic relationship have a history and this history is very important for way and speed of their economic integration.

assumption is needed. The number of companies in the economy is fixed at λ, which is the number of companies in pure national company equilibrium before the first company becomes an MNE. In the short run, the zero-profit condition does not necessarily hold. The economy is not in a general equilibrium. Profits must not be zero. Only in the long run, the zero-profit condition holds. Assuming symmetry of both countries is maintained. The number of MNEs, m, based in H equals the number of MNEs based in F. m_H and m_F and n_H and n_F add up to λ. With m larger than zero, Γ changes to

$$\Gamma = n\left(\frac{c^N}{\rho}\right)^{-\frac{\rho}{1-\rho}}\left(1 + e^{-\tau_M \rho/1-\rho}\right) + m\left(\frac{c^M}{\rho}\right)^{-\frac{\rho}{1-\rho}} + m\left(\frac{c^N}{\rho}\right)^{-\frac{\rho}{1-\rho}}$$

with $m = m_H = m_F$ and $2m + 2n = \lambda$ and λ fixed.

As argued above, Γ changes with the number of MNEs m in the economy:

$$\frac{\partial\Gamma}{\partial m} = -\left(\frac{c^N}{\rho}\right)^{-\frac{\rho}{1-\rho}}\left(1 + e^{-\tau_M \rho/(1-\rho)}\right) + \left(\frac{c^M}{\rho}\right)^{-\frac{\rho}{1-\rho}} + \left(\frac{c^N}{\rho}\right)^{-\frac{\rho}{1-\rho}}$$

$$= \left(\frac{c^M}{\rho}\right)^{-\frac{\rho}{1-\rho}} - \left(\frac{c^N}{\rho}e^{\tau_M}\right)^{-\frac{\rho}{1-\rho}}.$$

Plugging in the relationship between the costs of a foreign affiliate and a domestic company, $c^M = c^N e^{\tau_M (1-\theta)}$, yields

$$(42) \qquad \frac{\partial\Gamma}{\partial m} = \left(e^{-\tau_M (1-\theta)\rho/(1-\rho)} - e^{-\tau_M \rho/(1-\rho)}\right)\left(\frac{c^N}{\rho}\right)^{-\frac{\rho}{1-\rho}} > 0.$$

An increase of the number of MNEs in an economy affects the weighted price index positively. This results from the fact that although the price of an affiliate's product is lower than the import price of the same good would be, demand of the good is expanded so that the weight of the good in the consumption basket increases. Sales of the good increase, consumers substitute this good for the other goods. The sales of the other goods fall. The profitability of foreign production relative to exports is therefore negatively affected by an increase in the number of MNEs. The decision of one company to set up an affiliate in the foreign country decreases the profitability to do the same for every national competitor in this symmetric model through the change in the weighted price index as long as the total number of companies is fixed at λ.

In the symmetric situation assumed here all companies have the same costs and all products have the same elasticity of substitution. Hence, every company has an incentive to internationalize production at the same time. However, this incentive falls with a national competitor setting up a foreign affiliate. All other companies incur losses. Some might drop out, since the zero profit condition holds in the long run. The new equilibrium with one MNE and an endogenous number of national companies settles if no (negative) profits are made. Given the adjusted weighted price index, Γ, with one MNE and a number of national companies in a general equilibrium with zero profits for all companies, another company sets up an affiliate in the foreign country, since it is profitable to do so.

The long-run dropout is hardly imagined to materialize immediately. However, if it is assumed to take a finite time span, this adjustment interferes with the changes that result from falling distance costs over time. Then, the observed effects in equilibrium are not separable. The profitability of foreign production relative to exports depends then on the slope of the trigger curve at this particular distance cost level. If the relative profitability of foreign production increases in a wider neighborhood around the particular point, the internationalization process of production only stops when all companies have become MNEs. During the adjustment from the pure national company equilibrium towards a pure MNE equilibrium, there might exist a mixed equilibrium with national companies and MNEs coexisting at a range of distance cost levels. With falling distance costs, the number of MNEs increases while the number of national companies and the total numbers of companies fall. When all companies in equilibrium are MNEs, the economy enters again a path where each distance cost level characterizes an equilibrium. Then, the equilibrium consists of only MNEs. The economy continues to move from equilibrium to equilibrium with falling distance cost levels until exporting becomes the dominant strategy again, when distance costs have fallen further.

3.1.5   Welfare

Welfare in an equilibrium with free market entry and exit and without activities of a state reduces to utility of the consumers. The utility level depends according to (1) on the amount of agricultural and manufacturing goods they can consume given the budget constraints in (3) and the composition of the bundle of manufacturing goods in (2). Since consumers love variety, the number of goods, which equals the number of companies in equilibrium, affects consumers' utility. Changes in the utility level of consumers can therefore stem from two sources: the affordability of larger amounts of the goods and the availability of more goods. Both sources of welfare changes are affected by exogenously falling distance costs. With falling distance costs, companies increase exports and gain market share in the foreign market. However, companies experience stronger competition from imports in their home market. Given the symmetry in the model, their sales at home, $p_i^H q_i^H$, fall as much as the foreign sales, $p_i^F q_i^F$, rise, and total sales, $p_i q_i$ remain unchanged (see Appendix A for derivation).

$$(43) \quad \frac{\partial(p_i q_i)}{\partial \tau_M} = -\frac{\dfrac{\rho}{1-\rho} n \left(\dfrac{c^N}{\rho} \right)^{-\frac{2\rho}{1-\rho}} e^{\tau_M \left(-\frac{\rho}{1-\rho} \right)}}{\Gamma^2} \mu Y_H$$

$$-\frac{\dfrac{\rho}{1-\rho} n \left(\dfrac{c^N}{\rho} \right)^{-\frac{2\rho}{1-\rho}} e^{\tau_M \left(-\frac{\rho}{1-\rho} \right)}}{\Gamma^2} \mu Y_F = 0$$

with $\quad \Gamma = n \left(\dfrac{c^N}{\rho} \right)^{-\frac{\rho}{1-\rho}} \left(1 + e^{\tau_M (-\rho/(1-\rho))} \right)$.

However, foreign sales include distance costs which are part of the consumer prices, but not relevant for companies' profits. Foreign c.i.f. sales are therefore less profitable for companies; the foreign sales rise cannot make up for the home sales losses in terms of the generation of (variable) profits which pay the fixed costs. Profits fall with falling distance costs, except for very small distance costs (Appendix A):

$$(44) \quad \frac{\partial \pi_i}{\partial \tau_M} = n \left(\frac{c^N}{\rho} \right)^{-\frac{2\rho}{1-\rho}} \mu Y / \Gamma^2 \left(\rho e^{\tau_M \left(-\frac{\rho}{1-\rho} \right)} - e^{\tau_M \left(-\frac{1}{1-\rho} \right)} \right).$$

With falling distance costs, losses in profits from sales at home are larger than increases of profits from export sales if $\rho e^{\tau \rho} > 1$. Distance costs must be very close to zero to allow companies to generate more profits abroad than they lose at home. For higher distance cost levels, companies incur losses for the given number of companies. Hence, some companies exit. The economy settles at a new equilibrium with more trade and less companies. Whereas larger quantities of cheaper imports increase consumer utility, the smaller number of varieties in equilibrium decreases utility. Consumers could have bought the same bundle of goods as before at new prices, but they decide not to do so and substitute a certain amount of domestic goods by imports. This substitution does not necessarily mean that the total effect on utility must be positive. Consumers spend not only the money they saved due to the price change of imported goods on purchases of higher import quantities; they additionally cut their expenses on domestic goods in favor of imports. In this decision they take the numbers of companies as given. Doing so, they realize utility gains, which are (at least partly) lost when some companies drop out and the number of available goods decreases. The size of both effects is shown in a numerical simulation solution in the next section. The results of this example are parameter-dependent. However, for all parameter constellations, the love-of-variety effect decreases with falling distance cost level as can be seen from (44). Only for very low distance costs, it turns positive.

A welfare analysis of the process of internationalization of production must assume the long-run adjustment to take place in a (infinitely) small time span to separate the effects which are due to falling distance costs. Only equilibria at the same distance cost level are compared with each other. The equilibria differ in the number of MNEs and in the (endogenously determined) number of national companies, in prices, quantities, and export levels. As discussed above, sales of the affiliate good increase, those of the other goods fall. Again, consumers could buy the "old" bundle at new prices and realize a utility gain. They can buy even more of the affiliate good and hold the sales per company constant. However, given prices and the number of varieties, they decide not to do so. They increase the sales fraction on the affiliate good at the expense of other goods. That leaves national companies producing these goods with losses. Some of them exit the market. Whether the positive or the negative effect on welfare prevails I discuss in the next section using numerical simulations.

Consumer utility in pure national company equilibria and pure MNE equilibria are different. If the utility level in pure national company equilibria is higher at distance cost levels which allow for stable MNE equilibria, a ban of internationalization of production is welfare improving. Lower prices, and therefore higher quantities of affiliate goods relative to imports, generate a consumption pattern which is more equalized in the pure MNE equilibrium. Contrarily, domestic products are bought much more extensively than imports in the pure national company equilibrium. Since consumers love variety, they prefer a more even distribution. Furthermore, there is a large income effect related to the switch from the c.i.f. price of an imported good to the price of an affiliate good. These effects favor MNE equilibria in terms of consumer utility. However, the total number of varieties in the pure MNE equilibrium is smaller than in a national company equilibrium. This favors the national company equilibrium over the MNE equilibrium.

The sum of these effects is parameter-dependent. In particular, the effects change with the distance cost level (Appendix A). The income effect of falling distance cost is larger in a MNE equilibrium for high and medium levels of distance costs. Although the fall in prices per unit in imports is larger than in affiliate goods (for affiliate goods, a price drop arises only because of cheaper intermediate inputs), price drops of affiliate goods apply to much larger quantities than those of imports. As long as the larger basis (quantity) effect outweighs the smaller price effect, the income gain is larger in the MNE equilibrium. In a national company equilibrium, the total numbers of varieties changes only in reaction to falling distance costs. It decreases first and rises later (at a low distance cost level). In equilibria that consist of MNEs only, the number of goods is constant with respect to distance cost changes.

3.1.6   Numerical Simulations

To demonstrate the mechanism of the general equilibrium model and quantify some effects, I apply numerical simulations. Therefore, the exogenous parameters have to be determined (for a discussion of the choice of parameters, see Appendix B). Using these exogenous parameters, the 14 equations, seven for each country, which define the pure national company general equilibrium are solved simultaneously. These are: the factor markets equilibrium given in (33), the pricing rules for the agricultural good in (34), the final manufacturing goods in (24), and the intermediate goods in (12), the zero-profit conditions for the final and the intermediate goods in (27) and (13), and the income equation in (35). In a mixed equilibrium with national and multinational companies, the pricing rule for the MNE in (24) is also needed.

This simultaneous solution describes together with the other equations a general equilibrium for a particular parameter constellation. Consumers cannot increase utility by changing their consumption bundle, companies cannot increase profits by variation of prices, all factor and goods markets are cleared, and there is no current account imbalance. Prices, quantities, and utility levels can be given explicitly in units of the numeraire, the agricultural good. This equilibrium is altered by a change of the exogenous distance cost level. Prices, quantities, and the number of companies in equilibrium adjust. The new equilibrium reflects the new conditions of competition. Utility and trade levels change, as does the incentive to internationalize production. As argued above, the resulting equilibria are parameter-dependent. The remainder of this part of Chapter 3 illustrates the general analysis by using one example. To a certain extent, the next chapters can be understood as sensitivity analysis.

The idea of this example is to mimic globalization (of two symmetric economies) by reducing the exogenous distance costs from initially very high levels to lower levels, and to let the system adjust to these changes and to discuss the results. For "historic" reasons, the initial equilibrium is modeled as pure national company equilibrium, since one of the phenomena of the globalization process is the emergence of MNEs on large scale. This equilibrium is checked for the incentive of a company to internationalize production. If deviation from the pure national company equilibrium is not profitable, the equilibrium is stable under the initial conditions. Over time, distance cost have fallen (they fall monotonously in this analysis). A particular distance cost level can, therefore, define a particular point in time in this approach, since earlier points in time are characterized by higher distance cost levels, later by lower distance costs. Thus, falling distance costs are employed as the driving force of the globalization process. With falling distance costs, the economy "moves" from equilibrium to equilibrium.

Falling distance cost levels stimulate trade in final goods. Consumers substitute imports for domestic products to satisfy their desire for variety in demand of the final good. That leads to a rise in exports of foreign companies which can be seen in Figure 7. Since both economies are symmetric in this basic version of the model, there is no interindustry trade. Furthermore, trade in intermediate goods and in services is bound to activities of MNEs. As long as there are no MNEs in equilibrium, there is no trade in intermediate goods and no trade in services. Figure 7 gives the exports of one country in symmetric equilibria with only national companies for falling distance cost levels.

Exports increase with falling distance costs at an increasing rate. In a world without distance costs, sales abroad equal sales at home. There is no home bias anymore. However, the trade levels shown here are calculated under the assumption of pure national company equilibria. But, since for high and medium distance cost levels, the incentive to internationalize production increases with falling distance costs as shown in Section 3.1.3, the pure national company equilibria might not be stable over the whole range of distance costs. The trigger curve, which is derived in Section 3.1.3, provides information about the stability of the national company equilibrium. It is given in Figure 8.

The national company equilibrium is stable until the distance costs level has been fallen to $\tau_M = 1.12$. At this point it is profitable for a company to deviate. The price index changes and the curves in Figures 7 and 8 are not valid anymore. After the adjustment is completed, there are only MNEs in equilibrium. Exports of final goods have fallen to zero, because the foreign market is supplied by foreign affiliates. But exports of intermediate goods and (headquarter) services pick up. The relationship of exports and production abroad is discussed in Chapter 5, using a more realistic version of this model. Here it is only concluded that in a world of falling distance costs, the observed pattern of globalization with increasing exports preceding growing importance of international production can be explained by using the framework proposed here.

The example allows to demonstrate the welfare effects of an internationalization of production in this symmetric equilibrium. Since no state is modeled

Figure 7:
The Effect of Falling Distance Costs on Exports

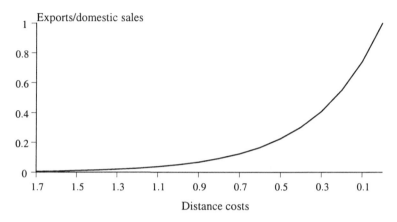

$\mu=0.6, \rho=0.75, \varepsilon=0.9, \theta=0.7, L_1=150, L_2=150, fz_1=fz_2=0.3, r_1=r_2=1.5, f_1=f_2=0.5$

Figure 8:
Trigger Curve

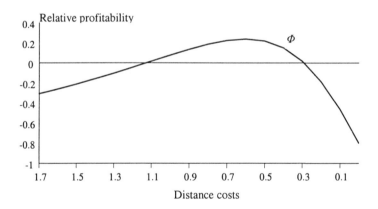

$\mu=0.6, \rho=0.75, \varepsilon=0.9, \theta=0.7, L_1=150, L_2=150, fz_1=fz_2=0.3, r_1=r_2=1.5, f_1=f_2=0.5$

and the zero-profit condition holds in equilibrium, welfare is determined by consumer utility. Consumer utility is given in Figure 9. It rises with lower distance costs due to increased foreign activities of companies. Internationalization of production reduces utility in the short run but lifts it to levels above the national

Figure 9:
Welfare in the Symmetric Equilibrium

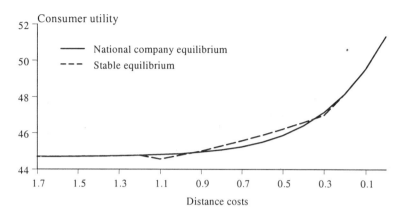

$\mu=0.6, \rho=0.75, \varepsilon=0.9, \theta=0.7, L_1=150, L_2=150, fz_1=fz_2=0.3, r_1=r_2=1.5, f_1=f_2=0.5$

company equilibrium for lower distance cost levels. Internationalization of production is therefore welfare-improving in this symmetric equilibrium. In terms of welfare, companies switch too late back to a national company equilibrium.

Changes of consumer utility result from two effects: from the change of the prices of the differentiated final goods, and from the number of goods available in equilibrium. To get an idea about the size of these effects, Figure 10 shows the price indexes and the number of companies in both equilibria for the different distance cost levels. The (rather small) increase in utility at high distance cost levels is driven by a falling price index. The effect of falling prices is almost offset by lower utility because of fewer companies in equilibrium. With falling distance costs the price effect outweighs the variety effect more and more. The variety effect decreases relatively and absolutely.

Higher welfare in the equilibrium with MNEs results from lower prices and a more balanced consumption of the available goods. The short-run fall in utility is due to the fall in variety and a short-run rise in the price index. Although prices of the "foreign" goods drop from import prices to affiliate-goods prices, consumer substitute "expensive" affiliate goods for "cheap" domestic goods. Affiliate goods get a higher weight in the consumption basket. In total, the price index increases. Throughout the time when MNEs exist in equilibrium, the number of companies (and therefore of goods) is lower in these equilibria than in national company equilibria. As pointed out in the discussion in Section 3.1.5, the number of companies increases with falling distance costs at very low levels of

Figure 10:
Price Effect and Variety Effect in the Symmetric Equilibrium

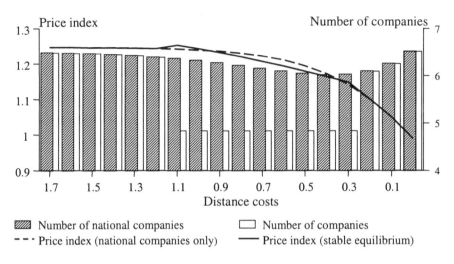

Number of national companies

- - - Price index (national companies only)

Number of companies

—— Price index (stable equilibrium)

distance costs. Hence, at very low distance costs levels, welfare increases for both effects: price and variety.

3.1.7   Conclusions

A general equilibrium model of trade and production in foreign affiliates is set up and analyzed with regard to the effect of falling distance costs. The model includes the use of intermediate goods in the production of final goods. Intermediate goods are specific to the final good or the production process, and are, therefore, not easily substitutable. Foreign affiliates import these intermediate goods from their home country. This raises the price of the affiliate product relative to the domestic producers because exported intermediate goods incur the same distance costs as final goods. However, affiliate goods are cheaper than imported ones, their sales (net of distance costs) are larger. It may, therefore, be profitable to save on the distance costs by changing the strategy to serve the foreign market, although this requires additional fixed costs at the plant level. An equilibrium with national companies or with MNEs may emerge.

Assuming an equilibrium with only national companies in the initial situation, effects of exogenously falling distance costs on this equilibrium are analyzed. Stability of the market structure with only national companies is given as long no company has an incentive to change its mode of serving the foreign market from exports to production abroad. Since the incentive to internationalize production depends on the level of distance costs, stability of the equilibrium depends on the distance cost level. For high levels of distance costs, the establishment of an affiliate is not profitable since its output is too small to generate variable profits large enough to make up for the additional fixed costs at the plant level. With falling distance costs, however, the profitability of foreign production first increases stronger than the profitability of exports, later less. The relative profitability, therefore, describes an inverted U-shape. At intermediate distance costs levels, the emergence of MNEs might be profitable. For low distance cost levels, export is always the preferred mode of serving the foreign market.

An adjustment path to the new equilibrium which includes MNEs is modeled. In the adjustment process, companies set up affiliates in the foreign market to supply their goods to consumers at lower prices. However, the adjustment forces some companies to exit the market. The number of goods in equilibrium falls. The number of MNEs in a pure MNE equilibrium is lower than the number of companies in a pure national company equilibrium. Whereas the first effect raises welfare, the second decreases welfare. The total effect can go either way and depends on the exogenous parameters. Welfare can therefore be lower in a world with strong tendency towards internationalization of production. However, the numerical example showed that there might be reasons to believe that welfare is higher in a world with a higher share of affiliate production. The welfare effect of globalization over time is unambiguously positive. Reductions in the separation of markets lead to rising welfare levels of both economies. Increased international activities of companies from both countries make these rises possible.

This analysis reveals that the observed pattern of increasing intraindustry trade preceding the internationalization of production in globalization can be explained in a trade model which allows for the endogenous emergence of MNEs. The consideration of specific intermediate goods in the production function is essential for deriving the results of the model. The second part of this chapter is therefore devoted to an empirical test of the assumed specificity of the intermediate goods in the production process of MNEs. In the next chapters, I analyze how sensitive these results from the numerical simulation are to particular parameter constellations. That is not only important because we do not know these parameters exactly but also because they might vary for countries, industries, and individuals.

3.2   Trade in Intermediate Goods and Multinational Enterprises Networks

The discussion in Chapter 2 argues and the model introduced in the first part of this chapter assumes that trade and the internationalization of production are not independent of each other. There are at least two links between both. First, they are different strategies of a company to serve the foreign market. Often, exports precede foreign production of a particular good in a foreign country. Companies use multiple internationalization strategies with production of some goods in some countries, exports of other goods, and licensing in third cases (Stehn 1992). Baldwin and Ottaviano (1998) offer an explanation for the simultaneous use of different strategies of multiproduct companies. Second, trade in intermediate goods might be necessary for the internationalization of production. This relationship has not been discussed so often because trade has almost exclusively been thought of as trade in final goods, in theoretical as well as in empirical analyses. This is surprising, given the large share of world trade which is trade in intermediate goods. It accounts for roughly one-half of the total imports of developed countries. This share proved to be remarkably constant over the 1980s and 1990s. Given the stronger growth in trade relative to production, the share of imported intermediate goods in total inputs increased strikingly over this period.

In order to remedy the lack of attention given to trade in intermediate goods and to test the assumption used in the model, part two of this chapter uses input-output data from six OECD countries and German time-series data to study the relationship of trade in intermediate goods and the internationalization of production. Three hypotheses are tested: (i) growing trade in intermediate goods results from the fact that companies use foreign cost advantages more intensively by buying inputs from the cheapest supplier (global sourcing), (ii) growing trade in intermediate goods is related to companies' outward FDI activities (outsourcing), and (iii) growing trade in intermediate goods results from an increasing importance of MNE networks.

The global-sourcing hypothesis for growing trade in intermediate goods implies that companies buy the intermediate goods which they use as inputs, by arm's length transactions, wherever the best conditions are offered. The increasing use of imported intermediate goods is, therefore, due to the decreasing prices of imported intermediate goods as result of decreasing distance costs between countries. Furthermore, by reducing information asymmetries and deficits, globalization could generate a growing propensity to import intermediate goods from abroad. This is not different from trade in final goods. Global sourcing, therefore, is the default hypothesis in this analysis. If there is nothing special about the strong increase in trade in intermediate goods, nothing that differs from trade in final goods, the global-sourcing hypothesis fits best. It reflects the deeper integration of world intermediate goods markets in 2000 compared to the 1960s or 1970s.

However, trade in intermediate goods could differ from trade in final goods in its characteristics if it is bound to foreign direct investment (FDI). Then, it would be important to analyze intermediate-goods trade separately. The outsourcing hypothesis (Feenstra and Hanson 1996) is one possible candidate to explain increasing intermediate-goods trade as being the result of the growing importance of production in foreign affiliates. According to this hypothesis, increasing imports of intermediate goods result from companies' strategies to relocate a part of their production to foreign countries with comparative advantages in the production of particular products. Thus, companies in industrialized countries shift labor-intensive stages of their production processes to labor-abundant countries with lower wages. Therefore, FDI of companies from developed countries is necessary in low-wage countries. The increasing use of imported intermediate goods in production in the developed countries is, according to the outsourcing hypothesis, related to growing outward FDI stocks of companies in industrialized countries.

In contrast, the MNE network hypothesis implies that it is not outward FDI but rather inward FDI that drives increasing imports of intermediate goods in developed countries. The increasing use of these imports is due to trading networks of MNEs. Intense trade between MNEs' affiliates in foreign countries and companies in the home country (including of course the MNE parent company) lead to higher imports of intermediate goods. This means there might exist a border effect, as has been found in trade between countries (McCallum 1995), for companies too. They trade relatively more within their networks than with outside parties. Affiliates import specific intermediate goods from home for processing and selling in the foreign country. Increased importance of networks of foreign MNEs, i.e., increasing inward FDI stocks, leads to growing imports of intermediate goods.

This part includes five sections. In Section 3.2.1, I review the related literature. In Section 3.2.2, I present three theoretical hypotheses of the growing importance of imported intermediate goods. In Section 3.2.3, I test these hypotheses by using an econometric cross-section model which includes 24 industrial sectors in six OECD countries. These six countries (Australia, France, Germany, Japan, the United Kingdom, and the United States) account for about two-thirds of world GDP and about one-half of world trade. Following the cross-section analysis, I present in Section 3.2.4 time-series evidence on the change in imported intermediate goods in the last 25 years. In Section 3.2.5, I conclude.

3.2.1   Related Literature

Trade in intermediate goods has been discussed in the international business literature for more than two decades. The transaction cost approach as a framework to study MNEs aims to explain the advantages and disadvantages of internalizing international markets within a company. It is concerned with the coordination of two activities which are located in two different countries and connected by the international trade of intermediate goods (Casson et al. 1986).

In contrast, trade theorists have not paid much attention to trade in intermediate goods until recently. In theoretical and empirical research, trade was thought of as trade in finished goods. With the increasing international division of labor through disintegration of the production process, which increased strongly in the 1980s and 1990s, trade in intermediate goods called for more attention (Jones and Kierzkowski 2000; Krugman 1995a). When Campa and Goldberg (1997) collected facts on the external orientation of particular industries in four countries (Canada, Japan, the United Kingdom, and the United States) they presented, besides export and import figures, shares of imported intermediate goods relative to total inputs used in domestic production. Their work points to a growing dependence on imported intermediate goods in the production of nearly all manufacturing industries in Canada, the United Kingdom, and the United States. There are sectoral as well as national differences. Almost all Japanese sectors, for instance, do not rely very heavily on imported intermediate inputs. Furthermore, the share of imported intermediate goods in Japan's total imports has declined over the last 25 years (Campa and Goldberg 1997).

Due to data constraints, empirical analysis of intermediate goods trade is quite rare. Sectoral studies (Campa and Goldberg 1997; Hummels et al. 1998) find increasing international trade in inputs in recent years. Next to increasing export and import levels and increasing FDI flows, increasing international integration can also be seen in the increasing use of imported inputs. Both studies cited above point to national and sectoral differences, with smaller countries being more dependent on imported inputs. Machinery and chemicals are the sectors that lead international integration regarding the use of imported intermediate goods. Differences in the trade of intermediate and finished goods are also found in studies which rely on company data (Andersson and Fredriksson 2000).

3.2.2   Theoretical Considerations

Globalization, with decreasing distance costs, and technological progress, both of which ease changes in production processes (shorter product cycle, smaller production series), lead to an increase in the use of imported intermediate goods relative to domestic inputs. The catchword "global sourcing" has been coined to express this phenomenon. The global-sourcing hypothesis states that the elasticity of imported intermediate goods demand with respect to output is increasing with increasing global integration. This should show up in a conditional demand function which can be estimated. Equation (45) gives the conditional demand function derived from a CES production function[4] with four input variables: labor L, capital K, domestic inputs D, and imported intermediate inputs I:

$$(45) \quad I = \frac{\partial C}{\partial p_I} = \alpha_4^{1-\rho} Y p_I^{\rho-1} \left[\left(\frac{w}{\alpha_1} \right)^\rho + \left(\frac{r}{\alpha_2} \right)^\rho + \left(\frac{p_D}{\alpha_3} \right)^\rho + \left(\frac{p_I}{\alpha_4} \right)^\rho \right]^{\frac{1-\rho}{\rho}} ,$$

where w stands for wage, i.e., the factor price of labor, r for interest rate, i.e., the factor price of capital, and p_D and p_I for the price for domestic and imported intermediate goods, respectively. The production output is denoted by Y. For the global-sourcing hypothesis to hold, α_4 must increase.

Growing trade in intermediate goods may also be a phenomenon which is bound to the internationalization of production. Mostly, trade in intermediate goods is then related to vertical integration, and vertical integration is related to factor proportion theories. Intermediate-goods trade, therefore, is expected to exploit country differences. This is the outsourcing view of intermediate goods. Labor-intensive stages in the value chain are relocated to labor-abundant low-wage countries. Intermediate products are imported for further manufacturing or selling in the developed country (Feenstra 1998). According to the outsourcing hypothesis, growing imports of intermediate goods point to growing vertical trade on the basis of factor proportion theories.

Feenstra and Hanson (1995) illustrate this process by using a Heckscher–Ohlin model with a continuum of intermediate goods, z, but only a single final good. There are three factors of production: unskilled and skilled labor, L and H, and capital, K, employed in production in two countries: the North and the South. The South is assumed to be unskilled-labor-abundant. Feenstra and Hanson (1995) interpret all activities as within one industry. The intermediate inputs are produced according to

$$(46) \quad x(z) = A_i \left[\min \left\{ \frac{L(z)}{a_L(z)}, \frac{H(z)}{a_H(z)} \right\} \right]^\theta [K(z)]^{1-\theta} ,$$

---

[4] A CES production function is used because it is fairly general and includes other often-used production functions as special cases, depending on the value of ρ.

where A_i is a constant that can differ between the North and the South, and $a_L(z)$ and $a_H(z)$ give the fraction of unskilled and skilled labor for the production of one unit of the intermediate input, z. The ratio $a_H(z)/a_L(z)$ is assumed to increase in z. Given these intermediate inputs, the final good is assembled free of cost according to the production function

$$(47) \quad \ln Y = \int_0^1 \alpha(z)\ln x(z)dz \quad \text{with} \int_0^1 \alpha(z)dz = 1 .$$

Factor price equalization cannot be achieved, since factor endowments and technologies are assumed to be sufficiently different. In equilibrium, the South produces and exports a range of inputs up to some critical ratio of skilled to unskilled labor, which characterizes the intermediate z^*, while the North produces the remaining inputs. Taking the location of the production of intermediate inputs into account, (47) changes to

$$(48) \quad \ln Y = \underbrace{\int_0^{z^*} \alpha(z)\ln x(z)dz}_{I} + \int_{z^*}^1 \alpha(z)\ln x(z)dz .$$

The second term on the right-hand side expresses the intermediate inputs produced in the North. These are more skilled-labor-intensive than the imported intermediate inputs, I (produced in the South), which are given in the first term on the right-hand side. By using (46), the imported inputs, I, can be written as

$$(49) \quad \ln I = \int_0^{z^*} \alpha(z)\theta \ln\left[A_i \min\left\{ \frac{L(z)}{a_L(z)}, \frac{H(z)}{a_H(z)} \right\} \right] dz + (1-\theta)\int_0^{z^*} \alpha(z)\ln K(z)dz .$$

Growth in the relative capital stock in the South or neutral technical progress relative to the North raises the critical ratio, z^*, dividing the Northern and Southern activities. Outsourcing occurs with relocation of production from the North to the South if z^* rises. Although FDI in the low-wage country is not mandatory for this phenomenon to occur, since it results more generally from any neutral increase in relative supply from the low-wage country (Feenstra and Hanson 1995), developed countries' outward FDI in low-wage countries is seen as being driven by outsourcing motives and as being likely to generate imports of intermediate goods by the North.

But it might also be that inward FDI drives the import of intermediate goods. In the model introduced in the first part of this chapter, growing trade in intermediate goods is explained by activities of foreign MNEs in a market. For their production in the foreign country, MNEs need to import specific intermediate goods. The production function, which mirrors the assumed cost function (18) of an MNE's affiliate in a foreign country in the model above, is given by

$$(50) \quad q_i = F_P + L^\theta I^{1-\theta} .$$

The first term on the right-hand side, F_P, shows the fixed input factors on the plant level. The production elasticity θ is given by the technology. The output of the company is denoted by q_i; the inputs, labor and intermediate goods, are denoted by L and I, respectively. Modern production generally relies on many intermediate goods which are supplied by independent companies and/or by affiliates and subsidiaries of the parent company. Many of these intermediate goods are specific to the company's product or production process. When a company internationalizes its production process, production in the foreign affiliate depends, at least partly, on the supply of intermediate goods from the MNE's home-country supplier network. The establishment of a supplier network in the host country is time-consuming. Many adjustments of the production process are necessary. Hence, it is cheaper for the foreign affiliate to import intermediate goods from the home country.

3.2.3   Evidence from Cross-Section Analyses

In the following two sections, I test the three hypotheses in a cross-section and a time-series framework. The outsourcing and MNE network hypotheses are tested directly by using outward and inward FDI stock data. I test the global-sourcing hypothesis in a more indirect manner in some of the cross-section regressions and directly by actually estimating the elasticity of demand for imported intermediate goods with respect to output in three regressions. The indirect test uses the fact that the size of the intercept contains information about the global-sourcing hypothesis: a positive intercept points to the importance of global sourcing, a growing positive intercept to an increasing propensity to source globally. The global-sourcing hypothesis of increasing use of imported intermediate goods thus shows up in increasing intercepts. In the time-series regressions in Section 3.2.5, I interpret the test of significance of the trend variable as "test" of the global-sourcing hypothesis. If there is a tendency towards a more intense use of imported intermediate goods independent of FDI stocks, this should be seen in the time trend variable.

I test the outsourcing hypothesis by estimating (49). The dependent variable on the left-hand side is the logarithm of imported inputs which is available from the OECD input-output table as described in Appendix C. For the six

OECD countries under consideration (the North), I use sectoral disaggregated imported input data for the analysis. In a cross-section analysis, the first term on the right-hand side, ($\int_0^{z^*} \alpha(z)\,\theta \ln[A_i \min\{L(z)/a_L(z), H(z)/a_H(z)\}]\,dz$), can be seen as a constant that is likely to vary among different sectors. It is not necessary to calculate proxies for this integral. It is sufficient to control for the sectoral differences. The second term is the product of an unknown coefficient (between zero and one) and the logarithm of the capital stock used in the production of the imported inputs: $(1-\theta)\int_0^{z^*} \alpha(z) \ln K(z)\,dz$. This capital stock is employed in the foreign country (South). The foreign capital stock can neither be calculated nor proxied by using outward FDI of the inputs-importing countries, but outward FDI is the appropriate variable to test the role of globalization in outsourcing. Since FDI in other countries is thought to be the reason for the increasing use of imported intermediate goods in domestic production in many developed countries, this should show up in the data. Outsourcing in this test is bound to outward FDI and therefore different from Feenstra and Hanson's definition, but in accordance with their reasoning. Sectoral outward FDI stocks of the intermediate-goods-importing country are used as an explanatory variable. For estimation, (49) is changed to

$$(51) \quad \ln I = c + \beta_1 \ln FDI_{Outward} + \beta_3 Dummy_{Sector} + \beta_4 Dummy_{Country} + u.$$

For the outsourcing hypothesis to hold, β_1 must be positive ($\beta_1 > 0$). Country dummies are included to control for national differences among the six countries which are pooled in these regressions and together called the North. Australia, for instance, is likely to import fewer intermediate goods because of its larger distance from its trading partners, the United States because of its economic size.

The test for the MNE networks is also straightforward. Companies in the model above are all symmetric. Aggregate intermediate-goods imports depend on the foreign affiliates' output and the number of foreign affiliates in a country. In reality, number and size of the affiliates in countries differ. The importance of foreign MNEs for a country is proxied here by the inward FDI stock. However, the exclusive use of this data would imply equal intermediate input shares and equal capital coefficients in all sectors. Thus, sector dummies shall control for differences among the various sectors. Logs are taken and a constant is included, which allows for imports of intermediate goods independent of FDI by host country companies. The estimated equation is given in (52):

$$(52) \quad \ln I = c + \beta_2 \ln FDI_{Inward} + \beta_3 Dummy_{Sector} + \beta_4 Dummy_{Country} + u.$$

The MNE network hypothesis implies $\beta_2 > 0$. The country dummies are included for the same reason as in (51). In addition, a third equation is estimated which includes both outward and inward FDI stocks:

$$(53) \quad \ln I = c + \beta_1 \ln FDI_{Outward} + \beta_2 \ln FDI_{Inward} + \beta_3 Dummy_{Sector}$$
$$+ \beta_4 Dummy_{Country} + u.$$

In some specifications, sectoral output is included as exogenous variable. A change of the inferred coefficient (i.e., the demand elasticity of imported intermediate goods with respect to sectoral output) over the three points in time the cross-section regressions are estimated gives a test of the global-sourcing hypothesis. The coefficient corresponds to $\alpha_4^{1-\rho}$ from (45). The term in square brackets and the price of the intermediate goods are included in the sector dummies. According to the global-sourcing hypothesis, FDI is not a determinant of imported intermediate goods, neither inward nor outward FDI.

Equations (51), (52), and (53) are tested using sectoral data for three points in time: the late 1970s/early 1980s, the mid-1980s, and 1990. The late 1970s/early 1980s are tested with sectoral data from only three countries: Germany (1978), Japan (1980), and the United States (1982), which are pooled. France and the United Kingdom did not report FDI stocks at that time; for Australia, no input-output table is available for the early 1980s. The number of observations is rather low, with very few Japanese sectors available. The other analyses are conducted using data from all six countries. The mid-1980s data range from 1984 (United Kingdom) to 1986 (Australia and Germany). French FDI stocks are calculated by using the late eighties stock data and subtracting the flow data, which are reported in OECD (1993).

Table 20 reports the estimation results for the late 1970s/early 1980s.[5] All regressions are run by using the White (1980) correction for heteroskedasticity. Columns I to III give the estimates without any dummy variable, in IV to VI dummies are included to allow for sectoral differences. Columns VII to IX include the value of the sectoral output in order to control for differences in the size of the sectors. Since larger sectors are supposed to import more inputs, the output variable is expected to have a positive sign. Furthermore, these regressions allow a test of the global-sourcing hypothesis since the output coefficient is the elasticity of the demand for imported intermediate goods with respect to output.

---

[5]   All estimations are conducted by using the software package EViews 3.1.

Table 20:

Imported Intermediate Goods and Outsourcing vs. MNE Networks in 1980[a]

	I	II	III	IV	V	VI	VII	VIII	IX
Constant	6.602***	5.788***	5.708***	7.057***	6.220***	6.187***	1.613	1.544	1.061
ln(Output)							0.628***	0.494***	0.601***
ln(FDI$_{Outward}$)	0.206***		0.038	0.153***		0.045	−0.047		−0.158
ln(FDI$_{Inward}$)		0.335***	0.307**		0.283***	0.237*		0.164*	0.232*
Textiles							0.295	0.647**	0.671**
Electrical equipment				−0.448**				−0.191	
Nonmetallic minerals				−0.728**	−0.845**	−0.768**	−0.686**	−0.552*	−0.718**
Petroleum				1.620***	1.131***	1.226***	1.607***	1.338***	1.262***
Mining				−1.206**	−1.164**	−1.153**	−1.060***	−1.046***	−0.976***
Metal							−0.468		
Other transport				−1.065			−0.709**		−0.421***
Adjusted R²	0.11	0.25	0.23	0.39	0.40	0.40	0.64	0.64	0.68
F-statistic	6.54**	15.30***	7.57***	6.40***	6.84***	6.65***	10.40***	11.90***	12.62***
Jarque–Bera Prob	0.55	0.92	0.93	0.22	0.45	0.53	0.47	0.64	0.27

*, **, *** significant at the 10 percent, 5 percent, and 1 percent level.

[a]Dependent variable: ln(imported inputs); method: least squares; number of observations: 44; White-heteroskedasticity-consistent standard errors and covariance. Data for Germany from 1978, for the United States from 1980, and for Japan from 1982.

Table 20 gives support to the outsourcing hypothesis as well as to the MNE network hypothesis. The outward FDI stock has a positive effect on imported intermediate goods in regression I and in regression IV, which includes dummy variables to control for sectoral differences. In regression VII, which includes the value of outputs to control for sectoral size effects, the outward FDI stock fails to exert a significant influence. The same holds for the regression which includes both inward and outward FDI stocks (III, VI, and IX). The insignificant coefficients in these regressions might result from multicollinearity between explanatory variables.

The correlation coefficient between the log of outward and inward FDI stocks is 0.633 which exceeds the critical value for 44 observations of 0.302. The correlation between the log of outward FDI and the production output is 0.627, which is rather high, too. That could explain the insignificant coefficient of outward FDI in regression III, VI, VII, and IX as multicollinearity inflates the standard error.

The coefficient of the inward FDI stock variable proves to be more robust against specification changes. The inward FDI stock variable always exerts a significant positive effect on imported intermediate goods in this sample. A 10 percent increase in the inward FDI stock increases imports of intermediate goods between 1.6 percent and 3.3 percent. The explanatory power and the F-statistic are higher (regression II) than in the outward FDI stock equation (regression I).

Including some sectoral variables increases the explanatory power strongly. Equations (45) and (49) derived from theoretical models pointed to sectoral differences which must be controlled for. Regressions IV to IX point to large sectoral differences. Not surprisingly, the petroleum- and coal-products sector (Petroleum) imports significantly more inputs (oil and gas) than other sectors. The reliance on imported intermediate inputs in production in this sector was at 19 percent for the United States, 78 percent for Germany, and 82 percent for Japan in the early 1980s, far above sector averages (8 percent, 18 percent, and 14 percent, respectively). Other significant dummy variables confirm the sectoral differences. Including more sectoral dummy variables does not change the coefficients of FDI stocks in regressions IV to IX. Finally, the output variable adds further to the explanatory power and the F-statistics of the estimated equations. The coefficient is significantly positive for all three regressions. The size of the constant drops if output is included as explanatory variable.

The analysis for the mid-1980s includes six countries (Australia, France, Germany, Japan, the United Kingdom, and the United States). The numbers of observation increases to 75. An outlier, the French nonmetallic mineral sector, was excluded from the mid-1980s and 1990 regressions to ensure normal distribution of the residuals. The results, which confirm those in Table 20, are given in Table 21.

The country dummy for Australia was included to ensure normally distributed residuals. By using data from six instead of three countries, the estimation results improve (even without the Australia dummy), as seen in higher R^2 and F-statistics.[6] This indicates that the results from Table 20 do not only apply to the three largest economies. Again, the MNE network hypothesis gains stronger support than the outsourcing hypothesis.

F-statistic and R^2 are higher in all regressions run with mid-1980s data. The coefficient of the FDI_{Inward} variable is of higher significance. Again, significant sectoral differences are found. Dummy variables and production output in regressions IV through IX control for these sectoral differences. Furthermore, the country dummy for Australia is significant. Australian companies import significantly less intermediate goods than other countries in this sample which can be explained by Australia's geographic location.

The third cross-section results apply for 1990, the last year for which OECD input-output data are available (Table 22). The sample includes the same six

---

6   The R^2 and F-statistics presented here are not comparable to the early 1980s regression, because the regressions of Table 21 include the Australia dummy.

Table 21:
Imported Inputs and Outsourcing vs. MNE Networks in 1985[a]

	I	II	III	IV	V	VI	VII	VIII	IX
Constant	7.533***	6.118***	6.149***	7.470***	6.190**	6.311***	2.726***	3.165***	3.010***
ln(Output)							0.512***	0.357***	0.394***
ln(FDI$_{Outward}$)	0.085**		−0.019	0.099**		−0.018	−0.004		−0.073**
ln(FDI$_{Inward}$)		0.295***	0.310***		0.301***	0.296***		0.180***	0.219***
Australia	−1.50***	−1.65***	−1.69***	−1.38***	−1.62***	−1.63***	−0.70***	−0.96***	−1.05***
Nonmetallic minerals				−0.620*	−0.715**	−0.720***	−0.630***	−0.606***	−0.720***
Petroleum				0.938**		0.218	0.860***	0.535**	0.208
Metal				−0.645**	−0.670**	−0.623**	−0.437	−0.523*	−0.463*
Electrical equipment				−0.430***			−0.209		
Adjusted R^2	0.40	0.56	0.55	0.47	0.61	0.60	0.64	0.68	0.70
F-statistic	25.4***	47.7***	31.5***	14.3***	24.2***	19.4***	22.6***	23.9***	25.4***
Jarque–Bera Prob	0.22	0.65	0.71	0.15	0.48	0.65	0.24	0.16	0.21

*, **, *** significant at the 10 percent, 5 percent, and 1 percent level.

[a]Dependent variable: ln(imported inputs); method: least squares; number of observations: 75; White-heteroskedasticity-consistent standard errors and covariance. Data for the United Kingdom from 1984, for France, Japan, and the United States from 1985, and for Australia and Germany from 1986.

Table 22:
Imported Intermediate Goods and Outsourcing vs. MNE Networks in 1990[a]

	I	II	III	IV	V	VI	VII	VIII	IX
Constant	7.270***	6.751***	6.579***	7.281***	7.014***	6.799***	3.875***	3.655***	3.774***
ln(Output)							0.373***	0.376***	0.352***
ln(FDI$_{Outward}$)	0.198***		0.068	0.210***		0.099	0.109**		0.052
ln(FDI$_{Inward}$)		0.270***	0.220**		0.253***	0.180**		0.136***	0.101*
Australia	−1.510***	−1.880***	−1.740***	−1.330***	−1.800***	−1.580***	−0.860***	−1.090***	−1.010***
Nonmetallic minerals				−1.130***	−1.249***	−1.200***	−0.960***	−1.000***	−0.996***
Petroleum				1.156***			1.152***	0.928***	0.987***
Metal				−0.570**	−0.462**	−0.520***	−0.520**	−0.450**	0.478**
Professional goods				−1.030***	−1.070***	−1.070***	−0.800***	−0.800***	−0.819***
Mining				−0.940***	−0.610***	−0.740***	−0.750***	−0.560**	−0.631***
Adjusted R^2	0.56	0.61	0.62	0.72	0.71	0.72	0.80	0.80	0.80
F-statistic	47.7***	58.4***	39.4***	28.1***	30.7***	27.5***	36.3***	37.9***	33.9***
Jarque–Bera Prob	0.51	0.92	0.87	0.42	0.97	0.78	0.39	0.20	0.27

*, **, *** significant at the 10 percent, 5 percent, and 1 percent level.

[a]Dependent variable: ln(imported inputs); method: least squares; number of observations: 76; White-heteroskedasticity-consistent standard errors and covariance.

countries as the mid-1980s regression. The lack of Japanese FDI stock data for petroleum and rubber products and nonmetallic products reduces the number of observations to 73.

Table 22 confirms the results of the earlier points in time. As in the mid-1980s' regressions, the country dummy for Australia was included to ensure normally distributed residuals. The coefficient of $FDI_{Outward}$, although larger than in the mid-1980s regressions, is still highly sensitive to specification changes, whereas the FDI_{Inward} coefficient is more robust and improves the specification of the equations. The MNE network hypothesis is supported in all regressions. Notwithstanding multicollinearity with the output variable, which is used to control for sector size, the coefficient remains significant. Its size changes only little in all specification changes. Furthermore, it proves to be remarkably stable over time.

3.2.4   Discussion of the Results

Cross-section estimations give strong support to the hypothesis that international production plays a role in explaining the remarkable increase in intermediate-inputs imports of developed countries. Although hard to separate because of multicollinearity, the joint effect of outward and inward FDI stocks is significant and of considerable size. The hypothesis that the increasing use of imported inputs is triggered by a worldwide production network of MNEs is not rejected in any regression. The result seems to be robust to specification changes and holds for different points in time. Unfortunately, the last input-output table which includes imported transactions is published for 1990, a time when the latest wave of economic integration had just started. Given the strong increase in FDI by MNEs in the 1990s, the importance of MNE networks is likely to have increased. The stable coefficient of the elasticity of imported intermediate goods to changes in inward FDI stocks even in a period with drastically increased FDI flows points to a very stable economic relationship between the production of MNEs in a host country and their propensity to import intermediate goods.[7] Given the large home bias which has been found in the trade of nearly all countries, it is very likely that the bulk of the imports of MNEs are drawn from their home countries. Unfortunately, this hypothesis cannot be tested, since the imported-transactions table of the input-output matrix allows no distinction by countries from which inputs are imported.

---

[7]   The results are consistent with those of Andersson and Fredriksson (2000) and complementary to those of Blomström et al. (2000) and Rauch (1999).

Evidence for outsourcing as a major driving force of an increasing use of imported intermediate goods is somewhat weaker. However, the coefficient of outward FDI stock gained robustness over time. With the last regression results for 1990 it may be too early to judge the role of outsourcing. Beside that, the imported intermediate goods variable and the explanatory FDI stocks are aggregated over all countries. The share of developing countries in the aggregates is rather low, but developing countries are the likely candidates for outsourcing to occur. It would be very interesting to estimate the model with imported intermediate goods and FDI stocks exclusively from developing countries. FDI stocks could be calculated, but import data of intermediate goods is not available.

Furthermore, outsourcing does not necessarily depend on outward FDI (Feenstra and Hanson 1995). However, in this cross-section analysis, the share of outsourcing that does not depend on outward FDI is not distinguishable from global sourcing. The latter is represented in the intercept of regressions I to VI in Tables 20–22 which is significantly positive for all three points in time. Companies made substantial use of the advantages of global sourcing over the analyzed period. But the intercept did not change over time. It is not statistically different at the 10 percent level for the estimation of the three points in time. This is, of course, a very weak test, since the intercept collects a wide range of effects. In regression VII to IX, the estimated coefficient of the output variable can be interpreted as elasticity of imported intermediate-goods demand with respect to output. The elasticity should rise for global sourcing to hold. However, in a test for equality of the coefficients, unchanged parameters over the analyzed time period could not be rejected at the 10 percent level. Although there has been significant global sourcing, this analysis cannot present evidence that global sourcing is the dominant driving force behind the increase in imported intermediate goods used in production.

3.2.5   Time-Series Evidence

The sectoral data analyzed in the last section points to a robust relationship between the inward FDI stocks and imported intermediate goods used in production. The outsourcing theory receives some support, too. In this section, I explore the relationship between imported intermediate goods and outward or inward FDI stocks further by using annual time-series data from Germany between 1976 and 1998. The period is chosen for the reason of data availability; the number of observations is rather low. German FDI stock data (inward and outward) are reported by the Deutsche Bundesbank (1999, 2001) back to 1976. The foreign FDI stock invested in Germany increased over this period from DM65.8 billion to DM332.6 billion. The increase in the FDI stock of German companies in foreign countries was much more impressive: in 1998, the outward FDI stock was DM619.5 billion, which was more than 12 times higher than in 1976 (DM49.1 billion).

Imported inputs are also taken from the Bundesbank. Since 1973 the Deutsche Bundesbank (various issues) has reported imported manufactured inputs in its *Balance of Payments Statistics*. These manufactured goods, imported to be used as inputs in manufacturing, more than tripled within the sample period: from DM31.5 billion to DM98.3 billion.

Since the increase in the imported manufactured inputs did not keep pace with the increase in total imports since the mid-1970s, their share in total imports declined from 14.5 percent in 1976 to 12.1 percent in 1998. The category (imported manufactured inputs reported by the Bundesbank) is much smaller than the roughly 50 percent of imports which are imported intermediate goods according to the input-output data. Adding raw materials and semi-finished products (also taken from Deutsche Bundesbank various issues) to the imported manufactured inputs increases their joint share on total imports to approximately one-third, still less than the 50 percent from the input-output tables. Manufactured goods which are final goods but are used as inputs account for the remaining difference. In the absence of alternative data, it is assumed that these final-goods inputs are affected in the same way by the exogenous variables as the imported manufactured inputs, which are used here for the time-series analysis.

Worldwide economic integration has increased remarkably during the last two decades. FDI and trade have grown strongly. The aim of this section is to test whether intermediate-goods imports and FDI stocks (inward and outward) form an economically meaningful, stable, long-run relationship: Does the value of imported inputs depend on inward or outward FDI stocks in the long run? Therefore, I analyze equations (49) and (50) derived in Section 3.2.2. As in Section 3.2.3, I estimate the equations in the log-linear form.

Since both FDI stocks and imported inputs are I(1) variables (Table A1 in Appendix C), a meaningful economic relationship depends on cointegration of inward or outward FDI stock and the imported intermediate goods. Cointegration yields an I(0) process. In general, the linear combination of two or more integrated variables is also integrated. However, two variables that are I(1) may be related in an economically meaningful way, so that the linear combination of the variables is I(0).[8] Then the variables are called cointegrated.

Cointegration is tested for both pairs of variables, inward FDI and imported intermediate goods and outward FDI and imported intermediate goods, using the Johansen cointegration test (Johansen 1991). This procedure assumes all

---

[8]   This could stem from the fact that the source of their nonstationarity is the same or that one of the variables is the source of the nonstationarity of the other variable.

Table 23:

Johansen Cointegration Test for Two Specifications[a]

	Cointegration rank	Trace statistic	5 percent critical value
Model (i)	r=0	22.602	19.96
$\ln(I)\ \ln(FDI_{Inward})$	r=1	5.893	9.24
Model (ii)	r=0	33.480	25.32
$\ln(I)\ \ln(FDI_{Inward})$	r=1	11.445	12.25
Model (i)	r=0	16.442	19.96
$\ln(I)\ \ln(FDI_{Outward})$	r=1	3.981	9.24
Model (ii)	r=0	17.248	25.32
$\ln(I)\ \ln(FDI_{Outward})$	r=1	5.657	12.25

[a]Lag length: 2.

variables to be endogenous and tests for linearly independent cointegration relations. With only two variables, there can be none or one cointegration relationship. Since the critical values of the test statistics depend on the specification of the test, a choice has to be made about the inclusion of a constant and/or a trend in the specification of the cointegration equations. Table 23 gives the results of the Johansen cointegration test for two specifications: (i) constant, no trend in the long-run relationship, and no trend in the data, and (ii) constant, a trend in the long-run relationship, and a trend in the data.

The Johansen cointegration test suggests that there is a stable long-run relationship between imported intermediate goods and the inward FDI stock but none between imported intermediate goods and the outward FDI stock. The LR test (Table 23), which uses the trace statistic, only rejects the hypothesis of no cointegration between inward FDI and imported intermediate goods. One co-integration could not be rejected.

In the next step, an error correction model (ECM) is set up to infer an estimate of the long-run relationship of imported intermediate goods and the inward FDI stock. Furthermore, the ECM provides another test for cointegration of the variables. Given the low number of observations, another cointegration test can yield some information about the robustness of the results obtained. Therefore, equations (51) and (52) are transformed into an ECM. That gives the outsourcing hypothesis a second chance:

$$(54) \quad \Delta\ln(I_t) = \lambda\left[\ln(I_{t-1}) - c - \beta_1 \ln(FDI_{Outward,t-1}) + Trend\right]$$

$$+ Dynamics + Dummy + u_t,$$

(55) $\Delta \ln(I_t) = \lambda \left[\ln(I_{t-1}) - c - \beta_2 \ln\left(FDI_{Inward,\,t-1}\right) + Trend \right]$

$$+\, Dynamics + Dummy + u_t \,.$$

From an economic point of view, the error correction term is of special interest, since it gives the long-run relationship. Short-run dynamics and dummies are only included to produce well-behaved error terms, u_t. If imported intermediate goods deviate from their long-run equilibrium, the error shows the correction made in the future. For stability, this implies a negative loading coefficient λ. A high t-value of the loading coefficient points to cointegration. Banerjee et al. (1998) compute the critical values for the loading coefficient which indicate a cointegration relation in single-equation models with one co-integration vector and weak exogeneity of all right-hand side variables. Table 24 presents the results of the estimations of equations (54) and (55). The long-run relation included a trend variable which was dropped because of its insignificance. The short-run dynamics ensure normally distributed residuals. The lagged differences ($t-1$ and $t-2$) of the endogenous and the exogenous variables were included next to the unlagged difference of the exogenous variables and a dummy variable ($R93$) which controls for the sharp decrease in imported inputs during the 1993 recession in Germany. Insignificant variables were dropped after conducting an omitted variables test. Since the number of observations is very low, the dynamics are kept to a minimum. Tests for autocorrelation up to the fourth order, for heteroskedasticity, for structural breaks, and for normality were carried out to ensure that the residuals are well-behaved. Interestingly the trend variable proved to be insignificant. This could be seen as the rejection of global sourcing as an explanation for increasing imports of intermediate products.

Like the Johansen cointegration test, the ECM points to a stable long-run relationship between imported intermediate goods and the inward FDI stock[9] but not between imported intermediate goods and outward FDI. The loading coefficient λ in ECM (54) is not significantly different from zero, λ in ECM (55) is significant at the 5 percent level. The long-run effect of inward FDI on imported intermediate goods is given by $\ln(FDI_{Inward,\,t-1}) = \beta_1/\lambda$. The coefficient and the standard deviation of the exogenous variable in the error correction term can be directly estimated in the Bewley transformation of the ECM, a reformulation of the ECM which is given in the third column. The coefficient of

---

[9]   The estimated coefficients of model (i) using the Johansen procedure are not statistically different from the long-run ECM coefficients (without dummy $R93$) at the 10 percent level (standard deviations in parentheses):

$\ln(I) = 8.921 + 0.232 \ln(FDI_{Inward})$.
    (0.71)   (0.164)

Table 24:

Outsourcing and MNE Networks in Germany in a Time-Series Analysis

	ECM (54)	ECM (55)	Bewley (55)
λ^a	−0.273	−0.299[**]	
Constant	2.493	2.642	8.826[***]
β_1	0.086		
β_2		0.098	
$\ln(FDI_{Inward,\ t-1})$			0.326[***]
$\Delta\ln(I_{t-2})$	−0.348[**]	−0.310[***]	
$\Delta\ln(FDI_{Inward})$		0.825[***]	
$\Delta\ln(FDI_{Outward,\ t-2})$	−0.203		
R93	−0.217[***]	−0.18[***]	
Adjusted R^2	0.66	0.84	0.80
F-statistic	8.45	20.57	18.52

[**], [***] significant at the 5 percent and 1 percent level.
[a]Banerjee t-statistic.

$\ln(FDI_{Inward,\ t-1})$ equals β_1/λ. The influence of inward FDI is positive and significant at the 1 percent level. A 10 percent increase of inward FDI increases imported intermediate goods by 3 percent according to this estimation. Furthermore, a test of weak exogeneity was carried out. Weak exogeneity of inward FDI for imported intermediate goods could not be rejected at the 1 percent level.

Certainly, the FDI stock is not the only determinant of imported intermediate goods. Imports also react to changes in aggregate demand and prices. The Johansen cointegration test points to two cointegration equations among imported intermediate goods, the demand variable and the inward FDI stock (Table A2 in Appendix C). Thus, the single-equation approach (ECM) is not efficient; a system should be estimated (Harris 1995). Given the small number of observations, I refrain from estimating the Johansen procedure. Cointegration relationships found in small systems survive in larger systems.

3.2.6   Conclusions

The reason for growing trade in intermediate goods has been analyzed in the second part of this chapter. Therefore, three hypotheses—outsourcing, increasing importance of MNE networks, and global sourcing—have been discussed and tested using cross-sectional data from six OECD countries and German time-series data. The outsourcing hypothesis predicts a positive relationship of outward FDI to imported intermediate goods, whereas the MNE network hypothesis predicts a positive relationship of inward FDI stocks to imported intermediate goods. Global sourcing is the default case. It remains as an explanation if the other two hypotheses are rejected by the data. Growing propensities to use imported inputs should show up in a positive trend in the time-series analysis and in increasing elasticities of imported intermediate-goods demand in the cross-section regressions.

The MNE network hypothesis could not be rejected by the data, neither in the cross-sectoral estimations nor in the time-series analysis. There is a positive effect of inward FDI stocks on imported intermediate goods. Foreign affiliates tend to import significantly more intermediates than domestic companies. Furthermore, significant sectoral and national differences became obvious. It would, therefore, be very interesting to run time-series regressions with sectoral disaggregated data, which is unfortunately not available. National differences, as found in Barrell and te Velde (1999), should be examined by repeating the time-series analysis for other countries. This is left to further research.

There is less evidence for outsourcing in the data. The German time-series data rejects a long-run cointegration relationship between the outward FDI stocks and imported intermediate goods. The cross-section regressions did not always find a significant effect of outward FDI on imported intermediate goods. The regressions which use outward FDI stocks as explanatory variable are less robust to specification changes. However, the importance of outsourcing is generally believed to differ strongly between sectors. The significant differences between the industries found in the cross-section analysis support this belief. Again, a sectoral disaggregated time-series analysis could be very fruitful.

There is also evidence for global sourcing in the data. There is a large share of imported intermediate goods which cannot be explained by FDI stocks. However, global sourcing is rejected as an explanation of growing trade in intermediate goods by the cross-section and the time-series analysis. Certainly, there is global sourcing and outsourcing, but these might not be as important as growing and deepening MNE networks in explaining the growing trade in intermediate goods. The perceived increase of global sourcing in recent years results mainly from the ability of MNEs to use inputs from their wide international networks. Global sourcing takes place within MNEs.

For the model presented in the first part of the chapter, these results are supportive. Evidence for the importance of production abroad as a determinant of trade flows in intermediate goods backs the assumption that next to trade in headquarter services it is trade in intermediate goods which links affiliates with the parent company. The assumption of specific intermediate goods imported by foreign affiliates from the network of the parent company seems to be justifiable. Foreign affiliates of MNEs import more intermediate goods than an average company. This is assumed in the model framework and the empirical tests support this assumption.

4 Explaining Country Differences in the Internationalization of Activities and the Wave Behavior in Globalization

In order to allow for an analytical solution, Chapter 3 proposed a model of MNEs in globalization which relied on very strong symmetry assumptions. Companies are modeled symmetrically, although not identical, since they produce differentiated goods. Individuals are identical with regard to their supply of labor and their productivity. But they are heterogeneous in consumption. However, in aggregate a representative consumer can describe their consumption. Thus, symmetry among companies and among individuals is assumed. Furthermore, in Chapter 3 the countries are assumed to be equal. That makes an analytical solution possible but abstains from decisive differences of countries which might affect the internationalization strategies of companies in a particular country. With only one factor of production in the model, countries cannot differ in relative factor endowment. Differences in productivity are also assumed away.

The approach of Chapter 3 models the internationalization of activities of companies in developed countries. These countries are relatively homogeneous with respect to relative factor endowments and productivity levels to justify continuing to abstain from differences in these characteristics. However, the developed countries are certainly not all of the same size. This chapter relaxes, therefore, the assumption of equal country size and shows that the resulting internationalization pattern comes close to the observed pattern since the early 1960s. The price for this more realistic model is the reliance on numerical simulations for solution. However, the discussion of the basic model provides guidance in discriminating the various effects and evaluating their direction and size.

In the first part of this chapter, I study the internationalization of activities of companies based in two countries of different size.[10] More interesting trade and international production patterns emerge, because the effects on competition are different in both countries. That stems from the fact that the companies based in the two countries differ in size. Companies in the larger countries are larger. They can better exploit scale economies and have the advantage of a wider range of intermediate goods to choose their inputs from. Their average prices are lower than those of the (smaller) companies from the smaller country. Competition

---

[10] The first part of Chapter 4 is partly based on Kleinert (2001).

within the group is still symmetric, but companies from different countries compete at different terms. This influences the trade pattern and the choice of companies about their internationalization strategy. Companies in a larger country choose to set up an affiliate in the foreign country earlier than in a smaller country.

In the second part of this chapter, I analyze the adjustment to a new equilibrium after one company internationalized production. The adjustment is asymmetric; the number of companies, price levels, and utility might change in different directions in the two countries during this adjustment process. Internationalization of production of one company increases the incentive to internationalize production of any national competitor, whereas it decreases the incentive to internationalize for any foreign rival. This is caused by the differences in the change of the price indexes in both countries during the adjustment. The positive effect of the internationalization of production on the incentive for national competitors to do the same creates the wave behavior in internationalization, which has been often observed and widely discussed.

In the third part of this chapter, I analyze equilibrium trade patterns after the adjustment process of companies from the larger countries is completed. Because of the positive effect of one company's internationalization decision on the decision of its national competitors, all companies from the larger country decide to internationalize their production at the same time. They produce in both countries. In contrast, companies from the smaller country remain national, exporting companies. The emerging trade pattern involves interindustry trade of three groups of goods: agricultural goods and final manufacturing goods exported by companies from the smaller country and intermediate good exported by companies in the larger country to foreign affiliates of larger countries' MNEs. Furthermore, trade in headquarter services takes place between the parent companies in the larger country and their foreign affiliates.

4.1   Internationalization Activities When Countries Differ in Size

Economic size matters a lot. Even among developed countries, the sectoral structure and specialization, the degree of openness, the market structure in particular sectors, and many other economic variables differ with the size of the country. The sectoral structure of larger countries is more diversified. They can support more stages of production of many goods than smaller countries (Hummels et al. 1998). In contrast, large countries' degree of openness is smaller. The USA and Japan, the largest countries in economic terms, are the least open ones. Relatively more trade takes place within the countries, relatively less with other countries. This is different for small countries as Singapore, Luxemburg, the Netherlands, and Switzerland which show much higher openness indicators. Since internationalization activities are the focus of this study, the analysis should account for these differences.

The number of individuals, L, equals the labor force size and defines the size of a country in the model introduced in Chapter 3. For different L_i $(i=H,F)$, the gross domestic product, Y_i, varies, since Y_i, given in (35), is the product of wage rate, w_i, and the size of labor force, L_i. A larger labor force, therefore, implies a higher GDP. This translates into more product variants which are produced (equations 29 and 30). These product variants can also be consumed by foreign consumers but at a higher price and, hence, at a lower quantity. The weight of imports in the consumption bundle of consumers from the smaller country is higher. Their utility level in equilibrium is lower. Price indexes of (26) are different, too. The larger country's price index is lower since the weight of imported goods (and therefore the weight of distance costs) is lower. The quantities sold domestically (see first term in (19) and (20)) are not necessary the same for companies from the two different countries. Market size and price indexes differ. Sales abroad might also be different (see second term in (19) and (21)).

There is a second effect which lowers the price of a differentiated final good in the large country relative to a competitor in the small country: cheaper supply of intermediate goods. While single intermediate-goods prices are the same in both countries, the price index of (9) is lower in the large country, since it decreases with the number of intermediate goods. The number of intermediates is higher in the large country because the market for intermediate goods, I, is larger. A lower price index of intermediate goods leads to lower marginal costs of the final-goods producers in the larger country. There are therefore two sources of different output, domestic sales and export volumes of companies from two countries which differ in size.

Different export volumes of companies from different countries lead to different incentives to save on distance costs. At the same distance cost level, companies with higher export sales have a higher relative profitability of foreign production than their rivals from the other countries in spite of the fact that all use the same production technology. The trigger curve of companies from the two countries is not the same anymore. If companies in one country rely more heavily on exports than those in the other, their trigger curve lies above the trigger curve of companies from the other country. The trigger curve in (40) which gives the profitability of foreign production relative to exports for two identical economies changes to

(56) $\quad \Phi_1 = (1-\rho)\left(p_{1,1}^M q_{1,1}^M + p_{1,2}^M q_{1,2}^M - p_1^N q_1^N\right) - w_2 f_2,$

(57) $\Phi_2 = (1-\rho)\left(p_{2,2}^M q_{2,2}^M + p_{2,1}^M q_{2,1}^M - p_2^N q_2^N\right) - w_1 f_1$.

Φ_1 shows the incentive for a company from country 1 to invest in country 2. Φ_2 is the incentive for a company from 2 to invest in 1. Φ_1 and Φ_2 are positive if companies' profits are increased by an internationalization of production. A company sets up a foreign affiliate if Φ is greater than zero, since companies are assumed to maximize profit. The analysis follows the same line as in Chapter 3 where the market equilibrium is described. A succession of general equilibria is studied which differ because the distance cost level separating the economies falls exogenously. This leads to adjustments of individuals and companies which end in a new equilibrium. It is assumed that distance costs fall continuously over time.

A particular distance cost level characterizes, therefore, each equilibrium. Higher distance cost levels characterize equilibria earlier in time, lower distance cost levels equilibria occurring later. For the analysis, a simulation technique is applied, because more effects appear in the asymmetric case compared to the model in Chapter 3 which can hardly be analyzed analytically. Market structure, i.e., degree of competition and the number of companies in each economy, differ in this model. However, market structure emerges endogenously and affects the pricing and output decision of companies, which are themselves important to determine the market structure. The model consists of a system of 14 equations which need to be solved simultaneously, because the markets are interrelated. This is done using the software package Mathematica 3.0.

As in Chapter 3, the analysis assumes that early equilibria (at high distance cost levels) include only national companies. Their deviation from the exporting strategy depends on the profitability of international production relative to exports. This is shown in Figure 11 for two economies which differ in size. Country 2 is assumed to have only 80 percent of the size of country 1. Country 1 is seen as benchmark. The symmetric benchmark case, with two countries of the same size, is calculated with both countries having the size of country 1.

All trigger curves increase with falling distance costs until distance costs fall below a particular point, $\tau_M \approx 0.6$, and decrease thereafter. Φ_1, the larger country's trigger curve, lies above Φ (dashed line, the trigger curve of the symmetric case). The foreign affiliate's production is profitable at an earlier point in time for companies based in the larger country 1, $\tau_M \approx 1.55$, compared to those in the smaller country 2, $\tau_M \approx 1.50$, because they save more on their larger exports. These larger exports result from the cost advantage they enjoy because of cheaper intermediate goods and from the lower degree of competition in the smaller country 2. The trigger curves shown in Figure 11 are derived with only national companies in equilibrium. They are, therefore, only valid until the first company from the larger country 1 sets up an affiliate in the smaller country 2 at

Figure 11:
The Influence of Distance Costs on the Relative Profitability of Production
Abroad and Exports, When Countries Differ in Size

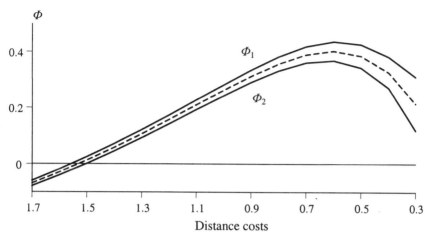

$\mu=0.6, \rho=0.75, \varepsilon=0.9, \theta=0.7, L_1=150, L_2=120, fz_1=fz_2=0.3, r_1=r_2=1.5, f_1=f_2=0.5$

$\tau_M \approx 1.55$. At this point, MNEs based in country 1 emerge. This changes the price
index according to (26) and, therefore, the trigger curves (equations 56 and 57).
The rest of the trigger curves in Figure 11 remains valid only if the companies of
country 1 do not internationalize their production.

Exports are more profitable than production abroad at any distance cost level
left of the point where the trigger curve crosses the zero line. Companies serve
the foreign market through exports, which are affected by falling distance costs.
Lower distance costs reduce the consumer's price of imported goods. Sales
increase. Hence, exports of final goods increase with falling distance costs as can
be seen from (43). For the numerical example, this is shown in Figure 12. Exports of the agricultural good are not affected by distance costs, because they are
traded without cost. Nevertheless, they are affected through the current account.
The smaller country 2 imports more final goods than it exports to country 1. A
balanced current account is assured by agricultural exports of country 2. The
smaller country 2 specializes (partly) in the production of the homogeneous
agricultural good for exports.

At very high distance cost levels, there is almost no trade. If there were fixed
costs in exporting, both economies would be autarkic. There would be no trade
in spite of consumers' love of variety. This was the situation of the world economy in the early 1950s. Companies operated mostly at national scale, there was

Figure 12:
Influence of Distance Costs on Exports

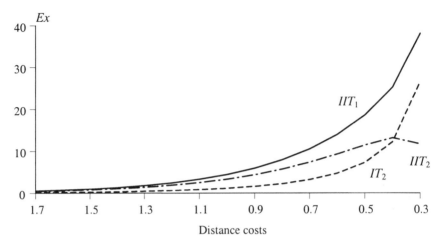

$\mu=0.6$, $\rho=0.75$, $\varepsilon=0.9$, $\theta=0.7$, $L_1=150$, $L_2=120$, $fz_1=fz_2=0.3$, $r_1=r_2=1.5$, $f_1=f_2=0.5$

very little international trade. The trade of the early 1950s was not intraindustry and not predominantly between developed countries. It was more motivated by differences in endowments. This kind of trade, however, is excluded here by assumption (one factor, same productivity in both countries).

With falling distance costs, exports increase. At high distance costs, intra-industry exports (*IIT*) are higher than interindustry trade (*IT*) in both countries. Due to the larger home market, more companies in the manufacturing sector are located in the larger country 1. Country 2 runs increasingly a trade deficit in manufacturing goods. Production of the agricultural good is relatively larger and increases in the smaller country 2. This is necessary in order to balance the current account. This phenomenon has been examined in Krugman and Venables (1995).

The growth of trade has been impressive in the last thirty years. In absolute terms, this can be seen in Table 12. Relative to industrial production, the more dynamic rise of trade in real terms can be seen in Figure 1. Figure 12 gives the world growth of trade derived by the model. Krugman (1995a) or Feenstra (1998), for instance, present figures on the growth of trade relative to production in the manufacturing sector. In Figure 13, manufacturing goods export levels of the model are shown relative to domestic sales in the manufacturing sector. Furthermore, total exports are shown relative to production in the manufacturing sector.

Figure 13:
Exports Relative to Overall Domestic Sales and Manufacturing Production

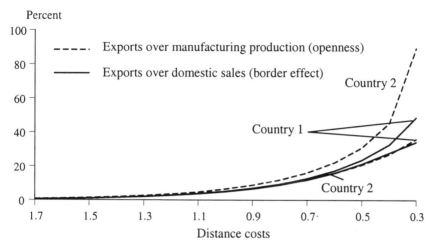

$\mu=0.6$, $\rho=0.75$, $\varepsilon=0.9$, $\theta=0.7$, $L_1=150$, $L_2=120$, $f_{z_1}=f_{z_2}=0.3$, $r_1=r_2=1.5$, $f_1=f_2=0.5$

Openness, here measured as total exports over domestic production in the manufacturing sector (broken line), increases with falling distance costs. The smaller country 2 is more "open" to trade because of relative smaller domestic production of differentiated final goods (fewer varieties). Trade, in contrast, is balanced. A higher degree of openness of small countries is consistent with the empirical evidence. The other lines show the relation of exports to domestic sales, which could be interpreted as economic integration of the two countries. This is the relation which measures border effects: the reduction of sales (foreign relative to domestic) by the existence of a border when all other influences are controlled for. A relation of zero indicates completely separated markets, a relation of one points to perfect integration. Real world border effects are still surprisingly high. McCallum (1995) inferred that, other things equal, trade between two Canadian provinces is more than 20 times larger than trade between a Canadian province and a U.S. state. Hence, the existence of the border between these two countries reduces trade to 5 percent of the volume of a borderless North America (minus Mexico). This is equal to the degree of integration the two model economies have achieved at a distance cost level of $\tau_M \approx 1.1$.

McCallum's (1995) study of U.S.-Canadian trade was soon followed by others. Helliwell (1997) confirmed McCallum's results. Anderson and Smith (1999) showed that Canadian border effects with the United States are as high as those with the rest of the world and vary strongly across provinces. For Australian-New Zealand trade, border effects of approximately the same magnitude are found. In spite of its common market, border effects remain high even for Europe. Nitsch (2000) found a reduction of trade to 10 percent for Europe in the mid-1990s. Over time, these border effects have decreased. Decreasing border effects show up as an increase in the exports over domestic sales ratio in the graphs in Figure 13. Intermediate values of the border effects shown in Figure 13 are, therefore, quite in line with the empirical finding for the late 1980s and 1990s.

But not only exports increase. With falling distance cost levels, the profitability of foreign production increases even more than that of exports. At every point in time after $\tau_M = 1.55$, it would be profitable for country 1 companies to internationalize production as Figure 11 shows. The graphs of Figures 12 and 13 are only valid if no company decides to produce abroad. Figures 12 and 13 show the increase of international activity through exports up to this point. Then, new graphs must be calculated which depict the international activities of companies in economies that include MNEs in equilibria. I accomplish this in Section 4.3. The economic integration of the two countries seems to be fairly modest at the time when an internationalization of production of the large country's companies becomes profitable ($\tau_M \approx 1.55$). Integration is lower than the empirical estimates on economic integration at the beginning of the last globalization round in the mid-1980s. With respect to this point, the model is, therefore, consistent with the real internationalization process, where companies from the large country, the United States, started their internationalization already in the 1950s and 1960s. Other (smaller) developed countries started their phase of internationalization of production later, i.e., in the mid-1980s.

In Section 4.2, the adjustment path from an equilibrium with only national companies, which is stable only until distance costs have fallen to a level of $\tau_M = 1.55$, to a new stable equilibrium is analyzed. As in Chapter 3, time is stopped during the adjustment. The distance cost level remains at $\tau_M = 1.55$. The adjustment process differs from that in Chapter 3, because the price indexes in both countries divert in the asymmetric case studied here. This leads to asymmetric adjustments of the two economies. An internationalization decision of one company from the large country 1 increases the incentive of any national competitor to internationalize its production, too. An internationalization wave emerges, with many companies from one country internationalizing their production at the same time.

4.2 Adjustment to a New Stable Equilibrium

As argued above, the trigger curves in Figure 11 are stable only until the distance costs have fallen to a particular level ($\tau_M = 1.55$ for the parameter constellation used for these simulations). At this time, internationalization of production becomes more profitable than exporting for companies in the larger country 1. If one company decides to set up an affiliate abroad, the market structure changes. Markets in the smaller country 2 are served by domestic companies, imports from the larger country 1, and a foreign affiliate of an MNE based in country 1. The foreign affiliate offers its good cheaper to country 2 consumers than it could offer it when the company was exporting its good before internationalizing production. At the lower price, consumers increase the fraction of the income they spend on this good as shown in Chapter 3. This increase is at the expense of other goods the sales of which fall. Given the symmetry in the model, all other companies realize losses. Some drop out.

This dropout is not symmetric. To see this, the weighted price indexes Γ of both countries are examined. Setting up of an affiliate has a positive effect on the weighted price index Γ_2 of country 2 as can be seen by (42). This stems from the lower price of this good, which initially lowers the price index. However, due to the increase in sales, its weight in the price index increases. This increases the price index, since the weight increase comes (partly) at expense of cheaper domestic goods. The total effect on the price index must be negative, otherwise the weighted price index change would not be positive ($P_{M,2} = \Gamma_2^{-(1/y)}$). This weighted price index change is calculated assuming an unchanged number of companies in both economies. The price index in the host country 2 decreases, therefore, with the decision of a company from country 1 to internationalize production. This increases competition. Profits of all other companies fall. This fall is stronger for country 2 companies, since home sales generate more profits than foreign sales because of lower costs in the absence of distance costs. In contrast, the weighted price index Γ_1 of country 1 is unaffected by the internationalization decision of country 1 companies.

This situation is not an equilibrium, because all companies but the one MNE incur losses. These losses are more severe for country 2 companies. Hence, more country 2 companies than country 1 companies exit the market. This lowers the price index in 1 and raises it in 2. After the dropout, $P_{M,1}$ is lower than before the internationalization of production of the first company; $P_{M,2}$ is higher. The weighted price index, Γ, changes in the opposite direction. This affects the trigger curves of both countries' companies. Since $\delta\Phi/\delta\Gamma < 0$, as can be seen from the derivation of (40) with respect to Γ, Φ_1 increases whereas Φ_2 decreases. This leads to more companies in country 1 to internationalize their production. In an adjustment process where the number of MNEs (all based in the larger country 1) is exogenously given and the numbers of national companies in both countries is endogenously determined (applying the zero-profit condition) the trigger curves for both countries are plotted in Figure 14. The x-axis shows the number of MNEs, the y-axis the profitability of internationalization of production relative to exports for any remaining exporting company.

The trigger curve of companies from country 1 starts at zero. A company is indifferent between exporting and internationalizing production. After the first MNE emerged, the trigger curve rises. This shows the gain which could be realized by the remaining national companies from country 1 when setting up an affiliate in the foreign country. Whereas the zero-profit condition holds for national companies, MNEs make profits. The profits increase in the internationalization process. One company's internationalization has, therefore, a positive effect on the decision of a national competitor to internationalize production. Internationalization waves emerge. The trigger curves of Figure 14 show that no equilibrium with national and multinational companies headquartered in country 1 is stable. At any fictitious point in time during the adjustment, it is profitable for any national company to become an MNE. When the adjustment is complete, all companies of the larger country 1 are multinationals.

The trigger curve of companies from the smaller (host) country 2 falls. For those companies internationalization of production has not been a profitable strategy at the beginning of the internationalization process of country 1 companies and becomes even less profitable during this process. These changes in the trigger curves of the companies of the two countries result from the change in the price indexes, $P_{M,1}$ and $P_{M,2}$, which are shown in Figure 15. Whereas the price index $P_{M,1}$ decreases in the larger country, the price index in the smaller country, $P_{M,2}$, increases. Internationalization of production leads to gains of consumers in the home country relative to those in the host country through cheaper goods from the manufacturing sector.

The change in the market structure from a pure national equilibrium toward an equilibrium which includes MNEs leads to market exit of many national country 2 companies. Their exit lowers the weight of cheap domestic goods in the consumption bundle of consumers in 2, where the overall price level is measured by $P_{M,2}$. Although MNE's affiliate goods sell at lower prices than imports, which they replace, they also force cheap country 2 companies to exit. The total effect is a rising price index in country 2 in the internationalization process. Country 1's price index falls, since with a lower number of country 2 companies, and therefore goods, their weight in country 1's consumption bundle falls. The change of the number of companies is shown in Figure 16.

Figure 16 shows how drastic the adjustment is among (host) country 2 companies. Their number falls to two-thirds of its level before the internationalization wave of country 1 companies. The total number of companies in both coun-

Figure 14:
Trigger Curve during the Adjustment

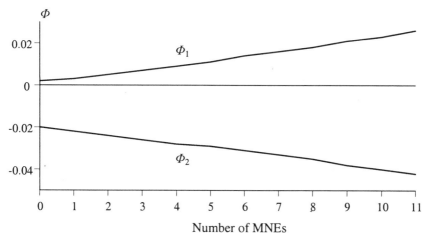

$\mu=0.6,\ \rho=0.75,\ \varepsilon=0.9,\ \theta=0.7,\ L_1=150,\ L_2=120,\ fz_1=fz_2=0.3,\ r_1=r_2=1.5,\ f_1=f_2=0.5$

Figure 15:
Change in the Price Index during the Adjustment

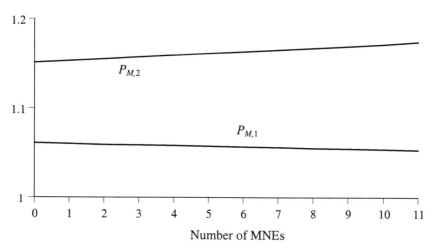

$\mu=0.6,\ \rho=0.75,\ \varepsilon=0.9,\ \theta=0.7,\ L_1=150,\ L_2=120,\ fz_1=fz_2=0.3,\ r_1=r_2=1.5,\ f_1=f_2=0.5$

Figure 16:
Change in the Number of Companies during the Internationalization Process

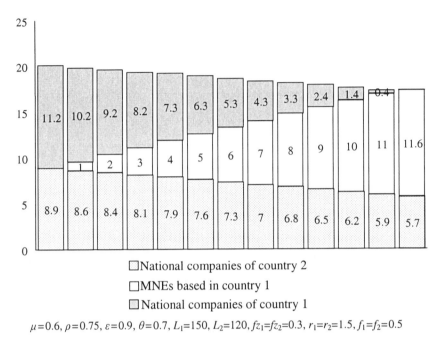

□National companies of country 2
□MNEs based in country 1
□National companies of country 1

$\mu=0.6$, $\rho=0.75$, $\varepsilon=0.9$, $\theta=0.7$, $L_1=150$, $L_2=120$, $fz_1=fz_2=0.3$, $r_1=r_2=1.5$, $f_1=f_2=0.5$

tries falls by about 15 percent. But while the number of home country 1 companies rises, the number of country 2 companies falls. The jump in the number of MNEs at the end of the adjustment points to the profits which could be realized by the MNEs in the adjustment process. The number of companies increases by about 2 percent when, in the long run, the zero-profit condition holds for MNEs and their number is endogenized.

Figure 14 offers an alternative explanation for wave behavior in companies' internationalization of production to the dominant oligopolistic reaction approach (Knickerbocker 1973; Graham 1978, 1996; Yu and Ito 1988; Cantwell and Sanna Randaccio 1992). According to this literature, companies internationalize production to counter the internationalization strategy of their competitors. As Graham (1996) has pointed out, the group of models based on interfirm rivalry has some power to explain the clustering in the internationalization activities but suffers from two shortcomings. First, the oligopolistic reaction theory depends on an exogenous triggering event: Why did the competitor invest in the first place? Second, it is not clear why companies internationalize production and cannot serve the foreign market through exports.

In the alternative approach presented here, wave behavior in the international-ization of production is driven by a changing degree of competition when com-panies decide to internationalize production when it has become more profitable than serving the foreign market by exports. Waves emerge endogenously, al-though there is still an exogenous trigger (falling distance cost) which changes the conditions continuously. When distance costs fall below a threshold, inter-nationalization of production of at least one company becomes profitable. The company sets up a foreign affiliate. This changes the foreign market structure and leads to an adjustment process in which the incentive of any national competitor to internationalize its production increases, too.

This approach does not suffer from the two shortcomings and matches the empirical facts even better. It explains the observations of Knickerbocker (1973) that internationalization of production occurs in temporal and sectoral clusters in specific national markets, and Flowers (1976), who pointed out that the FDI of European and Canadian companies into the United States came in clusters within three years after the initial investment of the leading firm in an industry, as well as oligopoly reaction models. Above this, the approach can make sense of Flowers' (1976) results which show temporal and sectoral clusters only of com-panies from one country. Internationalization activities of companies from differ-ent countries occur at different times. The clustering of investments disappears when different countries were examined. Companies seem to react only to activities of their national competitors.

In the model presented in this chapter, all companies of one country are symmetric. It is, therefore, clear that they reach the thresholds where production abroad becomes profitable at the same time. One company starts international-izing its production; the others follow, because their incentives increase with every national competitor who internationalizes production. Since all companies are symmetric, the internationalization wave only stops when all companies from this country have become MNEs. This is certainly not realistic. Companies of different characteristics can be observed in all industries: tiny domestic com-panies, companies relying on exports, MNEs with some affiliates and some export links, multiproduct firms of various kinds, and so on. They all have differ-ent trigger curves. In Chapter 5, the symmetry assumption between the com-panies in the same country is relaxed. Then, the internationalization wave stops before all companies have become MNEs. This leads to equilibria in which national companies and MNEs from the same country coexist in the same industry.

During the adjustment, time is stopped to separate the different effects. Hence, the distance cost level does not change. All activities result from the change in the market structure, which leads to changes in the degree of competition. Adjustment is assumed to be very fast, i.e., to occur immediately. The economies

Figure 17:
Trigger Curve of Country 2 Companies with Falling Distance Costs

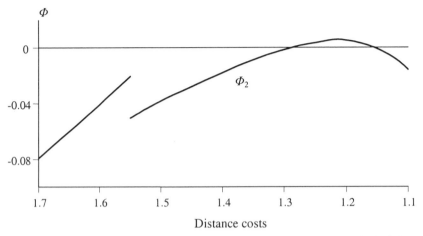

$\mu=0.6, \rho=0.75, \varepsilon=0.9, \theta=0.7, L_1=150, L_2=120, fz_1=fz_2=0.3, r_1=r_2=1.5, f_1=f_2=0.5$

jump from an equilibrium with only national companies to an equilibrium with national companies in country 2 and MNEs based in country 1. The trigger curves in Figure 14 are derived at the constant level of distance costs of $\tau_M = 1.55$. Since it is assumed that the economies adjust immediately, the trigger curves are discontinuous at $\tau_M = 1.55$. There are two levels of relative profitability of exports and production abroad at $\tau_M = 1.55$ which are given in the trigger curve of country 2 companies: one before the adjustment and one after (Figure 17).

After the slump during the internationalization of companies from country 1, the trigger curve of country 2 continues to increase, with further falling transport costs ($\tau_M < 1.55$). The price index now includes MNEs based in country 1 which produce in both countries, and national companies of country 2 which exclusively produce in country 2 and serve the larger country 1 through exports. Figure 17 shows that it is profitable for all companies of the smaller country 2 to internationalize production when distance costs have fallen to a level of $\tau_M = 1.3$. Note that this point is delayed compared to the time when internationalization becomes profitable in Figure 11 ($\tau_M = 1.5$). The change in the market structure brought about by the internationalization of country 1 companies forced companies from country 2 to postpone the internationalization of their production for a while. The internationalization process of U.S. companies in the 1950s and 1960s has only been countered since the mid-1980s, when the United States became the major host country.

Figure 18:
Trigger Curves during the Internationalization Process of Country 2 Companies

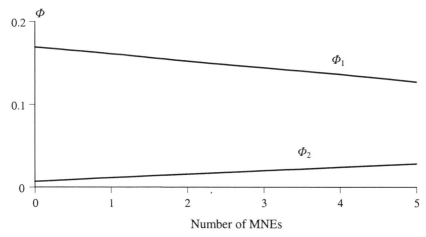

$\mu=0.6, \rho=0.75, \varepsilon=0.9, \theta=0.7, L_1=150, L_2=120, fz_1=fz_2=0.3, r_1=r_2=1.5, f_1=f_2=0.5$

At $\tau_M = 1.3$, internationalization of production becomes profitable for companies from country 2. If one company decides to establish a foreign affiliate in country 1, its good price falls in country 1. Sales increase in country 1, since consumer substitute this good for others. The profits of the internationalizing company increase, while the profits of all other companies (national and foreign competitors) decrease. Foreign (country 1) competitors suffer more, because their home sales decrease, and home sales are more profit-relevant than foreign sales. The adjustment is, therefore, more severe among country 1 companies. Their number falls. This reduces the competitive pressure on the remaining exporting companies from country 2.

As shown in Chapter 3, a change in the weighted price index affects the trigger curve of the companies. With the price index in the foreign country 1, $P_{M,1}$, rising and, hence, the weighted price index, Γ, falling, the trigger curve for country 2 companies, Φ_2, increases, since $\delta\Phi/\delta\Gamma < 0$. For companies based in country 1 the opposite is true, because the price index in their export market 2, $P_{M,2}$, falls. For the numerical example, the increase in the trigger curve Φ_2 can be seen in Figure 18. The trigger curves are calculated by exogenously setting the number of MNEs based in country 2. Country-1-based MNEs and national companies from country 2 are endogenously determined by applying the zero-profit condition.

Internationalization of production of country 2 companies occurs also in clusters, because one company's internationalization of production increases the

Figure 19:
Change in the Number of Companies during the Internationalization Process of
Country 2 Companies

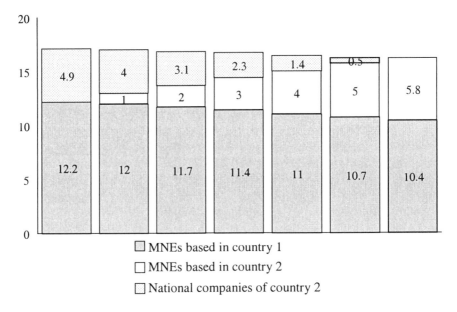

□ MNEs based in country 1
□ MNEs based in country 2
□ National companies of country 2

incentive to do the same for any national competitor. The profitability of production abroad relative to exports for companies from country 2, Φ_2, increases,
whereas Φ_1 decreases during the internationalization process of companies from
country 2. This change in relative profitability results from changing price
indexes which are due to adjustment of the number of companies based in each
economy. Market entries and exits can be seen in Figure 19. The opposite picture
of Figure 16 emerges with (aggregate) market exits of country-1-based companies and entries in country 2. The total number of companies decreases
modestly (5 percent).

Falling distance costs alter the conditions of competition over time. At any
distance cost level, an exogenous change in this level induces adjustments of
companies and individuals to the new conditions. These changes include adjustment of output, prices, export levels, market entry or exit by companies, and
the adoption of an optimized consumption bundle by consumers. With falling
distance costs over time, separation of market is reduced. Price indexes fall in
both countries; the degree of competition rises. This leads to a decreasing
number of companies in the two countries throughout time. There is continuous

adjustment in both economies as long as external conditions of competition change.

At some particular distance cost levels, the change in the two economies is more drastic. When a particular level is reached, the structure of the economies becomes unstable, because it is profitable for at least one company to rethink its internationalization strategy and serve the foreign market through a foreign affiliate instead of exports. This change in the market structure affects all companies by changing intensities of competition in both countries. In the host country, competition becomes fiercer. Companies realize losses. In the home country of the MNE, competition is initially unchanged, but is relaxed when some host-country companies quit to avoid the losses (in the long run).

This divergence in the change in the degree of competition leads to an increasing incentive of home country companies to also set up affiliates in reaction to the internationalization of production of the first company. The incentive to internationalize their production decreases for host country companies. Because every establishment of an affiliate in the host country increases the incentive for any home country company, an internationalization wave arises which only stops when all home country companies have become multinational. The market structure changes from an equilibrium with only national companies to an equilibrium which includes MNEs in one (the larger) country and national companies in the other. This change results only from the change in the price index. Distance costs are hold constant during the adjustment to separate the different effects. Holding distance costs constant means fixing time in this model. It is, therefore, assumed that the adjustment occurs immediately.

With further falling distance costs, the trigger curves of companies from both countries increase. When the distance costs have fallen beyond a particular threshold, it becomes profitable for a national company from the smaller country to internationalize production. Again, an internationalization wave occurs, this time from companies from the smaller country into the larger country. The market structure changes to a structure which includes only MNEs in equilibrium. Their competition is affected by the change in distance costs as well. Over the whole period, companies' trigger curves are altered by falling distance costs with two discontinuities at the points of the internationalization wave (Figure 20).

With falling distance costs, and therefore stronger economic integration, the number of companies in both countries falls. For equilibria with only national companies, this might lead, at very low distance costs, to very few companies in manufacturing. The decrease in the number of companies in the host country of the first internationalization wave following the change in the market structure is rather drastic. For the numerical example above, one-third of the companies quits. For a wide range of parameter constellations, the dropout is even more

Figure 20:
Trigger Curves over Time

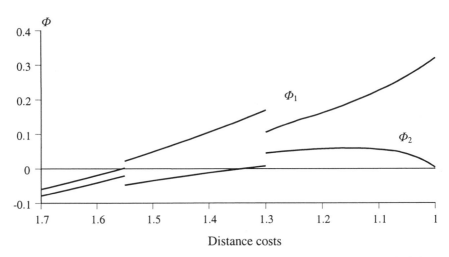

$\mu=0.6, \rho=0.75, \varepsilon=0.9, \theta=0.7, L_1=150, L_2=120, fz_1=fz_2=0.3, r_1=r_2=1.5, f_1=f_2=0.5$

severe. Is the difference in size between the countries larger or the differentiation of the intermediate goods more pronounced, the whole manufacturing sector of the (smaller) host country might disappear. Then, the market structure includes only MNEs from the larger country. Country 2 companies are only active in the perfectly competitive agricultural sector.

Although there might be cases of such a market structure, it is certainly not observed very often. Although no independent British carmaker survived, there is a British automobile industry including British companies. The drastic changes in the model result from the symmetry among all companies from the same country. This leads to an internationalization wave which only ends when all companies from one country have become MNEs. This is not realistic and creates the strong adjustment pressure on host countries' companies which leads to the sharp fall in the number of these companies. To tackle this problem, in the next chapter, some heterogeneity among companies from the same country is introduced.

Taking heterogeneity among companies from the same country into account solves another problem of the model version proposed in this chapter. According to the results presented above, there is no coexistence of national companies and MNEs from the same country. This is obviously not a matter of fact. In every bilateral economic activity, trade can be observed. This trade is not exclusively trade in intermediate goods and services if MNEs in an industry exist. Trade and production abroad might both be strategies of the same (multiproduct) company for the same foreign country at the same time. The model version in Chapter 5 allows for a coexistence of national companies and MNEs from the same country. Coexistence of national and multinational companies permits an even richer trade pattern than that analyzed in Section 4.3, because two market structures, which are studied now successively, are then occurring at the same time.

4.3 Trade Pattern under Different Market Structures

With the change in the (exogenous) conditions of competition brought about by falling distance costs, trade levels and patterns change over time. Levels change continuously, patterns suddenly with the change in the market structures. Falling distance costs lead to rising trade, especially in final differentiated manufacturing goods. These goods are traded even at very high distance cost levels because of consumers' taste for variety. This cannot be satisfied by the producers in one country alone, because required fixed costs in production of the final goods prevent companies in one country to produce all possible varieties of the differentiated final good. Additional varieties must be imported. Due to the imperfect substitution between final manufacturing goods, there is always an import market for differentiated final goods although import volumes might be very small at high distance cost levels. Trade in differentiated final goods is two-way intraindustry trade. Exports in final goods of companies from the larger country are larger, because more companies are based in the larger country. Since per company exports are approximately the same, there are higher export levels with more companies. With falling distance costs, the imbalance in final-goods trade increases, because the per company trade volume increases.

Although labor productivity and relative factor endowments are the same in both countries, there is a source of one-way trade in differentiated final goods which stems from a cost advantage of large country's companies relative to small country's companies. This advantage results from an agglomeration effect. A larger number of companies in the larger countries creates a larger market for intermediate goods with more companies and therefore more varieties of this differentiated intermediate good. A larger number of goods translates into a lower price level of the aggregate of intermediate goods which final-goods producers use as inputs. Lower input prices lead to lower final-goods prices in the larger market, since the optimal price is always a fixed markup over costs.

The price of every variety of the intermediate good is the same in both countries, but the larger number of intermediate goods leads to a lower price index for intermediate goods in the larger country. This is intuitive if the address approach, shortly discussed in Chapter 2, is used to motivate the CES aggregation. At the same price, the most preferred variety of the intermediate good is on average closer to the final-goods producer in the larger country than in the smaller one. The price advantage of larger countries' companies increases in the degree of differentiation, $1/\varepsilon$. The one-way trade of final goods which results from this price advantage is rather modest compared to two-way trade levels when the manufacturing sector in the smaller country is not too small.

Trade is always balanced in equilibria with only national companies. There is no intertemporal exchange between the two economies. The smaller country exports the homogeneous agricultural good to balance trade, since it imports more differentiated final goods from the larger country than it exports these goods. Larger imports result from the larger number of final-goods producers in the larger country and from the cost advantage companies from the large country possess. Homogeneous goods are traded without distance costs. Nevertheless, the one-way trade increases with falling distance costs to balance the increasing gap in two-way intraindustry trade of differentiated final goods. Homogeneous-good exports by the smaller country require a relatively larger homogeneous-good sector in the smaller than in the larger country.

Intermediate goods are specific to the final goods. They are, therefore, not internationally traded in equilibria with only national companies, because there is no possibility for companies to use intermediate goods from the foreign country. There is no positive price for foreign intermediate goods. Intermediate-goods trade arises with the emergence of MNEs. Foreign affiliates of MNEs produce the same good as their parent company. They use the same specific intermediate goods. Because foreign affiliates produce abroad, they have to import these intermediate goods from their home country. The volume of intermediate-goods trade increases, therefore, in the number and the production output of foreign affiliates of MNEs in equilibrium. If only MNEs from one country exist, there is one-way trade in intermediate goods from the home to the host country of the MNEs. Two-way intraindustry trade in intermediate goods arises if MNEs from both countries exist in equilibrium.

Like trade in intermediate goods, headquarter service trade is bound to the existence of MNEs. The service is produced in the parent company. It can be used in a nonrival way in both plants of one company. To use the headquarter service in the foreign affiliate, it must be exported to the foreign country. The amount of headquarter services which is used is independent of the output level of the parent company and the foreign affiliate. Exports in services of a country increase, therefore, only in the number of MNEs based in this country. Two-way trade in headquarter services emerges, if both countries are the home of MNEs.

In equilibria with only national companies, trade in differentiated final goods, Ex_1^M and Ex_2^M, dominates. Export of the homogeneous agricultural good from the smaller country, Ex_2^A, balances trade. In this framework, such a trade structure emerges at high distance cost levels. With falling distance costs, two-way intraindustry trade and one-way homogeneous-good trade increase (Figure 12). Intraindustry-trade coefficients are very high. There is only trade in final goods and in the agricultural good. Headquarter services are not traded, intermediate goods only within the countries. The model gives the same results as other models of the new trade theory which concentrate on trade in final goods (Krugman and Venables 1995; Schmitt and Yu 2002).

When distance costs haven fallen enough to make production abroad more profitable than exports for at least one company, the market structure changes. The exports in final goods of the internationalizing company are substituted by production abroad. Final-goods exports of the home country of the MNE, Ex_1^M, decrease. Trade in intermediate goods, Ex_1^{IG}, picks up. Intermediate goods from the home country are used in the foreign affiliate as inputs for production. These inputs must be imported. Trade volumes are not necessarily lower than those of final goods, although only inputs, and not the whole good, are traded, since sales of affiliates are much larger than export sales. For the production of this larger output, more intermediate goods are needed. Whether the merchandise trade volumes increase or decrease with the market structure change is parameter-dependent. Furthermore, headquarter services are exported from the parent company to the foreign affiliate.

At this time, trade patterns include larger country's exports of differentiated intermediate goods and headquarter services to the foreign affiliates, and smaller country's exports of differentiated final goods. Trade in the homogeneous good pushes in the direction of balancing international trade. The smaller country is exporter, the larger country importer of the homogeneous good. Trade in all groups of merchandise goods rises when distance costs fall further. Trade in headquarter services is not affected by distance costs and the change in affiliates output. It changes only with the number of companies, which is more likely to fall with falling distance costs. Trade in headquarter services might, therefore, fall until the second internationalization wave is reached. In the numerical example in Figure 21, trade in headquarter services is given as deficit of the trade balance.

Total trade in headquarter services jumps up when distance costs have fallen below the threshold where companies from the smaller country internationalize their production. With the emergence of small-country-based MNEs, trade in headquarter services becomes two-way trade. Headquarter service exports from the larger country decline, because the number of MNEs based in this country decreases. However, the growth in exports of headquarter services of the smaller

Figure 21:
Trade of Different Product Groups over Time

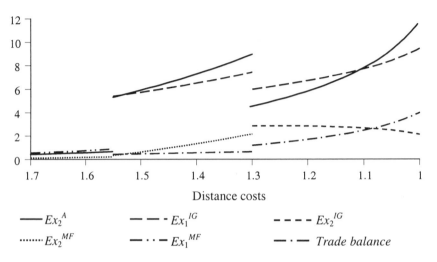

country overcompensates the larger countries' decline. The same holds for trade in intermediate goods, which also becomes two-way trade ($Ex_1^{IG}, Ex_2^{IG} > 0$). The total volume of trade in intermediate goods rises. The total volume of trade in manufacturing goods, ($Ex_1^{IG} + Ex_2^{IG} + Ex_2^{M}$), might rise or fall, because trade in final goods, Ex_2^{M} , disappears in an MNE equilibrium. Which effect prevails is parameter-dependent. Again, the smaller country's exports of the homogeneous agricultural good balance trade.

The continuous and the drastic changes in trade pattern of both economies can be seen in Figure 21. The numerical values seen on the y-axis of Figure 21 can be related to other model values for comparison. The GDP of the large country 1 in the model is 150; that of the small country 2 is 120. Exports of the homogeneous agricultural good, Ex_2^{A} , for instance, reach about 10 percent of the GDP of the smaller country 2 at a distance cost level of $\tau_M = 1$. At this time, openness, calculated as exports plus imports over GDP, stands at 25 percent for the smaller country 2 and 20 percent for the larger country 1.

The changes at the two points when the internationalization waves arise are much more drastic in the model than in reality. Certainly, there are structural changes in a particular industry of countries where significant restructuring is carried out within a short time period. This restructuring can be observed at home and in host countries. But the adjustment proposed by the model with an internationalization wave including all companies from one country and a complete change of the trade pattern in this process is certainly too severe. Although trade in intermediate goods has increased in recent years and this increase is related to the internationalization of production, a strong decrease of trade in final goods is observed by no means. Thus, even if the increase in internationalization of production occurs partly at the expense of the trade in final goods, it is by far not as drastic as the model proposes.

The symmetry assumption of all companies in a country causes this "unrealistic" result of the model. Internationalization waves include all (symmetric) companies. To model companies in the globalization process more realistically, differences between companies based in the same country are taken into account in the next chapter. This allows analyzing intersectoral differences in the internationalization of activities. More realistic patterns of trade and production abroad emerge, since different sectors reach their threshold at different points in time. In another interpretation, these differences reflect company differences within the same sector. Then, the coexistence of national companies and MNEs from the same sector in the same country becomes possible in stable equilibria.

4.4   Conclusions

Introducing country differences in the symmetric basic model proposed in Chapter 3 provides new insights in the globalization process. This process differs for countries of different absolute size. Companies from the larger country possess a cost advantage over their rivals from the smaller country which stems from the cheaper supply of the intermediate-goods aggregate and from the better usage of economies of scale. Large country's companies are larger than their small country's competitors. Allowing for country size differences in this (almost symmetric) model yields differentiation between the companies from both countries. The larger companies are more competitive. Regarding the export-versus-production-abroad decision, they react differently to falling distance costs. Companies from the larger country reach their threshold level for profitable internationalization of production earlier, i.e., at higher distance costs.

The analysis reveals that in an internationalization process which involves only companies from one country price indexes are affected in opposite directions. Competition increases in the (smaller) host country, so that some smaller country's companies exit the market. The price index increases, therefore, in the smaller market, since the weight of the foreign (larger) country companies' increases. Although these companies have a cost advantage, their consumer prices are higher than domestic companies' prices because of the distance costs their inputs incur. In the larger country, the price index decreases. This leads to opposite welfare changes during the adjustment process. Home country's welfare rises while host country's welfare falls. However, with further falling distance costs, welfare increases and even exceeds welfare levels in a pure trade equilibrium for most parameter constellations (as in the symmetric case in Figure 9). Only if very few country 2 companies survive after the adjustment, welfare falls in this country.

There is an incentive to internationalize production which grows with every national competitor which started production abroad. Hence, internationalization occurs in a wave, which only stops when the last national company from the larger country has become an MNE. The number of companies in the smaller country falls. In the larger country, the number of companies might rise or fall, depending on the condition of competition. The total number of companies falls. The adjustment to a new equilibrium requires severe restructuring in the host country, which partly specializes in the homogeneous-good sector. Home country companies must adjust to the new conditions, too, although with less pain. The market structure in the home country changes from an equilibrium with no MNE to an equilibrium which includes only MNEs from the larger country and national companies from the smaller one.

Trade patterns also change. In pure national equilibria, two-way intraindustry trade in differentiated final goods dominates. The trade balance is equalized by small country's exports of the homogeneous good. With falling distance costs, trade increases. When the market structure changes to the equilibrium which includes MNEs from the larger country and national companies from the smaller one, larger country's exports of differentiated final goods are completely substituted by production abroad. But exports of intermediate goods and headquarter services pick up. The smaller country continues to export differentiated final goods and the homogeneous good. With falling distance costs, trade in all product categories increase. After the second internationalization wave, companies from the smaller country have substituted their differentiated final-goods exports by production abroad as well. Then, two-way intraindustry trade in intermediate goods and headquarter services dominates.

Observed differences in the internationalization of activities by companies from different countries can be explained by differences in country size. U.S. companies started to internationalize their production in the 1950s and 1960s. Other developed countries have been the host countries. European and Japanese companies started to set up foreign affiliates in the mid-1980s. The United States has been the major host country in those days. Internationalization waves have often been noticed. Changes in the price indexes brought about by market structure changes explain internationalization waves in the model proposed here. One company's engagement in foreign production increases the incentive for any national competitor to do the same.

The next step is to introduce differences between companies from the same country to analyze sectoral concentrations, distinct sectoral internationalization patterns, and a market structure which allows for the coexistence of national companies and MNEs from the same country in the same industry. Furthermore, the richer trade patterns permit an analysis of the relationship of exports and foreign production. The model variant of Chapter 5 is employed to analyze whether trade and production abroad are substitutes or complements.

5 A Model with Different Sectors and Heterogeneous Companies within One Sector

The model versions proposed in Chapters 3 and 4 explain large parts of the observed pattern of MNEs in the globalization era quite well. The dominance of two-way intraindustry economic activity can be explained as well as its increase with decreasing distance costs. Further, by allowing for differences in country size, observed differences in the time pattern of the internationalization of activities could be explained. Further, the model could make sense of the widely discussed wave behavior of the internationalization process. Accounting for one aspect of real world heterogeneity, the differences in country size in the model version of Chapter 4, gives additional insights in real world phenomena. Chapter 5 follows this road by further differentiating the actors in the model. Heterogeneity in country size differentiates home and foreign companies with respect to their size, home and foreign consumers with respect to utility. However, companies in each country are symmetric. This assumption is dropped in Chapter 5 in taking heterogeneity between companies in the same country into account.

First, I introduce sectoral differences. Within sectors, I assume companies to be symmetric, but companies in different sectors may differ with respect to several characteristics such as their degree of product differentiation, their level and composition of fixed costs, or the share of intermediate goods they use in production. In such a setting, an analysis of the concentration of the internationalization of activities on some industries is possible. Empirical evidence points to distinct patterns of concentration on some industries. I use the multi-industry model version to explain sectoral concentration patterns in international activities and the differences in market structure between industries. Above that, I use the analysis in this chapter, which relies on many different parameter constellations, as a robustness check of the model. Internationalization patterns are parameter-dependent. Export levels and the particular location of the trigger curves differ with the parameters. This leads to many sectoral and national differences in the internationalization of activities. However, the explanation of the globalization process remains robust for a wide range of parameter constellations.

Second, this version allows the relationship between exports and production to be analyzed. Does export enhance or reduce production abroad and vice versa? The first relationship would imply a complementarity, the second one a substitution between these two strategies to serve the foreign market. At first glance, the model seems to favor substitution, but as Figure 21 in Chapter 4 demonstrates this is not necessarily the case. Whether substitution or complementarity prevails is parameter-dependent. Both outcomes are possible. Empirically, complementarity is more often found in aggregate studies, substitution is more likely in product-line-based studies. Real world trade and production abroad increase both in time. The multiindustry version of this approach pictures these developments, since both activities rise with falling distance costs.

Third, I take a slightly different perspective on heterogeneity of companies within each country. The different groups of companies from the multiindustry model are seen as different groups in the same industry. This leads to a different pattern of competition between companies. In the multiindustry model, competition takes place between symmetric companies from the same group (industry). In the heterogeneous company model, competition takes place between all companies in the manufacturing sector. An action of one company affects all companies, not only the companies from the same group. The market share of each group of companies is not exogenously given anymore. The markets of the groups are not disjunctive as in the multisector case. Thus, coexistence of national companies and MNEs can be found and studied. By modeling within-sector differences between companies, competition between companies which differ in size, costs and, therefore, prices can be studied more realistically. The establishment of an argument for coexistence is the most important result of Section 5.4.

5.1   A Multiindustry Version of the Model

The first step to account for the heterogeneity of companies is to model different industries within the manufacturing sector. I call a group of symmetric companies which differs from other groups of symmetric companies in at least one characteristic an industry in the following sections. Within an industry, there are many companies each producing one variety of a differentiated good. There are several goods in the manufacturing sector each of them with many different varieties, because there are several industries. Each company differs from other industry members, because it produces a different variety. In other respect, companies within an industry are identical. Companies from different industries differ in more than that. At least one (exogenously given) characteristic (degree of product differentiation, fixed costs, intermediate goods input share) differs. In equilibrium, companies from different industries set different prices and have different output levels. They are not symmetric.

Competition takes place only within industries. Interindustry competition between industries is assumed away by (exogenously) fixing the market share for each industry in the manufacturing sector. Thus, industries are isolated from each other. Price reductions in one industry, for instance, do not affect any (final-goods producing) company in another industry, because consumers spend by assumption always the same share of their income on goods of industry 1, for instance, regardless of price changes in other industries. This can be seen as the extreme case of the fact that competition within an industry is fiercer than between industries.

In contrast to the model versions in Chapters 3 and 4, the representative consumer splits further the share of her income which is spent on manufacturing goods, because she has to subdivide this amount on several industries. The representative consumer chooses, therefore, not only the amount to spend on each variety of the differentiated good but the amount to spend on each variety of several differentiated goods. As in (1), utility increases in the agricultural good and in the aggregate manufacturing good. However, this aggregated manufacturing good includes two sources of heterogeneity in this version: differentiated goods in different sectors. The utility function changes therefore to

$$(58) \quad U_j = Q_{A,j}{}^{\mu_A} \prod_{h=1}^{H} Q_{Mh,j}{}^{\mu_h} \ , \quad \mu_A + \sum_h \mu_h = 1 \ ; \ j{=}H,F.$$

The income share spent on the goods in one industry h in the manufacturing sector is given by μ_h. The aggregate Q_{Mh} is given by a CES function with λ_h different product varieties:

$$(59) \quad Q_{Mh,j} = \left[\sum_{i=1}^{\lambda_h} q_{i,j}^{h\ \rho_h} \right]^{1/\rho_h} , \quad \rho_h \in (0,1) \ ; \ j{=}H,F,$$

where ρ_h defines the degree of differentiation among the manufacturing goods in industry h. The aggregate in (2) of the whole group of final-goods producers changes to an industry aggregate in (59). The fraction of income spent on manufacturing goods μ is split into smaller μ_h for the different industries, with $\sum_h \mu_h{=}\mu$. Within each industry, consumers love variety. The number of products is endogenous. In contrast, the number of industries and their market shares are set exogenously.

Budget constraint and the agricultural sector are the same as in the basic model of Chapter 3. Intermediate-goods producers are also modeled accordingly. The only change in modeling of this group of companies applies to the calculation of their output which equals final-goods producer's demand for intermediate inputs I_j in each country j. This demand is the sum of the input demand of all companies in all final-goods industries in the manufacturing sector. This version of the model differs from that in Chapters 3 and 4 in modeling different groups of final-goods producers in the manufacturing sector. The former group of symmetric final-goods producers is decomposed into several groups, here called industries, where companies are symmetric within the industries but differ between industries.

Thus, companies from different industries differ in their variable or fixed costs or their markup. The cost functions for national companies in (16) and MNEs at home in (17) and abroad in (18) change, respectively, to

$$(60) \qquad C_{h,i,j}^N = w_j r_{h,j} + w_j f_{h,j} + \left(\frac{w_j}{\theta_h}\right)^{\theta_h} \left(\frac{Pz_j}{1-\theta_h}\right)^{1-\theta_h} q_{h,i,j}^N,$$

with $\theta_h \in (0,1)$, $j=H,F$; $h=1,2,\ldots,\kappa$,

$$(61) \qquad C_{h,i,j,j}^M = w_j r_{h,j} + w_j f_{h,j} + \left(\frac{w_j}{\theta_h}\right)^{\theta_h} \left(\frac{Pz_j}{1-\theta_h}\right)^{1-\theta_h} q_{h,i,j,j}^M,$$

with $\theta_h \in (0,1)$, $j=H,F$; $h=1,2,\ldots,\kappa$,

$$(62) \qquad C_{P,h,i,j,l}^M = w_l f_{h,l} + \left(\frac{w_l}{\theta_h}\right)^{\theta_h} \left(\frac{Pz_j^M}{1-\theta_h}\right)^{1-\theta_h} q_{h,i,j,l}^M,$$

with $\theta_h \in (0,1)$, $j,l=H,F$; $j \neq l$; $h=1,2,\ldots,\kappa$.

The first terms represent fixed costs on the company level, the second terms the fixed costs on the plant level. The fixed costs increase in the factor price of labor, w_j, and in $r_{h,j}$ and $f_{h,j}$. $r_{h,j}$ is the level of headquarter services produced by the companies in industry h and country j. $f_{h,j}$ is the amount of fixed input necessary for the production of the final good in industry h. $r_{h,j}$ and $f_{h,j}$ are given by the production technology and, therefore, exogenous to the company. Variable costs, the third terms, increase in the factor price of labor, w_j, in country j, the price index of the intermediates in country j, $Pz_j^{(M)}$, and the output level $q_{h,i,j}^k$ with $k=N,M$. The marginal costs $(w_j/\theta_h)^{\theta_h}(Pz_j^{(M)}(1-\theta_h))^{1-\theta_h}$ is denoted $c_j^{(M)}$.

Again, the costs of national companies and MNEs producing at home in each industry h differ only in the third term, the variable costs. Factor prices and technology used are the same, but MNEs produce at their home country plant only for the home market and not for exports. The output of a j-based national company and a j-based MNE in country j differ $(q_{i,j}^N \neq q_{i,j,j}^M)$. Different plants of an MNE have different variable costs in each country because of differences in the prices of the intermediate goods $(Pz_j^M \neq Pz_j)$ in both markets. The costs of production in the foreign country do not include costs at the corporate level which is due to the nonrivalry in consumption of the headquarter service. Headquarter services are produced at home and are used on a nonrival basis in both plants, at home in j and in the foreign country l at the same time.

The quantity of the intermediate-goods bundle used by a single final-goods producer can be calculated from the cost functions (60)–(62) by taking the partial derivatives with respect to the price index, Pz_j, (Shephard's Lemma):

$$(63) \quad qz_{h,i,j}^N = \frac{\partial C_{h,i,j}}{\partial Pz_j} = \left(\frac{w_j}{\theta_h}\right)^{\theta_h}\left(\frac{1-\theta_h}{Pz_j}\right)^{\theta_h} q_{h,i,j}^N, \quad j,l=H,F; \ l\neq j,$$

$$(64) \quad qz_{h,i,j}^M = \frac{\partial C_{h,i,j,j}^M}{\partial Pz_j} + \frac{\partial C_{P,h,i,j,h}^M}{\partial Pz_j^M} = qz_{h,i,j,j}^M + qz_{h,i,j,l}^M$$

$$= \left(\frac{w_j}{\theta_h}\right)^{\theta_h}\left(\frac{1-\theta_h}{Pz_j}\right)^{\theta_h} q_{h,i,j,j}^M + \left(\frac{w_l}{\theta_h}\right)^{\theta_h}\left(\frac{1-\theta_h}{Pz_j^M}\right)^{\theta_h} q_{h,i,j,l}^M.$$

In equilibrium, the aggregate demand for intermediate goods given by $\sum_h \sum_{i=1}^{mh,j} qz_{h,i,j}^M + \sum_h \sum_{i=1}^{nh,j} qz_{h,i,j}$ equals the aggregate supply, Z_j. The amount which is spent on intermediate goods I_j equals their total costs $\sum_h \sum_{i=1}^{mh,j} (pz_{i,j} e^{\tau_M}) qz_{h,i,j}^M + \sum_h \sum_{i=1}^{nh,j} pz_{i,j} qz_{h,i,j}$, since companies make zero profits.

As can be seen from equations (60) to (62), costs differ for different industries h, since fixed cost levels, r_h and f_h, the degree of product differentiation, ρ_h, and the level of intermediate goods used in production, $1-\theta_h$, are industry-specific. Different costs in each industry h and/or different degrees of product differentiation translate into different prices, different output levels and, together with the exogenously given market share μ_h, into a different number of companies in each industry. Prices are given by

$$(65) \quad p_{h,i,j}^k = c_{h,j}^k / \rho_h, \quad j=H,F; \ k=N, M; \ h=1,2,\dots,\kappa.$$

The price of a single final good depends only on the good's marginal costs, $c_{h,j}{}^k$, and ρ_h, the parameters of differentiation in industry h. Marginal costs can easily be obtained from variable costs in (60)–(62). Since all companies in one industry use the same technology, their marginal costs differ only if the factor prices differ. But factor prices cannot differ within one country because of interindustry and intersectoral labor mobility. However, between different industries, prices differ if the degree of differentiation, ρ_h, differs even if companies produce at the same marginal costs. If prices between companies from different industries differ, outputs differ too. Given the utility function (58) and the composition of the aggregated manufacturing good in (59), equation (66) gives the demand for a single product $q_{h,i,j}^N$ of a national firm, which serves the foreign country through exports:

$$(66) \qquad q_{h,i,j} = \frac{p_{h,i,j}^{-(1+\gamma_h)}}{P_{M_h,j}^{-\gamma_h}} \mu_h Y_j + \frac{p_{h,i,j}^{-(1+\gamma_h)} e^{-(1+\gamma_h)\tau_M}}{P_{M_h,l}^{-\gamma_h}} \mu_h Y_l ,$$

$$j,l=H,F; \quad l\neq j; \quad \gamma_h=\rho_h/(1-\rho_h).$$

The optimal quantity of good i produced in industry h in j depends on: its own price $p_{h,i,j}$, the price indexes $P_{M_h,j}$ and $P_{M_h,l}$ in both final-goods markets, the size of the markets $\mu_h Y_j$ and $\mu_h Y_l$, and the distance costs, τ_M. The lower the price of good i relative to the price index in both countries, the higher the optimal output of this good. High distance costs decrease the optimal output by increasing the good's price in the foreign market. Consumers in the importing country l must pay the distance costs and, therefore, react by partially substituting imported goods by goods produced in their country l.

A multinational company in industry h headquartered in j produces in both countries. It supplies consumers with goods which are produced in the country in which they are consumed. The optimal output from the domestic plant

$$(67) \qquad q_{h,i,j,j}^M = \frac{p_{h,i,j,j}^{M\,-(1+\gamma_h)}}{P_{M_h,j}^{-\gamma_h}} \mu_h Y_j , \quad j=H,F; \quad \gamma_h=\rho_h/(1-\rho_h),$$

equals the demand in the home country. The price of a multinational company's good in the foreign market l is lower than the price for an imported good, since consumers do not have to pay distance costs. The output of an MNE's good is, therefore, higher:

$$(68) \qquad q_{h,i,j,l}^M = \frac{p_{h,i,j,l}^{M\,-(1+\gamma_h)}}{P_{M_h,l}^{-\gamma_h}} \mu_h Y_l , \quad j,l=H,F; \quad l\neq j; \quad \gamma_h=\rho_h/(1-\rho_h),$$

where $q_{h,i,j,l}^M$ is the output in l of a multinational company i in industry h with headquarters in j. The output is positively related to the price index $P_{M_h,j}$ and the market size $\mu_h Y_l$ in country l, and negatively related to its own price $p_{h,i,j,l}^M$.

From the utility functions (58) and (59), the price index, $P_{M,h,j}$, for each industry h in market j can be calculated:

$$(69) \quad P_{M,h,j} = \frac{\mu_h Y_j}{Q_{M h,j}} = \left[\sum_{i=1}^{\lambda_h} p_{h,i}^{-\gamma_h} \right]^{-\frac{1}{\gamma_h}}, \quad j=F,H; \; h=1,2,\ldots,\kappa; \; \gamma_h=\rho_h/(1-\rho_h).$$

As in the model described in Chapter 4, prices set by companies located in H and F differ as a result of different price indexes for intermediate goods in the two economies, when the countries differ in size. Prices set by national and multinational enterprises differ in their foreign market but not at home. There are, therefore, up to three different prices $p_{h,j,l}^k$ ($j,l=H,F; h=1,2,\ldots,\kappa$; and $k=N,M$) for goods of each industry h in each market l: the price of goods produced by l-based companies (nationals and multinationals), the price of imported goods, and the price of goods produced by a j-headquartered multinational's affiliate in l. The price of a national firm's good in the foreign market $p_{h,j,l}^N$ equals the home-market price multiplied by the distance costs, $p_{h,j,l}^N = p_{h,j,j}^N e^{\tau_M}$. Using the different product prices of the different companies, equation (69) changes to

$$(70) \quad P_{M,h,j} = \frac{\mu_h Y_j}{Q_{M h,j}}$$

$$= \left[\sum_{i=1}^{n_{h,j}} \left(p_{h,j,j}^N\right)^{-\gamma_h} + \sum_{i=1}^{n_{h,l}} \left(p_{h,l,j}^N\right)^{-\gamma_h} + \sum_{i=1}^{m_{h,j}} \left(p_{h,j,j}^M\right)^{-\gamma_h} + \sum_{i=1}^{m_{h,l}} \left(p_{h,l,j}^M\right)^{-\gamma_h} \right]^{-\frac{1}{\gamma_h}},$$

with $j,l=H,F; \; j\neq l; \; h=1,2,\ldots,\kappa; \; \gamma_h=\rho_h/(1-\rho_h)$.

$n_{h,j}$ is the number of national companies active in industry h and located in country j, $n_{h,l}$ the number of nationals located in l, and $m_{h,j}$ and $m_{h,l}$ are the numbers of MNEs headquartered in j and l, respectively. $n_{h,j}$, $n_{h,l}$, $m_{h,j}$, and $m_{h,l}$ added together equal λ_h.

Since there is free market entry and exit, the zero-profit condition holds in equilibrium for both, national and multinational companies:

$$(71) \quad \Pi_{h,j}^N = (1-\rho_h)p_{h,j}^N q_{h,j}^N - w_j\left(r_{h,j} + f_{h,j}\right) = 0, \quad j=H,F; \; h=1,2,\ldots,\kappa,$$

$$(72) \quad \Pi_{h,j}^M = (1-\rho_h)\left(p_{h,j,j}^M q_{h,j,j}^M + p_{h,j,l}^M q_{h,j,l}^M\right) - w_j\left(r_{h,j} + f_{h,j} + f_{h,l}\right) = 0,$$

with $j,l=H,F; \; j\neq l; \; h=1,2,\ldots,\kappa$.

The zero-profit conditions (71) and (72) are sufficient to determine the number of national companies in industry h, $n_{h,j}$, and multinational companies in industry h of country j, $m_{h,j}$, in equilibrium.

As above, all final-goods producers in all industries decide whether to serve the foreign market through exports or to become an MNE and produce abroad. If there are no restrictions to the internationalization of production, a company sets up an affiliate in the foreign country if it is profitable to do so. A national final-goods producer in industry h decides to produce abroad if the gains in variable profits are at least as high as the additional fixed costs at the plant level:

$$(73) \quad w_l f_{h,l} \leq (1 - \rho_h)\left(p_{h,j,j}^M q_{h,j,j}^M + p_{h,j,l}^M q_{h,j,l}^M - p_{h,j}^N q_{h,j}^N\right),$$

$$j,l = H,F; \quad j \neq h; \quad h = 1,2,\ldots,\kappa.$$

The lower the fixed costs at the plant level, $w_l f_{h,l}$, are, the more likely it is that a national company decides to build a plant abroad. The influence of ρ_h is not easily specified. The first factor on the right-hand side of (73) increases if product differentiation increases (falling ρ_h), which accelerates investment. But ρ_h enters the second term on the right-hand side in a highly nonlinear way. Numerical simulations below show that the investment speeds up with falling ρ_h. A smaller ρ_h increases the market power of all companies; their average size rises. This increases the opportunity to use economies of scale and makes internationalization of production more likely. If ρ_h is close to one, there is very little market power with very small variable profits for any company. In the case of perfect competition there is no room for MNEs. With falling ρ_h, product differentiation increases. Companies gain in market power and variable profits. The emergence of MNEs becomes more likely. Finally, distance costs, τ_M, enter (73) in a nonlinear way, too. The last term in the parenthesis on the right-hand side of (73) increases with decreasing distance costs because $q_{h,j}^N$ increases, but so do $q_{h,j,j}^M$ and $q_{h,j,l}^M$. Which effect prevails depends on the specific values of the parameters.

Due to the iceberg form of the distance costs, τ_M, a share t_j of final goods is lost in the case of export; tz_j represents the loss of intermediate goods due to distance costs:

$$(74) \quad t_{h,j} = \left(e^{\tau_M} - 1\right)\frac{\left(p_{h,j}e^{\tau_M}\right)^{-(1+\gamma_h)}}{P_{M,h,l}^{-\gamma_h}} \mu_h Y_l,$$

$$j,l = H,F; \quad j \neq h; \quad h = 1,2,\ldots,\kappa; \quad \gamma_h = \rho_h/(1-\rho_h),$$

(75) $tz_{h,j} = \left(e^{\tau_M} - 1\right)\dfrac{\left(pz_{h,j}e^{\tau_M}\right)^{-(1+\gamma_h)}}{Pz_{h,j}^{M\ -\gamma_h}} m_{h,j}qz_{h,j,l}^{M}pz_{h,j}^{M}\,,$

$j,l=H,F;\ j\neq h;\ h=1,2,\dots,\kappa.$

Factor demand is derived by using Shepard's Lemma. The cost functions (7), (10), (60) through (62) and the distance costs equations (74) and (75) are differentiated with respect to factor prices.

Full employment of all resources is assumed in both economies. For a given endowment of labor, L_j, the labor market condition is

(76) $L_j = L_{A,j} + \sum_h n_{h,j}\left(r_{h,j} + f_{h,j} + L_{h,j}^{N} + L_{t,h,j}^{N}\right) + s_j\left(fz_j + z_j + L_{tz,h,j}\right)$

$\qquad + \sum_h m_{h,j}\left(r_{h,j} + f_{h,j} + L_{h,j,j}^{M}\right) + m_{h,l}\left(f_{h,j} + L_{h,l,j}^{M}\right)$

with $j,l=H,F;\ j\neq l;\ h=1,2,\dots,\kappa;$
$L_{h,j}^{N}=(\theta_h/(1-\theta_h))^{1-\theta}{}_h(Pz_j/w_j)^{1-\theta}{}_h q_{h,j}^{N};\quad L_{t,h,j}^{N}=(\theta_h/(1-\theta_h))^{1-\theta}{}_h(Pz_j/w_j)^{1-\theta}{}_h t_j;$
$L_{tz,h,j}=(\theta_h/(1-\theta_h))^{1-\theta}{}_h(Pz_j/w_j)^{1-\theta}{}_h tz_{h,j};\quad L_{h,j,j}^{M}=(\theta_h/(1-\theta_h))^{1-\theta}{}_h(Pz_j/w_j)^{1-\theta}{}_h q_{h,j,j}^{M};$
$L_{h,l,j}^{M}=(\theta_h/(1-\theta_h))^{1-\theta}{}_h(Pz_j/w_j)^{1-\theta}{}_h q_{h,l,j}^{M}.$

The labor market clears if the fixed labor supply, L_j, in country j equals the sum of the labor demand of the agricultural sector, the labor demand of all stages of production of j's national and multinational companies in all κ industries, the labor demand of the intermediate-goods producers in j, the labor demand of the affiliates in j of MNE's headquartered in l, and the labor demand for the transport of final and intermediate goods.

Wages are set in order to clear factor markets in each country. The wage level determines the size of the agricultural sector because agriculture is a perfectly competitive sector. In both countries, the price of agricultural goods equals marginal costs. The income Y_j in each country is given by the sum of the incomes of all individuals.

The demand functions (4) and (5), the income equation (35), and the budget constraint (3) ensure that goods markets clear. The factor market clearance is given by (76). The value of the marginal product of labor (6) determines the wages in each economy.

The pricing rule (65) and the equations (66) to (68), (71) and (72) determine prices and outputs of the national and multinational companies and their number in each industry and country. The number of intermediate-goods producers and their production levels are given by (14), (63), and (64). The pricing rule (34) determines the agricultural goods output in each economy and, therefore, with demand equation (4) the level of interindustry trade. The free-of-cost one-way trade of the homogeneous good Ex_j^{A} leads to price equality of this good in both economies. If the countries are symmetric, there is no trade in the agricultural good, since each country satisfies its own demand for this good.

As long as not all companies have become MNEs, there is always intra-industry trade of final manufacturing products in each industry $Ex_{h,j}{}^{M}$ in this model, because the final goods are not perfect substitutes for one another:

(77)　　$Ex_{h,j}^{M} = n_{h,j} p_{h,j,l}^{N} q_{h,j,l}^{N}$,　　$j,l=H,F; \; j{\neq}h; \; h=1,2,...,\kappa$.

The final-goods export sales, $Ex_{h,j}^{M}$, rise with the number of exporting companies, the price of an exported good, and its quantity. The export quantity given by $q_{h,j,l}^{N} = p_{h,j}^{-(1+\gamma)}{}_{h} e^{-(1+\gamma)}{}_{h}{}^{\tau} / P_{M,h,l}^{-\gamma}{}_{h} \mu_{h} Y_{l}$ falls with rising distance costs and rises with the price index in the foreign market and the market size. If the distance costs are almost prohibitive, exported quantities can be very small. Trade in services depends on the existence of MNEs, since trade in services in this model is trade in headquarter services. It rises with the number of MNEs and the level of headquarter services.

Trade in intermediate goods is also bound to MNEs' activities. In the production in the foreign affiliate, MNEs use intermediate goods which they import from their home country:

(78)　　$Ex_{j}^{I} = \sum_{h} m_{h,j} pz_{j} e^{\tau_{M}} qz_{h,j,l}^{M}$,　　$j,l=H,F; \; j{\neq}h; \; h=1,2,...,\kappa$.

Since this is a static model, trade must be balanced, otherwise one country would be giving away goods for free:

(79)　　$Ex_{j}^{A} + \sum_{h} Ex_{h,j}^{M} + \sum_{h} Ex_{h,j}^{S} + Ex_{j}^{I} = \sum_{h} Ex_{h,l}^{M} + \sum_{h} Ex_{h,l}^{S} + Ex_{l}^{I}$.

Ex_{j}^{A} can be positive or negative, depending on whether j is an exporter or an importer of the agricultural good. Ex^{M} (more precisely: $\sum_{h} Ex_{h,j}^{M}$) must be positive for both economies except in the case of prohibitively high distance costs τ_{M} . Ex^{S} (more precisely $\sum_{h} Ex_{h,j}^{S}$) and Ex^{I} can be zero or positive for both countries depending on the existence of MNEs with headquarters in the exporting country.

5.2　Sectoral Concentration of the Internationalization of Activities

In this section, I use the multiindustry version of the model to explain sectoral concentration in exports and in the tendency to produce abroad. The main tool of the analysis is again the trigger curve, which differs for companies from different industries. To see how the decision of companies in different industries to export or to serve the foreign market by production abroad is influenced by changes in distance costs, I use τ_M, an industry-specific trigger curve, $\Phi_{h,j}$. $\Phi_{h,j}$ can be derived from the strategy decision in (73):

$$(80) \quad \Phi_{h,j} = (1 - \rho_h)\left(p^M_{h,j,j}q^M_{h,j,j} + p^M_{h,j,l}q^M_{h,j,l} - p^N_{h,j}q^N_{h,j}\right) - w_l f_{h,l},$$

$$j,l = H,F;\ j \neq l.$$

If factor endowment and technology used in an industry h in both countries are equal, the trigger curves, $\Phi_{h,j}$, for the companies in this industry in both countries are identical. If factor endowments of the two countries differ as in Chapter 4, trigger curves differ between the companies from the two countries. The trigger curves of two companies may, therefore, differ because of differences in country size and because of differences in industry characteristics. These industry characteristics include demand characteristics of their products (degree of differentiation) and characteristics of their production process (fixed cost level and composition, share of intermediate goods in variable costs). The characteristics determine the shape of the trigger curve. Thus, the point in time when internationalization of production becomes profitable depends on these country and industry characteristics.

Having analyzed the influence of country size in the last chapter, this part deals with the differences between industries. Product differentiation in an industry is an important characteristic of industry differences. This difference is one of the variables explaining differences in conduct and market structure between industries. The effect of a change in the degree of differentiation on the shape and level of the trigger curve is nonlinear and depends on the distance cost level. What could be said is that a decreasing degree of differentiation (ρ increases) flattens the curve. For perfect substitutes ($\rho \rightarrow 1$), neither exports nor production abroad would be profitable. The trigger curve is a flat line at the fixed costs at the plant level in the foreign country ($-w_F f_F$). Figure 22 shows the effect of differences in product differentiation in three industries on the trigger curves of the companies in these industries. The trigger curves are calculated for two countries which differ in size and three industries which are identical except for the degree of differentiation of the final manufacturing goods they sell. The first index of the trigger curve, $\Phi_{h,j}$, indicates the industry, the second the country.

As discussed in Chapter 4, trigger curves of companies from the larger country 1 lie always above those of companies from the smaller country 2. With respect to the degree of differentiation, industries show a pattern in which industries with more differentiated goods precede those with less differentiated

Figure 22:
Trigger Curve of Companies in Industries Which Differ in Their Degree of
Product Differentiation $1/\rho$

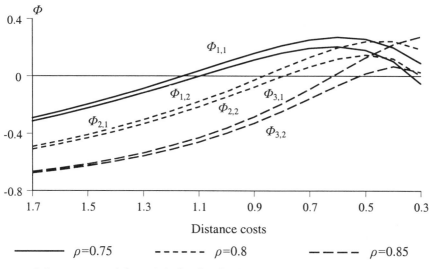

$\mu_A=0.4$, $\mu_1=\mu_2=\mu_3=0.2$, $\varepsilon=0.9$, $\theta_1=\theta_2=\theta_3=0.7$, $L_1=1000$, $L_2=800$, $f_{z_1}=f_{z_2}=0.3$,
$r_{1,1}=r_{2,1}=r_{3,1}=r_{1,2}=r_{2,2}=r_{3,2}=1.5$, $f_{1,1}=f_{2,1}=f_{3,1}=f_{1,2}=f_{2,2}=f_{3,2}=0.8$

goods in the change of the internationalization strategy. Companies in industries
with more differentiated goods decide earlier (at higher distance cost levels) to
internationalize production. Further, their trigger curves reach their maximum
earlier. The trigger curve shifts to the left with increasing degree of differentiation. Trigger curves from different countries become more similar, the run
of the curve more parallel, with increasing degree of differentiation.

One reason for the differences in the industry trigger curves stems from
differences in the export performance of companies from different industries.
This can be seen in Figure 22. A higher degree of product differentiation, $1/\rho$,
leaves companies with more market power. Their goods are not easily substituted by goods of competitors. Exports of more strongly differentiated goods
are, therefore, larger than exports of goods which are less differentiated from
goods of their competitors. A higher degree of differentiation, $1/\rho$, translates into
a lower elasticity of substitution, $\sigma=1/(1-\rho)$. For the same price increase in the
foreign market due to the distance costs, τ_M, the demand reduction in the foreign
market for more differentiated goods is smaller.

A high share of trade volumes in differentiated goods is intraindustry trade with imports and exports of goods in the same industry in both countries. The difference in countries size leads to an imbalance in intraindustry trade of all industries in the manufacturing sector. All industries in the small country 2 are net-importers ($Ex_{h,1} > Ex_{h,2}$) because of the smaller number of companies their smaller country hosts. This imbalance is equalized by small country's exports of the agricultural good, as discussed in Chapter 4. The level of exports of industry 1 is largest. Industry 1 is characterized by the smallest ρ, i.e., by the highest degree of product differentiation. Industry 1 is followed by industries 2 and 3, which are industries with a higher and the highest ρ, respectively. Industry 3, which comes closest to a homogeneous-good industry, exports the smallest amount. In the absence of any absolute or comparative advantages in this model, supply of unique varieties is the only reason for trade. Since the uniqueness falls with rising ρ, lower intraindustry export levels result (Figure 23). Note that the size of the industry, $\mu_h Y_j$, is the same for all three industries in the same country j and fixed over time.

The degree of product differentiation is an important factor in explaining sectoral concentrations of the internationalization of companies' activities. Industries which produce more differentiated goods are more active in export markets. Furthermore, companies in these industries rethink their internationalization strategy earlier and switch to foreign production. International activities fall with falling differentiation in goods. Industries which are characterized by more homogeneous goods are not so active in foreign markets, at least in this setting where all other reasons of trade than the love of variety in demand are assumed away. With lower product differentiation, market power of companies shrink and price competition becomes tougher. There is plenty of empirical evidence that trade, in particular intraindustry trade, is concentrated in industries which produce differentiated goods (Katseli 1992; Bruelhart and Trionfetti 2000; Hummels and Klenow 2002).

But product differentiation is not the only characteristic industries may differ in. The level and the composition of fixed costs are very decisive variables determining conduct and market structure of an industry. Furthermore, they affect the choice of the internationalization strategy. The graphs in Figure 24 depict trigger curves for companies from three different industries. The industries in one country differ only in the fixed costs at company level. All other parameters are the same. Countries differ again in size. Trigger curves of companies from the larger country 1 lie always above those of companies from the smaller country 2. As discussed in Chapter 3, increasing fixed costs at company level lift the trigger curves. With higher fixed costs at company level, economies of scope which give rise to multiplant production increase.

Figure 23:
Export Levels of Industries Characterized by Different ρ

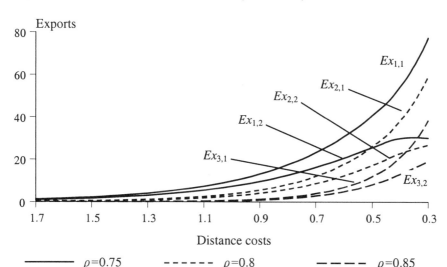

$\mu_A=0.4$, $\mu_1=\mu_2=\mu_3=0.2$, $\varepsilon=0.9$, $\theta_1=\theta_2=\theta_3=0.7$, $L_1=1000$, $L_2=800$, $f_{z1}=f_{z2}=0.3$, $r_{1,1}=r_{2,1}=r_{3,1}=r_{1,2}=r_{2,2}=r_{3,2}=1.5$, $f_{1,1}=f_{2,1}=f_{3,1}=f_{1,2}=f_{2,2}=f_{3,2}=0.8$

Trigger curves of companies from industry 1, the industry with the higher fixed costs at company level, are shifted upward relative to industries 2 and 3. Fixed costs at the company level affect the number of companies in an industry. Companies enter if profits in an industry can be made, i.e., if the variable profits exceed fixed costs at the company and at the plant level. With higher fixed costs, the number of companies in an industry is lower relative to other industries which have the same variable costs and apply the same markup factor (as in the example here). Companies' size in this industry is larger. Thus, total fixed costs spread over more units of output. Internationalization of production, however, depends on the level of plant fixed costs. This level is the same in all industries ($f_{h,j}=0.8$). The more expensive headquarter service, in contrast, can be used in a nonrival way in the foreign affiliate. This generates economies of scope in multi-plant production. The change of the internationalization strategy at the time when the trigger curve crosses the zero line depends on the share of fixed costs at plant level in total fixed costs. The effect of the composition of fixed costs on the decision about the internationalization strategy results also in the analyses of Brainard (1993), Markusen et al. (1996), and Markusen and Venables (1998).

Figure 24:
Companies' Trigger Curve for Different Fixed Costs at the Company Level

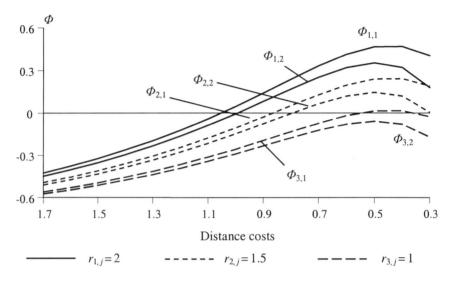

$\mu_A=0.4$, $\mu_1=\mu_2=\mu_3=0.2$, $\varepsilon=0.9$, $\theta_1=\theta_2=\theta_3=0.7$, $L_1=1000$, $L_2=800$, $fz_1=fz_2=0.3$, $\rho_1=\rho_2=\rho_3=0.8$, $f_{1,1}=f_{2,1}=f_{3,1}=f_{1,2}=f_{2,2}=f_{3,2}=0.8$

Empirical evidence supports this result. Proxy variables for headquarter activities as research and development, marketing and the maintenance of a brand name, or management and strategic planning are found to be important determinants of international production in many empirical studies (Horst 1972; Dunning 1973; Brainard 1997; Kleinert 1999).

Whereas the trigger curve is shifted upwards by increasing fixed costs at the company level, export levels are unaffected. Companies in the industry with high fixed costs are larger. Their per company exports are larger, too. But there are fewer companies in this industry in equilibrium. In industry aggregate, exports of industries which differ only in the level and composition of fixed costs are equal. A change in the level of the plant fixed costs is, therefore, as irrelevant for industry export levels as is a change in company level fixed costs. The trigger curves, in contrast, are affected by a change in the level of plant fixed costs (Figure 25). Given the important role plant level fixed costs play in determining the internationalization strategy (equation 73), this is obvious.

Fixed costs at the plant level are at the heart of the proximity-concentration tradeoff. Smaller fixed costs at the plant level reduce the concentration forces and

Figure 25:
Companies' Trigger Curve for Different Fixed Costs at the Plant Level

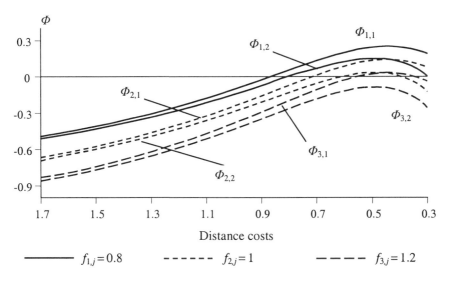

$\mu_A=0.4$, $\mu_1=\mu_2=\mu_3=0.2$, $\varepsilon=0.9$, $\theta_1=\theta_2=\theta_3=0.7$, $L_1=1000$, $L_2=800$, $fz_1=fz_2=0.3$,
$\rho_1=\rho_2=\rho_3=0.8$, $r_{1,1}=r_{2,1}=r_{3,1}=r_{1,2}=r_{2,2}=r_{3,2}=1.5$

ease the internationalization of production. This can be seen in Figure 25. Industry 1, the industry with the lowest fixed costs at the plant level ($f_{1,j}=0.8$),
internationalizes production first, followed later by industry 2. Fixed costs at
the plant level in industry 3 are very high. While companies from the larger
country 1 find it profitable to internationalize production, country 2 companies
always prefer exports. Their trigger curve does not reach the zero line at any
distance cost level. High fixed costs at the plant level force companies from
country 2 in industry 3 to rely always on exports.

   Next to level and composition of fixed costs, the share of intermediate goods
used in production, $1-\theta$, is important in determining internationalization activities of companies. This share stands for the complexity of the production of a
good. The larger the share of specific intermediate inputs in the production of a
good, the higher the complexity and, since specific intermediate goods must be
taken from the home country network of the company, the greater the relatedness
to the home country. A higher share in intermediate inputs, which must be
imported from the home country by the foreign affiliate, raises the cost and the

price of the affiliate's product. The profitability of production abroad relative to exports decreases. The trigger curve shifts downwards (Figure 26).

Industry 1, the industry with the lowest share of intermediate inputs in production, internationalizes production first, followed by industry 2. Again, in industry 3, only companies from the larger country 1 start production abroad. With a lower share of intermediate inputs, trigger curves shift up and to the right. The trigger curve reaches its maximum earlier. The shape of the trigger curve becomes less pronounced. If production does not depend on intermediate inputs as in Brainard (1993) and Markusen and Venables (1998), the trigger curves falls with falling distance costs. In their models, higher distance costs encourage the internationalization of production.

Among developed countries, the globalization process is characterized by a tendency of increasing internationalization of production driven by falling distance costs. MNEs emerge in many industries. Starting in industries with rather simple production processes as food processing and manufacturing of consumer good, which did not rely so heavily on the home country network of suppliers, the process spreads to other industries, which involves more complex production processes. For some developing countries following the import substitution strategy, MNEs started production without reliance on their home country network but sourced their inputs exclusively from the host countries. The Brainard (1993) and Markusen and Venables (1998) cases occurred. The profitability of this foreign production relative to exports falls with falling distance costs. A reduction of the high tariffs of these countries made exports to these countries more attractive. Foreign affiliates of MNEs lost in parts their importance.

In the multiindustry version of the model proposed here, the share of intermediate inputs in production of the final good affects the export volume of the final good. This is due to the different price levels of intermediate goods in both countries. In the larger country 1, the larger market for intermediate goods allows for more intermediate-goods producers and, therefore, more varieties. More varieties translate into a lower price in aggregate. Lower prices for their inputs mean lower costs for final-goods producers in the larger country 1. This price advantage yields higher export volumes relative to their competitors from the smaller country 2. Companies in industries which use a larger share of intermediate inputs export more than companies in industries with a smaller share of intermediated inputs used in production, because the price advantage over the competitors from the smaller country 2 is larger in industries which rely more heavily on intermediate inputs.

Higher export levels and lower prices in the larger country result only from an agglomeration effect. The larger market for intermediate goods generates a cost

Figure 26:
Companies' Trigger Curve for Different Shares of Intermediate Inputs Used in Production

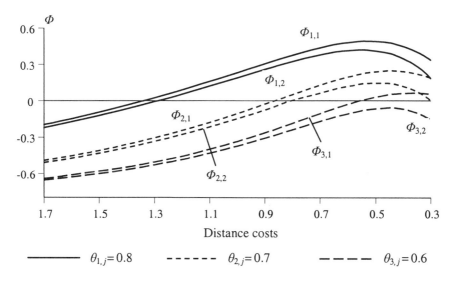

$\mu_A=0.4$, $\mu_1=\mu_2=\mu_3=0.2$, $\varepsilon=0.9$, $\rho_1=\rho_2=\rho_3=0.8$, $L_1=1000$, $L_2=800$, $fz_1=fz_2=0.3$, $r_{1,1}=r_{2,1}=r_{3,1}=r_{1,2}=r_{2,2}=r_{3,2}=1.5$, $f_{1,1}=f_{2,1}=f_{3,1}=f_{1,2}=f_{2,2}=f_{3,2}=0.8$

advantage. This translates into lower prices of every final good produced in the larger country. The aggregate price index is, therefore, lower. However, this aggregate price index in the larger country 1 includes as many final-goods varieties as the price index in the smaller country 2. Final goods are tradable and can be produced in the foreign country. Every consumer makes her choice from the same set of final goods. Although varieties may differ in price, they are available for all consumers. This is the difference to the intermediate goods, which are only available to final-goods producers from their home country.

The number of intermediate goods in each country and their effect on the price index of intermediate goods is influenced by the degree of differentiation of the intermediates, $1/\varepsilon$. This becomes clear if the CES aggregation function is seen as based on the optimal address approach. The distance between any two (optimal) varieties becomes larger with a smaller ε. Varieties are less substitutable. The advantage generated by a larger number of varieties is larger. The difference in the price indexes of intermediate goods in both countries increases with falling ε. The cost advantage of final-goods producers in the larger country 1 increases relative to their foreign competitors. Export volumes increase, therefore, with falling ε in the larger and decrease in the smaller country. The trigger curves of companies in the larger country are shifted upwards, those of companies in the smaller country downwards.

To sum up, the analysis reveals the reason for the industry concentration of the internationalization of activities when using the multiindustry version of the model. The extent of international activities in an industry can be explained by the technology used in the industry and by demand characteristics in this particular industry. Industries where companies produce more differentiated goods internationalize their activities earlier, with exports preceding foreign production. Their engagement in the foreign country is more pronounced. On the technological side, exports are only slightly affected by the share of intermediate goods in production of a final good and by the degree of differentiation of the intermediate goods. Fixed cost levels and composition does not affect exports. But all four technological parameters affect the point in time of the internationalization of production. High levels of fixed costs at the company level and a low degree of differentiation among the intermediate goods spur internationalization of production, as do low levels of fixed costs at the plant level and a low share of intermediate inputs in production of the final good.

So far, all results are derived from equilibria which included only national companies. Only the point in time when the trigger curve crosses the zero-line was discussed. In the next section, I do not restrict the analysis to such equilibria. I model and analyze periods of intense internationalization of production to examine the question of the relationship between export and production abroad. For this analysis, I compare equilibria which include MNEs to pure national company equilibria in order to generate a counterfactual situation to answer the question whether exports and production abroad are complements or substitutes.

5.3   Complementarity versus Substitutionality of Exports and Production Abroad

Whether exports and production abroad are complements or substitutes has been hotly discussed. The question is an important issue, because in the political debate activities of MNEs are often related to fears of a restructuring of their production process which might include dismissal of workers. Many people in developed countries are afraid that globalization leads to MNEs exporting jobs instead of goods. This is why it is a politically very important question whether the internationalization of production substitutes for exports or stimulates them. It touches people's attitude towards globalization, because it touches the income distribution among different groups in the developed countries. The fear is that globalization increases profits but decreases wages and/or employment through the reallocation of jobs.

These fears receive substantial support from economic theory. Various theoretical models predict substitution of exports by foreign production. Especially horizontal investment is expected to yield substitution, since companies save on distance costs and serve the foreign market by production abroad. Vertical investment would yield a complementary relationship. Given the dominance of horizontal investment (Markusen and Maskus 2002; Blonigen et al. 2002), substitution would prevail.[11] In empirical studies, however, another picture emerges. Most empirical work finds a complementary relationship between trade and foreign affiliates' output on the aggregate and on the industry level (Swedenborg 1979; Lipsey and Weiss 1981; Eaton and Tamura 1994).

Since the theory used to explain the emergence of MNEs deals mostly with the decision of one company, which decides whether to export or to produce abroad. From a theoretical point, studies which are based on more disaggregated data are more likely to yield substitution. However, studies based on company-level data also find a complementarity between costs and foreign production (Blomström et al. 1988; Head and Ries 2001). There are a few company- and product-level studies which find net substitution (Pfaffermayr 1996; Blonigen 2001). Blonigen (2001) argues that the use of product-level data allows for a test of a substitution effect separately from complementarity effects, such as those arising from vertical linkages.

Some explanation could be brought forward why trade and foreign affiliates' output should be substitutes on the most disaggregated level but complements when more aggregated data are used. One is the complex vertical structure of many industries with (foreign) trade occurring at the interface of any two stages of production which are based in different locations (countries). Foreign affiliates' production is necessarily trade-creating if production involves more than one stage. However, it is trade-reducing if the formerly exported goods are now produced in the same amount in the foreign country. Which effect prevails depends on the production function of the company. Another reason why trade and affiliates output appear to be complements in many studies might be that they are driven by the same force. If reduction of distance costs increases trade as well as affiliates' production, they appear to be complements because they react in a similar way to changes in distance costs. What seems to be a complementarity is a co-movement of the two time series.

---

[11] The terms complementarity and substitution are used differently in this literature than in a typical demand analysis, where these terms refer to a change of a quantity with respect to price changes. Here, the change in one quantity with respect to a change in another quantity is asked for.

Hence, trade and foreign affiliates' output would show substitution when very disaggregated (product-level) data are used, substitution or complementarity when more aggregated data (company-level) are used, and complementarity when industry or balance of payments data are used. This is exactly what is observed. Here, I analyze the relationship between trade and foreign affiliates' output theoretically by using the model extension developed in Section 5.1. Different industries are modeled to show product-level, industry-level, and country-level effects at work in a general equilibrium.

So far, the concentration of international activities on some industries has been explained by an analysis of the influence of exogenous technology and demand parameters on export volumes and the internationalization decision. The analysis revealed that some industries reach the point in time when internationalization of production becomes profitable earlier than other industries. There might also be industries which companies always rely on exports. However, with the first company deciding to set up a foreign affiliate the question of complementarity or substitutability arises. The effect of this decision on exports of other companies in the same industry, on exports of other final-goods-producing industries in the manufacturing sector, on intermediate-goods companies and their exports, and on total exports stands in the center of interest in the following analysis.

When one company decides to internationalize production, the trigger curves, like those depicted in Figure 22, lose their validity because the price indexes change. The equilibrium does not only include national companies anymore but also MNEs. The trigger curves change as discussed above. Since companies are only very indirectly affected (through the intermediate-goods producers) by an action of a company from different industries, market structure changes affect different industries very asymmetrically. The trigger curves can be seen in Figure 27. The change in industry 1, the industry where a company decided to internationalize production, is by far the strongest. Country 2 companies' trigger curves fall, while those of country 1 companies rise. The effect on the other two industries is only very indirect and, therefore, much weaker.

Output of foreign affiliates is much larger than export volumes. Hence, there are more intermediate inputs needed in production. This enlarges the market for intermediate goods in country 1 during the internationalization period. In addition, the number of final-goods producers in the home country increases. This enlarges the intermediate-goods market further. This market growth increases profits of intermediate-goods producers and provides an incentive for new companies to enter the intermediate-goods market. The number of intermediate-goods producers rises in country 1. With more varieties in the bundle, the aggregate price index of intermediate goods falls in country 1. Then, inputs are cheaper for companies in industries 2 and 3, their prices fall, and their goods

Figure 27:
Trigger Curves in the Multiindustry Model

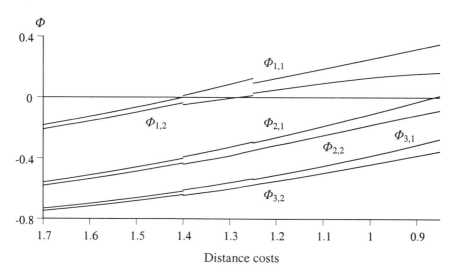

$\mu_A=0.4$, $\mu_1=\mu_2=\mu_3=0.2$, $\varepsilon=0.9$, $\rho_1=0.75$, $\rho_2=0.775$, $\rho_3=0.8$, $\theta_1=\theta_2=\theta_3=0.7$,
$L_1=1000$, $L_2=800$, $r_{1,1}=r_{1,2}=2$, $r_{2,1}=r_{2,2}=1.5$, $r_{3,1}=r_{3,2}=1$, $f_{1,1}=f_{1,2}=0.8$,
$f_{2,1}=f_{2,2}=f_{3,1}=f_{3,2}=1$, $fz_1=fz_2=0.3$

have an additional advantage over their small country rivals. Their trigger curves rise. Small country's companies experience the opposite. The number of final-goods producers in industry 1 falls. Since foreign affiliates do not use intermediate goods from the host country, the intermediate-good market shrinks. The number of intermediate-goods varieties falls. The aggregate price index of intermediate goods rises. Final-goods producers' costs and prices rise. The trigger curves fall during the internationalization process of companies from industry 1 in country 1. This effect is stronger for companies in industry 2 than for those in industry 3.

During the adjustment, the trigger curve of the companies from the internationalizing industry experiences a jump in the home country and a fall in the host country indicating a drastic change in the profitability of production abroad relative to the profitability of exports in both countries. This results from the change in the trade structure between the two countries, which leads to a changing market structure in both economies. When a final-goods producer sets up an affiliate in the foreign country, the company substitutes exports of the final good by production abroad. Exports in final goods decrease, therefore, but ex-

Figure 28:
Exports of Companies from Country 1 during the Internationalization Process

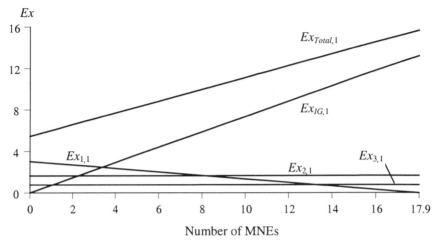

Number of MNEs

$\mu_A=0.4$, $\mu_1=\mu_2=\mu_3=0.2$, $\varepsilon=0.9$, $\rho_1=0.75$, $\rho_2=0.775$, $\rho_3=0.8$, $\theta_1=\theta_2=\theta_3=0.7$, $L_1=1000$, $L_2=800$, $r_{1,1}=r_{1,2}=2$, $r_{2,1}=r_{2,2}=1.5$, $r_{3,1}=r_{3,2}=1$, $f_{1,1}=f_{1,2}=0.8$, $f_{2,1}=f_{2,2}=f_{3,1}=f_{3,2}=1$, $fz_1=fz_2=0.3$, $\tau_M=1.4$

ports in intermediate goods increase. Whether the export-enhancing or the export-reducing effect prevails is parameter-dependent in the model and up to empirical evidence in applied economics. In Figure 28, it is very clear that the trade creation in intermediate goods outweighs the trade reduction in final goods in industry 1.

As in Section 5.2, the first subscript indicates the industry, the second the country. It is easy to see that internationalization of production has a positive effect on exports in this example. Total exports of country 1 companies, $Ex_{Total,1}$, increase by about 190 percent. The export reduction in final goods from industry 1, $Ex_{1,1}$, is by far overcompensated by the rise of exports in intermediate goods, $Ex_{IG,1}$. These stand at the end of the internationalization period at more than 4 times the size of intraindustry exports from industry 1, $Ex_{1,1}$, at the beginning of the internationalization. Export levels of companies from industries 2 and 3, $Ex_{2,1}$ and $Ex_{3,1}$, are nearly unchanged. They increase marginally because of falling prices of the intermediate-goods price index.

In empirical cross-section analyses with industries from a particular country as sample population, this internationalization pattern would yield the result of strong complementarity between exports and production abroad. The industry which hosts MNEs exports most, whereas industries without MNEs export less. According to input-output table analyses, intermediate goods are predominantly drawn from the own industry. Thus, in such an empirical study, a large fraction of intermediate-goods exports would be found to be industry 1 exports. However, there might also be complementary effects of production abroad of industry 1 companies on other industries' exports. Nevertheless, there is substitution of finals-goods exports by production abroad in industry 1, which would be found in product-level studies.

The graphs of Figure 28 are derived at a constant distance cost level of $\tau_M = 1.4$, the distance cost level at the point in time when companies from industry 1 in country 1 internationalize their production. However, substitution or a complementary relationship is often better discussed as process, i.e., in a framework which includes a time dimension. Using the multiindustry version of the model, an analysis of the relationship between exports and production abroad requires a comparison of export levels of both countries in a model world which includes MNEs and a model where internationalization of production is restricted. Thus, using the simulation techniques, it is possible to generate an as-if comparison. Everything being equal in both runs but the market structure (which changes with the existence of MNEs in one or both economies) yields different exports levels, as depicted in Figure 29.

Over time, exports and production abroad are complements in this example. In equilibria which restrict companies to be national companies, the level of exports, Ex^{NC}, lies below the export level in equilibria with MNEs, Ex^{MNE}. The one-time jump at $\tau_M = 1.4$ discussed above is very distinct. With falling distance costs, export growth is higher in equilibria which include MNEs than in pure national equilibria. However, in the internationalization period of country 2 companies from industry 1, export levels drop. With falling distance costs and MNEs from both countries in the MNE equilibria, exports increase parallel under both regimes. Since an equilibrium is characterized by a balanced international trade, the export levels shown in Figure 29 apply to both countries.

The fall in total exports, $Ex_{Total,2}$, during the internationalization period of companies from industry 1 in the smaller country 2 shows that exports do not necessarily increase with increasing foreign production. As can be seen in Figure 30, decreasing exports from the smaller country 2 are due to decreasing exports of the homogeneous agricultural good, $Ex_{AG,2}$. The trade balance deficit of country 2 shrinks with the internationalization of production of their companies. Homogeneous-good exports, $Ex_{AG,2}$, have to balance a smaller deficit. Hence, they fall. Exports of manufacturing goods increase, which results from increasing exports of intermediate goods, $Ex_{IG,2}$, overcompensating the decrease in final-goods exports from industry 1, $Ex_{1,2}$. Exports of companies from industries 2 and 3, $Ex_{2,2}$ and $Ex_{3,2}$, are almost unchanged.

Figure 29:
Export Levels over Time

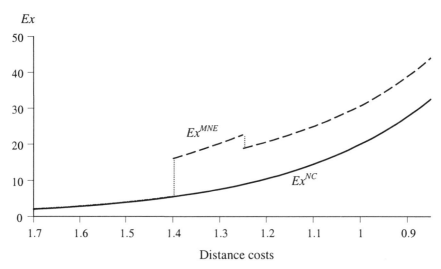

$\mu_A=0.4$, $\mu_1=\mu_2=\mu_3=0.2$, $\varepsilon=0.9$, $\rho_1=0.75$, $\rho_2=0.775$, $\rho_3=0.8$, $\theta_1=\theta_2=\theta_3=0.7$, $L_1=1000$, $L_2=800$, $r_{1,1}=r_{1,2}=2$, $r_{2,1}=r_{2,2}=1.5$, $r_{3,1}=r_{3,2}=1$, $f_{1,1}=f_{1,2}=0.8$, $f_{2,1}=f_{2,2}=f_{3,1}=f_{3,2}=1$, $fz_1=fz_2=0.3$

Internationalization of production and total exports of country 2 companies are substitutes in this example. With increasing production in foreign affiliates of MNEs from country 2, total exports of companies from country 2 decrease. However, this result stems from a balance of payments effect. Production abroad and exports are complements if only the manufacturing sector is analyzed. While $Ex_{2,2}$ and $Ex_{3,2}$ remain unchanged, the sum of intermediate-goods exports and intraindustry exports from industry 1, $Ex_{IG+1,2}$, increases with increasing number of MNEs in the economy (broken line). Thus, exports and foreign production in industry 1 and in the manufacturing sector are characterized by a complementary relationship.

Exports of companies from country 1, $Ex_{Total,1}$, decrease because the number of MNEs in industry 1 which are based in country 1 decreases during the internationalization process of country 2 companies as discussed in Chapter 4. The volume of intermediate-goods exports, $Ex_{IG,1}$, decreases therefore. There are very small effects on the exports of final goods from industries 2 and 3, $Ex_{2,1}$ and $Ex_{3,1}$, through the change in the costs of intermediate goods which stems from the price index changes due to the shrinking intermediate-good market in

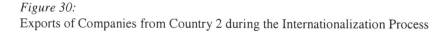

Figure 30:
Exports of Companies from Country 2 during the Internationalization Process

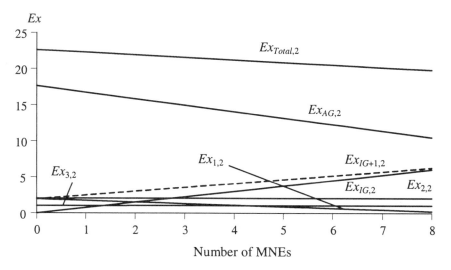

$\mu_A=0.4$, $\mu_1=\mu_2=\mu_3=0.2$, $\varepsilon=0.9$, $\rho_1=0.75$, $\rho_2=0.775$, $\rho_3=0.8$, $\theta_1=\theta_2=\theta_3=0.7$, $L_1=1000$, $L_2=800$, $r_{1,1}=r_{1,2}=2$, $r_{2,1}=r_{2,2}=1.5$, $r_{3,1}=r_{3,2}=1$, $f_{1,1}=f_{1,2}=0.8$, $f_{2,1}=f_{2,2}=f_{3,1}=f_{3,2}=1$, $f_{z1}=f_{z2}=0.3$, $\tau_M=1.25$

country 1. With falling distance costs, after the internationalization process has been completed, trade increases parallel in both regimes, which differ by market structures with or without MNEs (Figure 29).

Export structure and export level of both economies change strongly over time. At very high distance cost levels, there are very low levels of intraindustry trade in the three final-goods-producing industries of the manufacturing sector. In addition, there are low levels of agricultural-goods exports from the smaller country 2. With falling distance costs, these exports rise. In the internationalization process of country 1 companies (at $\tau_M=1.4$), large intermediate-goods exports arise which overcompensate the fall in final-goods exports from industry 1. Furthermore, (headquarter) services are exported from the home country of the MNEs. Companies in industries 2 and 3 engage in intraindustry trade, industry 1 shows intermediate-goods and service exports from country 1 and final-goods exports from country 2. Trade increases over time. In the internationalization process of companies from industry 1 in country 2, intermediate-goods and headquarter service exports from country 2 to country 1 arise. Then, industry 1 is characterized by bi-directional intraindustry trade in intermediate

Figure 31:
Changing Trade Pattern over Time

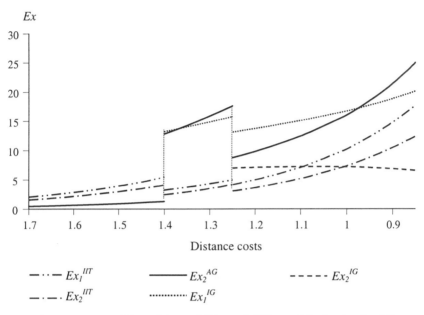

$\mu_A=0.4$, $\mu_1=\mu_2=\mu_3=0.2$, $\varepsilon=0.9$, $\rho_1=0.75$, $\rho_2=0.775$, $\rho_3=0.8$, $\theta_1=\theta_2=\theta_3=0.7$,
$L_1=1000$, $L_2=800$, $r_{1,1}=r_{1,2}=2$, $r_{2,1}=r_{2,2}=1.5$, $r_{3,1}=r_{3,2}=1$, $f_{1,1}=f_{1,2}=0.8$,
$f_{2,1}=f_{2,2}=f_{3,1}=f_{3,2}=1$, $fz_1=fz_2=0.3$

goods and services. Industries 2 and 3 continue to trade final goods. Trade volumes increase with falling distance costs. This complex trade pattern is depicted in Figure 31.

Market structure changes alter the trade pattern significantly. The discontinuities in Figure 31 indicate a drastic change in the trade pattern at the points in time of internationalization waves ($\tau_M=1.4$ and $\tau_M=1.25$). The largest effect results from changes in industry 1, the industry where the changes in market structure occur. The other industries in the manufacturing sector are only indirectly affected. But intermediate-goods companies are strongly affected. The demand for intermediate goods produced in the home country of the MNEs is increased by intermediate inputs demand of the foreign affiliates of MNEs. Intermediate-goods producers export their intermediate goods. Demand for intermediate goods in the host country of the affiliates of the MNEs is reduced, because the number of country 2 companies decreases. The same holds, the other way around, when country 2 companies in industry 1 internationalize their production at $\tau_M=1.25$.

Figure 32:
Trade Levels in Equilibria with and without MNEs

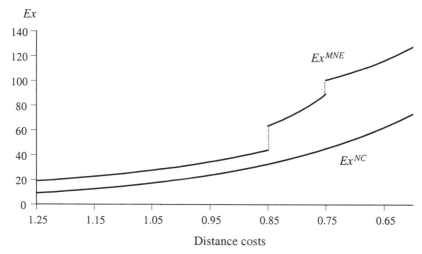

$\mu_A=0.4$, $\mu_1=\mu_2=\mu_3=0.2$, $\varepsilon=0.9$, $\rho_1=0.75$, $\rho_2=0.775$, $\rho_3=0.8$,
$\theta_1=\theta_2=\theta_3=0.7$, $L_1=1000$, $L_2=800$, $r_{1,1}=r_{1,2}=2$, $r_{2,1}=r_{2,2}=1.5$, $r_{3,1}=r_{3,2}=1$,
$f_{1,1}=f_{1,2}=0.8$, $f_{2,1}=f_{2,2}=f_{3,1}=f_{3,2}=1$, $fz_1=fz_2=0.3$

With further falling distance costs, internationalization of production becomes profitable relative to exports in industry 2 as well. The point in time where the trigger curve of companies in industry 2 from the larger country 1 crosses zero is reached at $\tau_M=0.85$ as can be seen in Figure 27. The internationalization process of industry 2 companies follows the same pattern. Intermediate-goods exports, $Ex_{IG,1}$, increase more than final-goods exports from industry 2 of country 1, $Ex_{2,1}$, decrease. Again, foreign production and exports are complements. The trade deficit of the manufacturing sector of country 2 widens, interindustry agricultural exports, $Ex_{AG,2}$, increase to balance the current account. Although the trade balance is not equalized, the current account is. There are net exports of headquarter services from country 1 to country 2. The intraindustry trade share in service trade falls, the one-way export share of country 1 rises. Figure 32 shows the development of trade for a medium range of distance costs.

The second discontinuity results from the change in market structure which is due to the exit of the last MNE from industry 1 based in country 2. With increasing integration of the two markets due to falling distance costs, the competitive advantage of country 1 MNEs increases. The number of MNEs based in country 2 decreases. At $\tau_M=0.75$, the last MNE exists, market structure in industry 1 changes. It only includes MNEs from country 1 which produce in both countries but have their headquarters in country 1. After the exit of country 2 companies, there is no intraindustry trade in industry 1 ($Ex_{IG,2} = 0$). However, total trade rises, since intermediate-goods exports of country 1, $Ex_{IG,1}$, rise. Country 2 increases its agricultural-goods exports, $Ex_{AG,2}$. Again, trade and production abroad are complements rather than substitutes. As discussed in Chapter 4, the strong fall in the number of host country companies results from the symmetry of the companies in each industry, an assumption which is relaxed in the next section.

The existence of MNEs has a positive effect on trade in this example. At all points in time, equilibria which include MNEs generate more trade than equilibria where international activities of companies are restricted to exports. Although, this seems to be in line with the empirical evidence, it must be tested whether this result is robust with regard to parameter changes. From the discussion on concentration of international activities on particular industries in the previous section in this chapter it should be clear that the share of intermediate goods in production is the most likely candidate to change the complementarity relationship between production abroad and exports. Figure 33 gives, therefore, equilibrium export levels for three different production processes. Production differs with respect to the share of intermediate inputs used. For comparison, trade levels in equilibria with only national companies are also given. For all three shares of intermediate inputs in production, trade in equilibria with MNEs exceeds trade in equilibria without MNEs.

Figure 33 shows that the complementary relationship holds for all three shares of intermediate input used in the production of the final goods. Export levels in equilibria with MNEs always lie above those in equilibria with only national companies. At high distance costs, export levels do not differ so much with respect to the share of intermediate inputs. The largest effect on export levels results from different market structures at the same distance costs level depending on the intermediate input share. At given parameters, there exist MNEs in industry 1 already at $\tau_M = 1.7$ if the share of intermediate inputs is low ($\theta_1 = 0.8$). In contrast, for high shares of intermediate inputs used in production ($\theta_1 = 0.6$), internationalization of production becomes profitable only at $\tau_M = 1$. For the same market structure, however, export levels are very similar. This is different for intermediate levels of distance costs. Although export levels in MNE equilibria are generally higher than those in pure national company equilibria, the extent of the positive effect of foreign production on exports depends on the share of intermediate goods used in production. The higher this share is, the stronger the complementary relationship between exports and production abroad is.

Figure 33:
Export Levels over Time for Different Shares of Intermediate Inputs

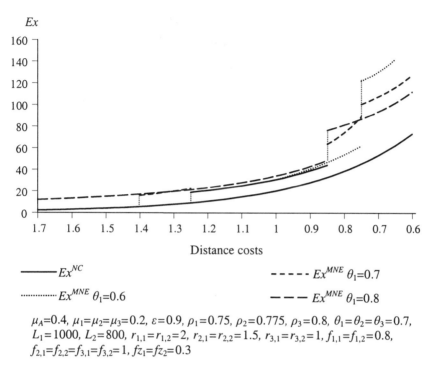

$\mu_A=0.4$, $\mu_1=\mu_2=\mu_3=0.2$, $\varepsilon=0.9$, $\rho_1=0.75$, $\rho_2=0.775$, $\rho_3=0.8$, $\theta_1=\theta_2=\theta_3=0.7$, $L_1=1000$, $L_2=800$, $r_{1,1}=r_{1,2}=2$, $r_{2,1}=r_{2,2}=1.5$, $r_{3,1}=r_{3,2}=1$, $f_{1,1}=f_{1,2}=0.8$, $f_{2,1}=f_{2,2}=f_{3,1}=f_{3,2}=1$, $fz_1=fz_2=0.3$

The analysis reveals why production abroad and exports are mostly found to be complements in empirical studies, although there is certainly substitution of the good produced in a foreign country and its export to this foreign country. This substitution is found in product level studies (Blonigen 2001). Blonigen uses product level data and analyzes only the bilateral effect of production abroad of Japanese companies in the United States on their exports to the United States. This is different from company level studies which often not only analyze multiproduct companies but also the relationship of production abroad and exports of these companies in total, i.e., with all business partners in many countries. There are, therefore, two components which contribute to complementarity: the multiproduct dimension and the multicountry dimension. The multiproduct dimension includes complementarity because at least some of the intermediate goods are produced within the company. Furthermore, each product has its own trigger function which might differ depending on taste and production parameters. Different trigger curves yield different points in time of setting up foreign production. Some products might precede others. However, over time production abroad and exports increase. Hence, a complementary relationship is inferred. The same arises for trigger curves of the same good for various countries, i.e., there appears to be complementarity, because the real world is a multi-country world. Trigger curves certainly differ, because the countries differ and because distance (which is always set to one in this analysis) differs between different countries. The setup of an affiliate in one country might precede those in others. Again, over time, production abroad and exports increase. Hence, a complementary relationship is inferred.

To sum up, studies of the export versus production abroad relationship which use data at industry level often find also a positive effect. According to the theory presented here, this is due to the intermediate-goods trade which over-compensates the export reduction of final goods. The complementary relationship seems to be robust to parameter changes in the model. Empirical analyses back this explanation (MITI 2000). For the whole economy, there might be periods with net substitution between exports and foreign production (inter-nationalization of companies from the small country) but export level in equilibria with MNEs lie always above those in pure national equilibria.

With regard to the fears presented at the beginning of this section, it can be concluded that not only for empirical but also for theoretical reasons, society in developed countries in general should not be afraid of the internationalization of production. Certainly, globalization is a form of structural change and therefore not without costs for some people or groups. However, the necessary adjustments on labor markets are not as costly as feared (Brainard and Riker 1997; Slaughter 2000). The costs of restricting the internationalization process are definitely much larger.

5.4   On the Coexistence of National and Multinational Companies

In contrast to the previous section which deals with a political debate, this section is more of academic interest. There is no doubt that national and multi-national companies coexist in many sectors of many economies. However, there is an argument whether models of MNEs can reflect this coexistence. Brainard (1993) discusses coexistence for a knife-edge solution of her model. Markusen and Venables (1998) claim coexistence of both types of companies, because under particular conditions there might be a national company or an MNE in equilibrium. However, the market structure is not explicitly given. The existence of a particular type of company might depend on the prevailing market structure. Moreover, there is no comparison of profits of both strategies. There is therefore no check whether it would be profitable to change the strategy. Whether the coexistence result prevails if such a comparison is made is unclear.

In the model presented in Chapter 3, coexistence is not possible. Since all companies are symmetric, they all internationalize production at the same time. The economy switches from hosting only national companies to hosting only MNEs when distance costs have fallen below a particular threshold. In the asymmetric country model in Chapter 4, this tendency is strengthened by the wave effect which results from the asymmetric change in the market structure in the home and host country. One country's companies are still symmetric and internationalize at the same time. In the multiindustry version in this chapter, national and multinational companies coexist but there are only national companies in one industry and only MNEs in another. Within one industry, companies internationalize at the same time. There is no coexistence within an industry in the model yet.

In the following part, the multiindustry model is changed slightly to reflect differences between companies within an industry. Between sectors, it was already hard to justify fixed income shares and no competition, but within an industry it is impossible to assume such a market structure. Generally, companies belonging to an industry are characterized by producing closer substitutes than companies of different industries. Competition within an industry should be fiercer than between companies from different industries. Seen from the address approach, each consumer chooses his most preferred variety in each industry in the multiindustry model. In the multigroup model, the consumer chooses one good from the different groups within the industry. This reflects competition between different groups of companies within one industry. The model version used to analyze different companies in one industry must reflect this.

An adjusted multiindustry model is used to analyze competition within one sector. Industries are reinterpreted as to reflect different groups of companies with different characteristics within an industry. The manufacturing sector consists, therefore, of one industry hosting several groups of different companies. These are symmetric within their group. The model structure with three industries without competition between companies from different industries and fixed income shares for each industry is changed by using a different utility function which accounts for the possibility of substitution between products of companies from different groups. Individuals choose their most preferred version of the differentiated final good in a two-stage process. First, one of the different nests is chosen depending on the price indexes of the nests. Second, the most preferred version from the chosen nest is taken. The CD-CES (Cobb-Douglas constant elasticity of substitution) structure utility function in (58) and (59) changes to a CD-nested CES structure in (81) and (82):

$$(81) \quad U_j = Q_{A,j}{}^{\mu} Q_{M,j}{}^{1-\mu}, \quad \text{with} \quad \mu \in (0,1); \quad j = H, F,$$

$$(82) \quad Q_{M,j} = \left[\sum_{h=1}^{\lambda} Q_{Mh,j}{}^{\varsigma} \right]^{1/\varsigma}, \quad \text{with} \quad Q_{Mh,j} = \left[\sum_{i=1}^{\lambda_h} q_{i,j}^{h}{}^{\rho_h} \right]^{1/\rho_h},$$

where $\varsigma, \rho_h \in (0,1)$; $j = H, F$.

Individuals choose a group h of products from the whole set of different groups of differentiated final goods. Groups of products are formed by similar companies which stand in fiercer competition between each other than final goods from two different groups. The idea is that within an industry like the automobile industry, for instance, there are different groups, like compact cars, sports cars, or pick-ups, which compete for customers. However, although there is certainly competition between a producer of a pick-up and a producer of a sports car,[12] the competition between two sports car producers is tougher. This requires the degree of differentiation $1/\rho_h$ of different members of a group h to be lower than the degree of differentiation $1/\varsigma$ between the different groups. After having chosen their preferred group, individuals choose the most preferred variety out of the group members in the second stage.

Given the change in the utility function, demand of the representative consumer changes. She chooses goods of the different groups depending on their prices. The income share which is spent on each group varies with the prices. It increases in the price index of manufacturing goods (the weighted sum of the price indexes of all groups of differentiated final goods), P_M, with the share of income spent on manufacturing goods, μ, and with total income, Y_j, and it decreases in the price index of the particular group of final goods, $P_{Mh,j}$. Equation (83) gives the demand for each group of final goods, Q_{Mh}, and (84) the price index of manufacturing goods, P_M, which can be calculated from (82):

$$(83) \quad Q_{Mh,j} = \frac{P_{Mh,j}{}^{-(1+\chi)}}{P_{M,j}{}^{-\chi}} \mu Y_j \quad \text{with} \quad \chi = \varsigma/(1-\varsigma); \quad j = H, F; \quad h = 1, \ldots, \kappa,$$

$$(84) \quad P_{M,j} = \left[\sum_{h=1}^{\kappa} P_{Mh,j}{}^{-\chi} \right]^{-\frac{1}{\chi}} \quad \text{with} \quad \chi = \varsigma/(1-\varsigma); \quad j = H, F; \quad h = 1, \ldots, \kappa.$$

---

[12] It is hard to maintain the single product company approach in this example, but for simplicity, the argument is still based on a single product company.

P_{Mj} increases in the price indexes, $P_{M_h,j}$, of the different groups and decreases in their number, κ. Each group consists of different (symmetric) companies which produce imperfectly substitutable final goods. The price indexes of these groups increase in the (identical) prices of the final goods and decrease in the number of goods in each group, λ_h. Prices of goods in different groups may differ; within each group, prices are identical, because companies are symmetric. The price index, $P_{M_h,j}$, of group h in the industry which constitutes the manufacturing sector is shown in (85):

$$(85) \quad P_{M_h,j} = \left[\sum_{i=1}^{\lambda_h} p_{i,h,j}^{-\gamma_h} \right]^{-\frac{1}{\gamma_h}} \quad j,l=H,F; \ j \neq l; \ h=1,2,\dots,\kappa; \ \gamma_h=\rho_h/(1-\rho_h).$$

Demand for a single variety of the differentiated good changes because of the variable market size, Ω_{hj} (more precisely: $\Omega_{h,j} = P_{M_h,j}Q_{M_h,j}$), of each group of goods. Demand for a single variety i of the differentiated good in group h increases in the market size for its group's goods, Ω_{hj}, and in the group price index, and decreases in its own prices. Demand may differ for companies from different groups. Within a group, demand differs for national companies and MNEs in the foreign market, because they are differently affected by distance costs. At home, they face the same demand. Output of an individual company, which equals demand in equilibrium, changes from (66)–(68) to (86)–(88). The output of a national company includes the supply of the home and foreign demand, since the foreign market is served through exports. Production takes place exclusively at home. MNEs produce in both countries to satisfy the local demand:

$$(86) \quad q_{h,i,j} = \frac{p_{h,i,j}^{-(1+\gamma_h)}}{P_{M_h,j}^{-\gamma_h}} \Omega_{h,j} + \frac{p_{h,i,j}^{-(1+\gamma_h)} e^{-(1+\gamma_h)\tau_M}}{P_{M_h,l}^{-\gamma_h}} \Omega_{h,l},$$

$$j,l=H,F; \ l \neq j; \ \gamma_h=\rho_h/(1-\rho_h),$$

where $\Omega_{h,j} = P_{M_h,j}Q_{M_h,j}$

$$(87) \quad q_{h,i,j,j}^M = \frac{p_{h,i,j,j}^{M-(1+\gamma_h)}}{P_{M_h,j}^{-\gamma_h}} \Omega_{h,j}, \quad j=H,F; \ \gamma_h=\rho_h/(1-\rho_h),$$

$$(88) \quad q_{h,i,j,l}^M = \frac{p_{h,i,j,l}^{M-(1+\gamma_h)}}{P_{M_h,l}^{-\gamma_h}} \Omega_{h,l}, \quad j,l=H,F; \ l \neq j; \ \gamma_h=\rho_h/(1-\rho_h).$$

Output of the national company, $q_{h,i,j}$, is larger than output of the home plant or the foreign plant of the MNE. MNEs' home plant output, $q^M{}_{h,i,j,j}$, is larger than that in the foreign plant, because prices abroad, $p^M_{h,i,j,l}$, are higher than prices at home, $p^M_{h,i,j,j}$, because of more expensive intermediate goods. Final goods produced by an MNE at home sell at the same price as goods of domestic national companies, $p^M_{h,i,j,j} = p_{h,i,j}$.

There is one more change compared to the multiindustry model: the number of companies in each group is affected by price index changes of the group in this multigroup version. In the multiindustry model, market shares of the industries are fixed. Now, market shares are variable. The size of the market is important for the number of companies in equilibrium. The number of companies in each group is determined by the zero-profit condition of each group of final-goods producers. For the special cases discussed in Chapter 3 (zero distance costs, symmetry between the two countries), the number of companies in each group can be calculated as the product of the market share and the share of variable profits of total revenue of a company, $1-\rho$, divided by the sum of the fixed costs, $w_j(f_j+r_j)$ or $w_j(f_j+r_j)+w_l f_l$. The number of companies changes with the variable market share. The number of companies is now given for a group h of only national companies by (89), and for a group h consisting of only MNEs by (90):

$$(89) \quad n_{h,j} = \frac{(1-\rho_h)\Omega_{h,j}}{w_j r_{h,j} + w_j f_{h,j}}, \quad j=H,F; \ h=1,\dots,\kappa,$$

$$(90) \quad m_{h,j} = \frac{(1-\rho_h)\Omega_{h,j}}{w_j r_{h,j} + w_j f_{h,j} + w_l f_{h,l}}, \quad j,l=H,F; \ j\neq l; \ h=1,\dots,\kappa.$$

This model framework has the advantage to allow more general substitution configurations across alternatives than the approach of Chapter 4 but has the drawback that results are quite sensitive to the grouping and it is not always clear how the industry should be partitioned. This is especially troubling in empirical studies. In theory, homogeneous groups can be assumed. Suppose, for instance, there are three groups in the industry which differ in product differentiation and fixed cost level and composition in the same way as the industries in the previous section did. Foreign and home companies with the same characteristics are grouped into one nest. They compete within the group on the same basis, regardless whether the competitor is a national or a foreign one. Competition with other group members is more indirect. The elasticity of substitution between two goods which are not grouped in the same nest is much lower.

In such a setup, the coexistence of national companies and MNEs emerges within the industry, because not all companies but only those of one group internationalize their activities at the same time. To see this, look at the trigger curve Φ in (80) again, which shows the profitability of exports relative to the profitability of production abroad for a company i in group h. The trigger curves are group-specific. However, groups affect each other (and therefore the trigger curves of the companies) through changes in the price indexes of the groups. Price index changes lead to changes in the market share a group holds. How important substitution between different groups is, depends on the degree of differentiation between the groups, $1/\varsigma$. For this value being low, goods from different groups are good substitutes. However, it is useful to assume that the degree of differentiation within a group, $1/\rho_h$, is smaller than the degree of differentiation between different groups, $1/\varsigma$. Figure 34 depicts the trigger curves for an example with three different groups of companies within an industry which satisfies the requirement of a smaller degree of differentiation within the group than between two groups.

The trigger curves look similar to the trigger curves in the multiindustry model for the same exogenous parameters, which are shown in Figure 27. The reason is that trigger curves are not affected by the market size. Group market sizes, however, differ strongly from the fixed market size multiindustry model in the last section. The market size of the first group is much larger than that of the other two groups. The number of companies differs in the groups compared to the industries. It is higher in the first and lower in the second and third groups. Furthermore, there is a change in the groups' market size with falling distance costs and changing market structure. The size of the first group increases whereas those of the other two decrease over time. In the internationalization period, the internationalizing group of companies gains market shares in the home country but loses in the host country of MNEs.

At distance cost levels lower than $\tau_M = 1.4$, national companies and MNEs from country 1 coexist in equilibrium (Figure 34). All companies from group 1 internationalized production but the other two groups of companies in the industry continue to produce only in one plant at home. At distance cost of $\tau_M = 1.25$, companies of group 1 in country 2 internationalize production. Group 2 and group 3 companies remain national companies. Hence, there is a coexistence of national and multinational companies in country 2 as well. For distance cost level below $\tau_M = 1.25$, there exist therefore MNEs based in both countries at the same time as national companies in both countries, which serve the foreign market by exports. By relaxing the symmetry assumption of companies in one industry, coexistence emerges naturally, because companies' profitability of foreign production does not exceed profitability of export at the same point in time. The trigger curves exceed zero at different distance cost levels.

As stated above, the results are sensitive to the grouping of the companies. In the example above, consumers decide whether they prefer a sports car to a pick-

Figure 34:

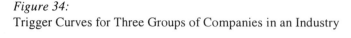

Trigger Curves for Three Groups of Companies in an Industry

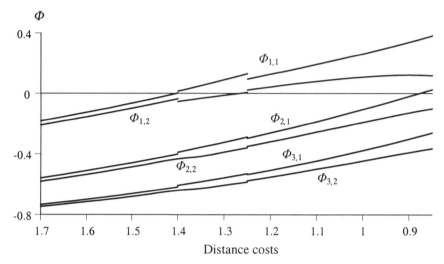

$\mu_A = 0.4$, $\mu_1 = \mu_2 = \mu_3 = 0.2$, $\varepsilon = 0.9$, $\rho_1 = 0.75$, $\rho_2 = 0.775$, $\rho_3 = 0.8$, $\theta_1 = \theta_2 = \theta_3 = 0.7$, $L_1 = 1000$, $L_2 = 800$, $r_{1,1} = r_{1,2} = 2$, $r_{2,1} = r_{2,2} = 1.5$, $r_{3,1} = r_{3,2} = 1$, $f_{1,1} = f_{1,2} = 0.8$, $f_{2,1} = f_{2,2} = f_{3,1} = f_{3,2} = 1$, $fz_1 = fz_2 = 0.3$

up or compact class car at the first stage and choose then their most preferred variety. They do not differentiate between a domestic and a foreign product, i.e., they do not care, for example, whether they buy a German or a Japanese car. They see two German cars as far from each other as two Japanese cars or a German and a Japanese car. This might be, but it is not necessarily the case. Consumers might also view the industry partitioned not in three but six groups, three from each country. Then, there would be a German and a Japanese pick-up group, a German and a Japanese compact class car group and a German and a Japanese sports car group.

This different grouping affects the trigger curves, because price indexes are changed. They do not include domestic and foreign products with the same characteristics anymore but only domestic or only foreign products. Given the high price of imported goods when distance costs are high, the market share of this group of goods is very low. Even if a company that internationalizes production can capture a large fraction of this group's market, the market is too small to reach the breakeven point. Choices at the first stage are made with respect to the price index of the whole group, which is assumed to be unaffected by the change of one companies' price in the monopolistic competition model à la Helpman and Krugman (1985). Trigger curves do not exceed zero for the parameters used in Figures 27 and 34. Foreign production is not a profitable alternative to exports at any distance cost level if consumers partition the total market in this way.

Coexistence of national companies and MNEs within one industry in one country emerges if the symmetry assumption between the companies in the industry is relaxed. Then, there are different groups of companies which reach the point when profitability of foreign production becomes profitable at different time. Relaxing symmetry between the companies requires a nested CES structure which allows for more realistic substitution patterns but has the disadvantage of necessitating a grouping of the companies which might predetermine results. It is therefore very important, especially for empirical studies, to analyze the market very carefully in order to model substitution patterns as close as possible to those observed in the market.

5.5 Conclusions

A multiindustry version of the model is developed in this chapter to analyze sectoral concentration and the relationship between exports and production abroad. The final-goods producers are divided into several groups which differ in the demand they face and the technology they use. The groups of symmetric companies are called industries. These industries differ between one another in their exogenous demand and technology parameters. Companies compete only with rivals from the same industries. There is no substitution of goods from one industry by a good from another industry. Market shares of the industries are fixed. Consumers spend always the same amount of income on one industry's goods regardless of changes in relative prices. This strong assumption is made for simplicity. It captures the fact that interindustry competition is weaker than intraindustry competition.

The multiindustry version is used to analyze the industry concentration of the internationalization of activities. The different level of international activities can be explained by the technology used in the different industries and by differences in demand industries face. Industries where companies produce more differentiated goods internationalize their activities earlier, with exports preceding foreign production. Their engagement in the foreign country is more pronounced. Four technological parameters spur the internationalization of production: (i) a high level of fixed costs at the company level, (ii) a low degree of differentiation among the intermediate goods, (iii) a low level of fixed costs at the plant level, and (iv) a low share of intermediate inputs in production of final goods. In contrast, exports are only slightly affected by the share of intermediate goods in production of a final good and by the degree of differentiation of the intermediate goods. Fixed cost levels and the structure of fixed costs do not affect exports. Given the different characteristics of industries (modeled by different industry-specific parameters), international activities of companies are concentrated on some industries and less pronounced in others.

The analysis of the relationship of exports and production abroad is motivated by the public debate on the effects of the internationalization of production on employment in developed countries. The fear is that exports of goods are substituted by exports of jobs. That claim stands in clear contrast to the empirical literature which mainly finds a complementary relationship of foreign production and exports. Substitution is found for product-level studies, but using higher aggregated data complementarity dominates. The analysis, which harnessed the multiindustry version of the model, reveals the two components which bring in complementarity: the use of intermediate goods and (headquarter) services, which may exceed exports of final goods which are substituted by foreign production, and the rise in exports and foreign production with falling distance costs. Each product has its own trigger function which might differ depending on demand and production parameters. Different trigger curves yield different points in time of setting up foreign production. Some products might precede others. However, over time, production abroad and exports increase. Hence, a complementary relationship is inferred in many empirical studies.

A slightly altered version of the multiindustry model is used to analyze coexistence of national and multinational companies in one industry in this framework. The different industries are reinterpreted as different groups of companies within one industry. In contrast to the multiindustry version where goods from companies in different industries do not compete with each other, since there is no substitution possible between any two of those goods, there is competition between the goods from different groups in the multigroup version. The industry, which contains groups of different companies, is characterized by a more general substitution pattern across alternatives. All the alternative varieties compete with each other. A higher degree of substitution between some goods defines a group in this approach. Within a group, substitution is higher than substitution between different groups which compose the industry. In such a setup, coexistence of national companies and MNEs emerges within the industry, because not all companies but only those of one group internationalize their activities at the same time.

Chapters 4 and 5 study the effect of a company's decision to internationalize its activities (exports and production abroad) on competitors in the home and host country. Wave behavior and concentration in internationalization of activities of similar companies in one country are found and explained. Foreign country companies are affected by fiercer competition which influences their international activities. However, globalization is not a bilateral phenomenon. Companies from a third country are affected by the decision of a company in one country to increase its engagement in another country. The next chapter focuses, therefore, on these third-country effects. For an analysis, all final-goods producers in the manufacturing sector are modeled symmetrically. This simpler structure eases focusing on the competition between companies from three different countries.

6   Modeling Globalization: The Three-Country Version

The theoretical analysis of the role of MNEs in globalization could explain large parts of the observed internationalization patterns. International activities are predominantly a developed-country phenomenon. They are intraindustrial to a high degree, and do not so much rely on factor costs differentials. With falling distance costs, international activities of companies (foreign trade, internationalization of production, and the transfer of knowledge and technology) has increased. Thereby, companies from larger countries internationalize their activities earlier than those from smaller countries. The increase in international activities occurs in sectoral and temporal clusters. Mostly, international activities are complementary; important trade links foster the internationalization of production and vice versa. Further, there is room for national companies and MNEs to coexist in an internationalizing industry.

The term globalization points to a phenomenon which exceeds a bilateral framework. In political debates and academic discussions, the term is used to characterize a multilateral interdependency among many players in many countries. U.S.-Japanese conflicts, for instance, affect Europe much stronger than twenty years ago. Certainly, with open markets for goods and investments, there are many more foreign influences. Competition by foreign companies might require earlier and fiercer adjustments with all the merits and problems. In a truly integrated world economy, the world market is the only existing market; national markets are not distinguishable. There is no home bias anymore. Border effects are insignificant. At the beginning of the 21st century, this is far from being the case. However, globalization names a process in this direction. We stand only at the beginning of this development. Nevertheless, the world today is already interrelated. This chapter is, therefore, devoted to an analysis of one possible channel of this interdependency.

To a certain extent, the year 1985 marks something as the beginning of the period of intensified economic integration. Foreign direct investment flows took off and outstripped foreign trade as most dynamic channel of economic integration (Figure 1). A large wave of internationalization of production started which included and still includes companies from many countries. Whereas in the 1950s and 1960s predominantly U.S. companies internationalized their production to build up an international network with activities in many countries, the 1980s and 1990s saw companies from much more countries internationalizing their activities (Table 3). U.S. companies were a source of FDI among others. Notice, however, that the United States became the largest recipient of FDI in these years (Table 2).

This chapter brings forward one explanation of the sudden rise of FDI from many developed countries in the mid-1980s. Using a three-country version of the framework developed in Chapter 3 and applied in Chapters 4 and 5, the simultaneous decision to internationalize production by companies from different countries is explained by changes in the degree of competition which results from internationalization waves of companies from one country. Internationalization waves, which are national originally, are passed on companies from third countries through changes in the degree of competition in the host country. Therefore, a third, seemingly unaffected, country is added to home and host country from the models in the chapters before.

6.1 The Three-Country Model Version

In this section, I explain the changes of the model used in this chapter. The framework remains the same. I alter the one-industry model structure applied in Chapters 3 and 4 to include three countries. I model these countries symmetrically. However, they differ in size. Different country size leads to different size of the symmetric companies of each country and yields different trigger curves of the companies from different countries. Trigger curves are calculated for international activities in both foreign countries separately. Each company has two trigger curves. One indicating the profitability of country 1 companies exports to country 2 relative to the profitability of production of country 1 companies in country 2, and one indicating the profitability of country 1 companies exports to country 3 relative to the profitability of production of country 1 companies in country 3. If countries 2 and 3 differ in size, these trigger curves differ. Hence, the point in time, when companies decide to internationalize production differs.

With three countries in the model world, consumers can choose among varieties from three instead of only two countries. Hence, their subutility function (2) includes goods from all three countries. The number of final goods λ is the same in each country. It is the sum of all final-goods producers in the three economies. Assuming the same number of final goods in each country which equals the total sum λ of all final-goods producers assumes every company active in all three markets. This requires either exports to both foreign markets or production of a foreign affiliate of the company in one or both foreign countries.

Demand for the variety of the differentiated final good of an exporting company, which equals output in equilibrium, changes, therefore, from (19) to (91):

$$(91) \quad q_{i,H} = \frac{p_{i,H}^{-(1+\gamma)}}{P_{M,H}^{-\gamma}} \mu Y_H + \frac{p_{i,H}^{-(1+\gamma)} e^{-(1+\gamma)\tau_M}}{P_{M,F_1}^{-\gamma}} \mu Y_{F_1}$$

$$+ \frac{p_{i,H}^{-(1+\gamma)} e^{-(1+\gamma)\tau_M}}{P_{M,F_2}^{-\gamma}} \mu Y_{F_2}, \quad \text{with } \gamma = \rho/(1-\rho).$$

Output of company i increases with increasing demand at home and increasing exports. The demand at home increases in the price index at home, $P_{M,H}$, and in the market size, μY_H, and decreases in the price of good i, $p_{i,H}$. Exports increase in the price indexes in both foreign markets, $P_{M,F1}$ and $P_{M,F2}$, and in the size of the foreign market, μY_{F1} and μY_{F2}. Exports decrease in the price of good i, $p_{i,H}$, and in distance costs, τ_M. Equation (91) applies to situations when a company serves both foreign markets by exports. This is just one possible strategy. Companies could also serve one foreign country by exports and produce in the other, or it could produce in both foreign countries. If a company exports to one foreign country and produces in the other, (91) changes to include only two terms as in (92). Equation (92) differs from (19) because the price indexes, P_M, contain companies from three countries instead of two:

$$(92) \quad q_{i,H} = \frac{p_{i,H}^{-(1+\gamma)}}{P_{M,H}^{-\gamma}} \mu Y_H + \frac{p_{i,H}^{-(1+\gamma)} e^{-(1+\gamma)\tau_M}}{P_{M,F_l}^{-\gamma}} \mu Y_{F_l}, \quad l=1,2; \; \gamma = \rho/(1-\rho).$$

The output of a plant in the home country H as given in (92) is that of an MNE, since the company operates with two plants: one at home producing the output given in (92) and one in one foreign country. Output of the affiliate in the foreign country is given in (93). It increases in the price index in this country, $P_{M,F}$, and in market size, μY_F, and decreases in the price of good i, $p^M_{i,F}$. Equation (93) differs from (21) only in the price indexes which contain companies from three countries:

$$(93) \quad q^M_{i,H,F} = \frac{p^M_{i,H,F}{}^{-(1+\gamma)}}{P_{M,F}^{-\gamma}} \mu Y_F, \quad \gamma = \rho/(1-\rho).$$

Production in the home plant is given in (20), when an MNE produces in two foreign affiliates and in a plant at home. Production output in the foreign affiliate in each country is given in (93). The difference to the model in Chapter 3 is the price index. Competition in the three-country version takes place among companies from three countries. The price index in the manufacturing sector contains, therefore, prices of final goods of companies from three countries. Hence, the price index (26) changes to (94) to account for the companies from the third country:

$$(94) \quad P_{M,H} = \frac{\mu Y_H}{Q_{M,H}} = \left[\sum_{i=1}^{n_H} \left(p_{H,H}^N \right)^{-\gamma} + \sum_{i=1}^{n_{F_1}} \left(p_{F_1,H}^N \right)^{-\gamma} + \sum_{i=1}^{n_{F_2}} \left(p_{F_2,H}^N \right)^{-\gamma} \right.$$

$$\left. + \sum_{i=1}^{m_H} \left(p_{H,H}^M \right)^{-\gamma} + \sum_{i=1}^{m_{F_1}} \left(p_{F_1,H}^M \right)^{-\gamma} + \sum_{i=1}^{m_{F_2}} \left(p_{F_2,H}^M \right)^{-\gamma} \right]^{-\frac{1}{\gamma}},$$

where n_H is the number of national companies located in H, n_{F_1}, and n_{F_2} are the numbers of national companies located in F_1 and F_2, respectively; m_H, m_{F_1}, and m_{F_2} are the numbers of MNEs headquartered in H, F_1, and F_2, respectively. n_H, n_{F_1}, n_{F_2}, m_H, m_{F_1}, and m_{F_2}, added together, equal λ. The price index $P_{M,H}$ increases in the prices of each kind of company and, therefore, in distance costs, since distance costs increase the prices of national exporting companies and MNEs in the foreign markets. The price index, $P_{M,H}$, decreases in the number of companies, λ, in market H.

The size of national companies (with one plant) is larger than in the two-country model in Chapter 3, because national companies produce for the home market and two export markets. Exports are less profitable than home sales because of distance costs. A certain amount of goods, which have to be produced, smelts without generating profits (iceberg transport costs). Under comparable conditions of competition (the same exogenous parameters), the share of exports in total sales is larger in the three-country case than in the two-country model. This leads to larger companies in equilibrium, where zero profits are required. The total number of companies increases by adding a third country but the number of companies based in each economy decreases. The zero-profit condition (27), which endogenizes the number of national companies, applies further. However, output q_H^N includes exports to two foreign countries. The zero-profit condition (28) for the pure MNE (only foreign production, no exports) must be altered to account for both foreign markets (95). Another zero-profit condition (96) applies for companies which serve one market by exports and produce in the other foreign country:

$$(95) \quad \Pi_H^M = (1-\rho)\left(p_{H,H}^M q_{H,H}^M + p_{H,F_1}^M q_{H,F_1}^M + p_{H,F_2}^M q_{H,F_2}^M \right)$$

$$- w_H (r_H + f_H) + w_{F_1} f_{F_1} + w_{F_2} f_{F_2} = 0,$$

(96) $\Pi_H^{X,M} = (1-\rho)\left(p_{H,H,F_{-l}}^X q_{H,H,F_{-l}}^X + p_{H,F_l}^M q_{H,F_l}^M\right) - w_H\left(r_H + f_H\right)$

$\qquad +w_{F_l} f_{F_l} = 0, \quad$ where $l=1,2.$

The demand functions (4) and (5), the income equation (35), and the budget constraint (3) ensure that goods markets clear in each economy. The factor market clearance is given by (33). The value of the marginal product of labor in (6) determines wages in each economy. The pricing rule (24) and the equations (20), (21), (91), (92), (27), (95), and (96) determine the output of the national and multinational companies and their number in each country. The number of intermediate-goods producers and their production levels and prices are given by (13), (11), and (12). The pricing rule (34) determines the agricultural-goods output in each economy and, therefore, with demand equation (4), the level of inter-industry trade. The costless one-way trade of the homogeneous good Ex_H^A leads to price equality of this good in the three economies.

Since this is a static model, trade must be balanced, otherwise one country would be giving away goods for free. The equalized trade balance condition (38) must hold for all three bilateral trade relations. Costless one-way trade of the homogeneous good, Ex_H^A, might be positive or negative, depending on whether H is an exporter or an importer of the agricultural good. There is always intra-industry trade in final goods: Ex_H^M is always larger than zero for all economies. As in Chapter 3, trade of intermediate goods and (headquarter) services is bound to the existence of MNEs.

6.2   Exports and Production Abroad in a Globalizing World

Competition in a three-country world takes place among companies from three different countries. All produce different varieties of the final good. Consumers, who love variety, opt for imported goods from foreign countries depending on their price. Imported goods are more expensive, since distance costs on these goods have to be covered. Except for prohibitive distance cost level, $\tau_M \rightarrow \infty$, all varieties are sold in every country, although quantities sold might be very low for high distance costs. All companies export, therefore, their final goods to both foreign markets. As stated above, this leads to higher export levels in the three-country equilibrium than in the two-country model in Chapter 3.

This can be seen in Figure 35. It shows export levels of one country in a two-country and in a three-country equilibrium. The countries are symmetric and of the same size to ease comparison. For very high distance cost, exports in a three-country model are about twice as high as in the two-country model. Export levels

Figure 35:
Export Levels of One Economy in a Two-Country and in a Three-Country World

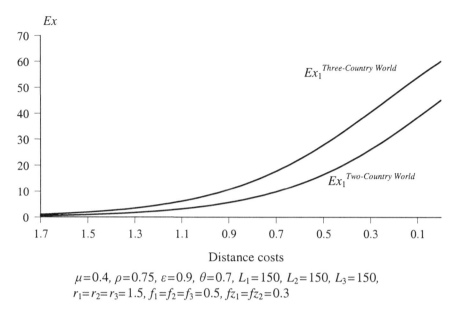

$\mu=0.4$, $\rho=0.75$, $\varepsilon=0.9$, $\theta=0.7$, $L_1=150$, $L_2=150$, $L_3=150$,
$r_1=r_2=r_3=1.5$, $f_1=f_2=f_3=0.5$, $fz_1=fz_2=0.3$

increase with falling distance costs in both model versions. This increase in absolute terms is higher in the three-country model, but in relative terms it is higher in the two-country model, because competition of two foreign countries decreases the number of (exporting) companies more strongly in the three-country model. For very low distance costs, exports of one country in the two-country model increases, therefore, to two-thirds of the levels of a country in the three-country model.

Relative to one country's GDP of 150, exports increase from 0.7 percent in the three-country model at $\tau_M=1.7$ to 40 percent at free trade ($\tau_M=0$). Since trade is balanced, the import to GDP ratio is as high. Openness, defined as exports plus imports over GDP, at free trade is, therefore, larger in a three-country world than in a two-country world, where only one trading partner could increase purchasable varieties for consumers. In a two-country world, exports over GDP increase from 0.4 percent to 30 percent. Half of all final goods in the manufacturing sector which are consumed in a country are also produced there, compared to only one-third in the three-country world. This is expected in a borderless symmetric world with trade only in differentiated manufacturing goods. The homogeneous agricultural good, which has a share of $\mu=0.4$ in the consumption bundle, is not traded in equilibrium, because countries are assumed to be symmetric. Exports and imports of differentiated final goods equal, and wages in all (in both in the two-country case) countries are the same. There is no room for trade in the homogeneous good.

Export levels in Figure 35 are derived for equilibria with only national companies. However, when production abroad becomes more profitable than exports, companies switch to production abroad to serve the foreign market. Decision rule (39), which specifies whether to internationalize production or to export, changes as well, because three markets have to be taken into account. There are more possible strategies, which have to be compared in the three-country case. One strategy is to export final goods to both foreign countries. Production takes place exclusively in the home country. This might, however, not be the most profitable strategy for all distance cost levels. The profitability depends on the condition of competition, i.e., consumers' demand and technology used in production. Production in one foreign country or in both might be a preferable strategy.

To visualize the relative profitability of exports and production abroad, trigger curves are used again. With three countries in equilibrium, there are three different trigger curves for each country which have to be compared. There is a trigger curve in the tradition of the analyses in Chapters 3 to 5 which compares profits from exports of the final good with those from production abroad. In the three-country case, this means profits from exports to both foreign countries are compared to profits from production in both foreign countries. This trigger curve is given in (97). It is also possible to internationalize production by producing in only one foreign country and serve the other market by exports. The trigger curve showing the profitability of exports relative to the profitability of this strategy is given in (98). Equation (99) gives the trigger curve for the comparison of the mixed strategy and the pure internationalization strategy:

$$(97) \qquad \Phi_j = (1-\rho)\left(p_{j,j}^M q_{j,j}^M + p_{j,g}^M q_{j,g}^M + p_{j,l}^M q_{j,l}^M - p_j^N q_j^N\right) - w_g f_g - w_l f_l,$$

with $j,g,l=H,F_1,F_2$; $j\neq g\neq l$,

$$(98) \qquad \Phi_j = (1-\rho)\left(p_{j,jg}^{MX} q_{j,jg}^{MX} + p_{j,l}^M q_{j,l}^M - p_j^N q_j^N\right) - w_l f_l,$$

with $j,g,l=H,F_1,F_2$; $j\neq g\neq l$,

$$(99) \qquad \Phi_j = (1-\rho)\left(p_{j,j}^M q_{j,j}^M + p_{j,g}^M q_{j,g}^M - p_{j,jg}^{MX} q_{j,jg}^{MX}\right) - w_g f_g,$$

with $j,g=H,F_1,F_2$; $j\neq g$.

Superscript *M* denotes a pure international company which produces all final goods in the market they are sold. Companies which produce at home for the home market and one foreign market, which they serve by exports, and in one foreign plant are denoted by *MX*. Superscript *N* denotes companies which produce exclusively at home and export to both foreign markets. The first two trigger curves show whether it is profitable to stop exporting to both or to only one foreign country in favor of starting production in this country. The third trigger curve depicts the profitability of producing in all three countries relative to production in two countries and serving one foreign market *g* by exports from the home country. The subscript of the national companies denotes the home country. MNE's home country is denoted by the first subscript, the second denotes the market they supply. For MNEs which serve one foreign market by exports the second subscript, *jg*, denotes the two markets which are supplied by the plant at home. By assumption, export markets are served from the home market. Foreign affiliates' exports to third countries are excluded.

For countries differing in size, companies' trigger curves differ. Companies from smaller countries internationalize their production later. In the three-country model, companies from the large country are expected to internationalize their production first. The analysis in Chapter 4 shows that it is not only the trigger curve of the smaller country, which is shifted down, but also the trigger curve of the larger one, which is shifted up. Both move by the same amount (in opposite direction) relative to the benchmark. It is therefore likely that companies from the large country internationalize their production first in the smallest country and then in the larger foreign country. Companies from the second-largest country are expected to internationalize their production later than companies from the largest country but earlier than companies from the smallest country. Further, second-largest country's companies also start to set up affiliates in the smaller country. Figure 36 shows the trigger curves for companies of the three countries of different size.

The first subscript denotes the home country. A comma separates locations of different plants of an MNE. Subscripts which are not separated by a comma are supplied from the same plant (in the home country). $\Phi_{23,1}$, for instance, denotes the trigger curve of a company from country 2 which serves country 3 by exports and produces in a second plant in country 1 to serve this market. Trigger curve $\Phi_{2,1,3}$ is that of a country-2-based MNE which produces in all three countries. Since the supply of a third country by a foreign affiliate of an MNE is excluded by assumption, a trigger curve like $\Phi_{2,31}$ is not possible. With equal distance between the three countries, the strategy to supply the third market by markets from the foreign affiliate cannot be profitable, anyway, since production in the foreign affiliate is more expensive than in the home plant because of the more expensive intermediate goods which must be used in the foreign affiliate.

Figure 36:
Trigger Curves in the Globalization Model

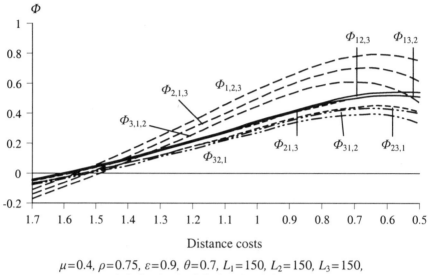

$$\mu=0.4,\ \rho=0.75,\ \varepsilon=0.9,\ \theta=0.7,\ L_1=150,\ L_2=150,\ L_3=150,$$
$$r_1=r_2=r_3=1.5,\ f_1=f_2=f_3=0.5,\ fz_1=fz_2=0.3$$

The trigger curves of national companies in a pure national company equilibrium in Figure 36 show the expected picture. Trigger curves of companies from the largest country 1 lie above those of the smaller country 2 and the smallest country 3. Furthermore, trigger curves of companies which serve the larger foreign market by exports and the smaller one by production abroad lie above those which produce in the larger foreign market and export to the smaller one. The existence of a third country shifts trigger curves up. $\Phi_{12,3}$ denotes the trigger curve of a company from country 1 which aims at producing in country 3 if possible but certainly serves country 2 by exports. This trigger curve is comparable to Φ_{12} in Chapter 4. The only difference is the existence of a smaller third country which is served by exports. Companies would decide earlier (at $\tau_M=1.59$ compared to $\tau_M=1.55$ in the two-country case in Chapter 4) to set up foreign affiliates in country 2. The same holds for the internationalization of country 2 companies to country 1. It would occur earlier, at $\tau_M=1.53$ instead of $\tau_M=1.51$.

However, these comparisons are made under the assumption that it is not possible, for whatever reason, to set up an affiliate in the smallest country 3. All trigger curves are derived for equilibria with only national companies. But the trigger curves of companies from countries 1 and 2 for a plant configuration with a foreign affiliate in the smallest country 3 and service of the larger foreign market by exports crosses the zero line already at $\tau_M = 1.61$ and, therefore, before companies from the larger country 1 start setting up affiliates in country 2 at $\tau_M = 1.59$. At $\tau_M = 1.61$, companies from the largest country 1 start to internationalize their production by establishing foreign affiliates in the smallest country 3. Up to a particular distance cost level, production in only one foreign affiliate (in the smallest country 3) and export to the larger country is more profitable than production in two foreign affiliates and the home country plant. This can be seen from the trigger curves in Figure 36, where all trigger curves of two-plant configuration lie above the trigger curves of the corresponding three-plant configuration for very high distance costs. It pays, therefore, for a company to establish its foreign affiliates sequential, starting with the one in the smallest partner country.

The decision of one company to start production abroad increases the profitability to internationalize production for any national competitor, as known from Chapter 4. This decision has, additionally, effects on the internationalization decision of companies from the third country. Both effects can be seen in Figure 37 which shows the movement of the trigger curves during the internationalization period of country 1 companies which set up affiliates in country 3. The positive effect on national competitors and the negative effect on the profitability of foreign production relative to exports on host country competitors (here from country 3) are extensively discussed in Chapter 4. The change in the trigger curves of national competitors, $\Phi_{12,3}$, is therefore only given for comparison and not further discussed. The trigger curve of companies from country 3, $\Phi_{32,1}$, $\Phi_{31,2}$, and $\Phi_{3,1,2}$, in the internationalization process of country 1 companies are not shown here. Instead, the effect on the relative profitability of country 2 companies which have an affiliate in country 1 and export to country 3 is shown here as an example.

The positive effect which the establishment of foreign affiliates of country 1 companies in country 3 has on the relative profitability of the establishment of foreign affiliates of country 2 companies in country 3 can easily be seen in the strong increase of the trigger curve $\Phi_{21,3}$, in Figure 37. From being negative at the beginning of the internationalization process of country 1 companies, the profitability to produce in country 3 relative to export to this country increases for companies from country 2, the relative profitability becomes positive over the internationalization process of country 1 companies. The internationalization wave of country 1 companies has a contagion effect. Profitability of production in country 3 is "passed on" country 2 companies.

The contagion effect is caused by changes in market structure with companies based in country 1 establishing affiliates in country 3, which increase price competition in this market. Country-3-based companies incur losses; some of them

Figure 37:
Trigger Curves during the Internationalization Process of Companies from
Country 1 by Setting up an Affiliate in Country 3

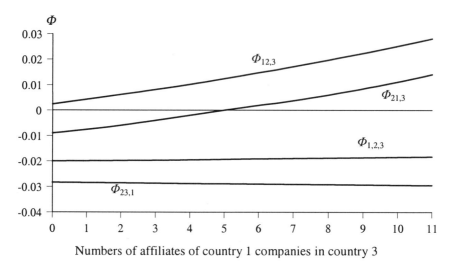

Numbers of affiliates of country 1 companies in country 3

$\mu=0.4$, $\rho=0.75$, $\varepsilon=0.9$, $\theta=0.7$, $L_1=150$, $L_2=120$, $L_3=100$,
$r_1=r_2=r_3=1.5$, $f_1=f_2=f_3=0.5$, $fz_1=fz_2=0.3$, $\tau_M=1.6$

have to exit the market. This creates larger sales opportunities for country 1 affiliates' production and country 2 companies' exports. The price index, $P_{M,3}$, increases. In contrast, price indexes in the other two countries, $P_{M,1}$ and $P_{M,2}$, decrease because of the lower fraction of imports in the consumption bundle which
is due to the reduction of the number of country 3 companies. The higher price
index in country 3 increases the relative profitability of production in country 3
which can be seen by an increase of trigger curve $\Phi_{21,3}$. This is because a higher
price index allows for larger sales per affiliate of country 2 companies in country 3 (equation 93). These larger sales are necessary to pay the additional fixed
costs at the plant level.

$\Phi_{23,1}$ decreases slightly. The profitability of a plant configuration of country 2
companies with production in the home country plant and in an affiliate in
country 1, and the supply of country 3 market by exports from the home plant is
less profitable than the configuration with the second plant in the smallest
country 3. However, the establishment of an affiliate in country 3 by a country 1
competitor of a country 2 company decreases the relative profitability for
country 2 companies to establish a second plant in country 1 even further. This is

shown by trigger curve $\Phi_{23,1}$. The reason is the fiercer competition in country 1 relative to that in the smallest country 3, which is further reduced by the setup of a foreign affiliate there and the following reduction of the number of country 3 companies.

$\Phi_{1,2,3}$ increases slightly. The establishment of foreign affiliates in country 3 by country 1 companies increases the profitability of a plant configuration with affiliates in all three countries relative to the just emerged configuration with two plants (in country 3 and at home) and exports to country 2. Note that the profitability given in $\Phi_{1,2,3}$ is not relative to exports to all countries but relative to the mixed configuration described above. The change in market structure in countries 1 and 3 increases the profitability of a three-plant configuration because of falling competitive pressure on the (potential) affiliates in country 2. This falling competitive pressure results from the lower exports from country 3 companies to country 2 which stem from the decline in the number of country 3 companies.

The changes in the three markets during the internationalization of production of country 1 companies by setting up affiliates in country 3 can be summarized as follows. Price indexes in countries 1 and 2 fall slightly, while the price index in country 3 rises. The effect on host country 3 is much larger than the effects on home country 1 and third country 2. The changes in the price indexes result from changes in the number of companies based in the three countries. The number of companies is altered by the internationalization process in a way that the number of companies rises in countries 1 and 2 and falls in country 3. The larger fraction of foreign companies in the consumption basket of country 3 consumers leads to the increase in the price index in this country. Hence, the relative profitability to set up an affiliate in country 3 increases for country 1 and for country 2 companies. Country 3 companies' incentive to set up an affiliate abroad decreases for both possible host countries. Furthermore, country 1 companies' incentive to produce in the third country 2 increases slightly.

These results from the three-country version of the framework developed above can be used to analyze the reason behind the sudden and strong increase of the internationalization of production around 1985. This strong increase can be seen remarkably clear in Figure 1 in Chapter 2. In the mid-1980s, exports were replaced by the internationalization of production as the most dynamic channel of global economic integration. Exports continued to rise faster than industrial production, but the internationalization of production, approximated by FDI in Figure 1, outpaced both by far. New countries entered world markets as exporters and importers and as host and home countries of MNEs, most notably countries in East and Southeast Asia. Only few years later, former socialist countries opened up their markets for trade and investment flows. This gave globalization an additional momentum. However, the takeoff of globalization occurred earlier and involved almost exclusively developed countries.

The mid-1980s boom of internationalization activities reflected the change in the pattern of the internationalization compared to the 1950s and 1960s. In that time, U.S. companies engaged in production in many developed countries. The most important countries were Canada and European countries as the United Kingdom, Germany, and France. U.S. MNEs served their foreign markets much more through foreign affiliates than through exports, while European countries and Canada relied mainly on exports (Dunning and Pearce 1985). In the second half of the 1980s, the internationalization pattern dominating up to this time reversed. The United States became the most important host country. Several developed countries held strong positions as home countries of FDI in this period (Graham 1996). Interesting is the simultaneous increase in the internationalization of production of companies from many countries.

This global wave can be explained by the contagion effect demonstrated above. There are certainly other explanations of the boom in international activities, but the one offered here seems, at least to me, very interesting, because the new integration period does not need any exogenous shock except for the trigger already introduced: falling distance costs. In the framework proposed in this study, the mid-1980s globalization wave emerges endogenously. As shown in Chapter 4, smaller companies which are based in smaller countries start later to internationalize their production. Thus, while U.S. companies had already set up affiliates in foreign countries, European and Japanese companies competed on world markets by exports against each other and U.S. MNEs which had already internationalized their production. However, falling distance costs raised exports of the European countries, Canada, and Japan to the United States and at the same time the relative profitability of production in the United States relative to exports. About the mid-1980s, some companies from Europe, Canada, and Japan reached the point where their large foreign activities in the United States generated enough (variable) profits to support the additional fixed costs of a foreign affiliate there. Their decision to internationalize their production initiated the globalization takeoff in the mid-1980s.

The setup of a foreign affiliate in the United States, let's say of a U.K. company, increases the relative profitability of any national competitor of this company to set up an affiliate in the United States as well. This national internationalization wave was discussed in Chapter 4. Similar companies from the same industry in the United Kingdom follow the first company in producing abroad. This affects the market structure in the United States. Competitive pressure on U.S. companies increases. Some companies exit. Market structure changes increase the incentives for companies from other European countries, Canada, or Japan in the same industry to internationalize their production in the United States as well. The internationalization takeoff arises because of the contagion of the "national" internationalization wave of one country's companies on another country's companies which ends in the emergence of a "global" internationalization wave of companies from various home countries in one host country.

Although no test of this theory exists so far, empirical results by Co (2001) support this explanation. In her study, Co analyzed the effects of imports and the setup of affiliates by foreign companies in the United States on market structure and industry performance in the United States during the 1980s. The results indicate a decisive influence of market concentration on the effects of increased competition by imports and production in the US. The way the market structure changes drives the profit changes in the industry. Market structure changes are themselves strongly affected by market exit and entry which occur in the adjustment process to increased foreign competition. Market structure changes are the key to an analysis of the effects of increased foreign competition. They should be accounted for in empirical assessments.

6.3 Different Distances between Countries in a Multipolar World

Throughout the whole analysis, the distance D between countries has been set to one. In the two-country case, this could be done without any loss in generality, because a change in distance D has the same effect as a change in the distance cost level between the two countries. To save on exogenous parameters, D was set to one. It was not worthwhile to look at pairs of countries which differ in distance, because there was nothing which could not have been learned from changes in distance costs, τ_M, as well. This is different in the three-country case, because there is no reason to assume all countries to have exactly the same distance from each other. Then, there are not only absolute differences, which could be reflected by a change in τ_M as well, but also relative differences of distance cost levels between country pairs.

European countries are much closer to each other than to the United States or Japan, for instance. Economic activities of a European company in foreign European countries are, therefore, higher than their activities in the United States or in Japan. This can be found in all gravity-equation-based research: economic activities, such as trade, FDI, bank lendings, technology transfer, or affiliate sales, decrease in the distance of two countries (Keller 2002; Kleinert 1999; Buch 2003). In sectoral studies on trade, for instance, it is found that a one percent increase in distance decreases on average the foreign activity of an industry by 0.6 percent (Leamer and Levinsohn 1995). These studies measure the relative distance of countries to one home or host country and are therefore well suited to motivate the analysis of the influence of different relative distances between country pairs on foreign activities in the three-country model version.

For an analysis of the influence of relative distance differences, the distance variable D is set to two for the distance between the largest country 1 and the two smaller countries 2 and 3, while distance D between the smaller countries 2 and 3 remains one. Countries are located at a triangle with two legs twice the size of the third. Distance cost levels per distance unit are the same: τ_M. Exports of goods from country 1 to one of the other countries incur twice as much distance costs than exports from country 2 to country 3. Of course, this affects the foreign activities of country 1 companies. Not surprisingly, their export levels are lower. This can be seen in Figure 38. For comparison, country 1's export level for an equal distance case between all countries is given as well (dotted line).

The export level of country 1, $Ex_{D=1}^1$, at shorter distance $D=1$ is much higher than the export level at longer distance $D=2$, $Ex_{D=2}^1$. For all distance cost levels, export levels of the more distant country lie lower. At a distance cost level of $\tau_M = 0.8$, for instance, exports stand at 1 percent of the GDP of country 1 for $D=2$ and at 10 percent for $D=1$. Hence, there is a huge difference in the absolute export levels depending on the remoteness of a country. Countries like Australia with a large distance to the most important trading partners show, therefore, smaller degrees of openness than European countries, for instance, which are situated in an area with many (potential) trading partners.

The absolute reduction of exports is rather obvious if consumers face higher distance costs which are passed through to the price of the imported good. Export levels relative to the other two countries compared to the benchmark case is more interesting. If the large country has the distance to the other two countries at $D=1$, it dominates the trade relationships between the countries. A deficit in manufacturing good's trade with the larger country 1 forces the smaller countries 2 and 3 to specialize partly on agricultural production. Agricultural goods' exports balance trade. This is different for a remote large country 1, e.g., $D=2$. Country 1 still exports more manufacturing goods than it imports but the trade surplus is small. The specialization on agriculture in the smaller countries is much less pronounced. The number of final-goods and intermediate-goods producers in the smaller countries is larger if country 1 is farer away.

Export levels of the largest (but remote) country 1 are lowest. The smaller countries 2 and 3 trade more between each other than with country 1. In the equal distance case, trade with country 1 dominates the foreign trade activities of the smaller countries. Export levels given in Figure 38 show, therefore, lower

Figure 38:
Export Levels When Countries Differ in Distance

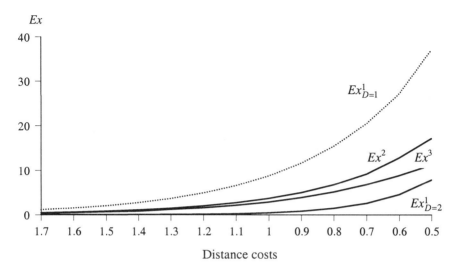

Distance costs

$\mu=0.4$, $\rho=0.75$, $\varepsilon=0.9$, $\theta=0.7$, $L_1=150$, $L_2=120$, $L_3=100$,
$r_1=r_2=r_3=1.5$, $f_1=f_2=f_3=0.5$, $fz_1=fz_2=0.3$, $D=2$

levels for countries 2 and 3 total exports compared to an equal distance equilibrium, because exports to country 1 are lower in the remoteness case. However, export levels between countries 2 and 3 are higher if country 1 is more remote. This results from the lower market share of country 1 companies in both foreign markets, which are supplied mainly by national companies and partly by companies from the smaller foreign country. For some distance cost levels, market structure differs substantially in both cases.

The remoteness of the large country 1 does not only affect exports. Production abroad, i.e., the alternative internationalization strategy, is also affected. The larger distance reduces the incentive to produce abroad for companies in the large country 1. Affiliates' sales are lower if the country is remote. This stems from the higher prices of affiliates' goods which result from higher distance costs for the intermediate inputs. Lower sales do not allow to cover the fixed costs in the foreign market. Hence, internationalization of production of companies from country 1 is delayed quite drastically as can be seen in Figure 39. Production in the smallest country 3 is profitable for a country 1 company at $\tau_M=0.78$, much later than in the equal distance case ($\tau_M=1.61$).

Figure 39:

Trigger Curves in the Globalization Model When the Largest Country 1 Is Remote

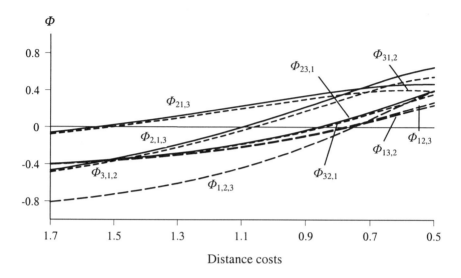

$$\mu=0.4, \rho=0.75, \varepsilon=0.9, \theta=0.7, L_1=150, L_2=120, L_3=100,$$
$$r_1=r_2=r_3=1.5, f_1=f_2=f_3=0.5, fz_1=fz_2=0.3, D=2$$

Furthermore, companies from the largest country 1 are not the first to internationalize their production. Instead, country 2 companies are first to internationalize production in country 3 at $\tau_M=1.55$. This is later than in the equal distance case. The reason is the stronger position of country 3 companies in equilibrium, which results from their larger market share due to the weakened competition from country 1 companies. A larger number of final-goods producers in a country attracts more intermediate-goods variants. This lowers the price index of intermediate goods, and, therefore, the costs for the final-goods producers in country 3. Country 3 companies' trigger curve for production in country 2, $\Phi_{31,2}$, crosses the zero line only slightly after that of country 2 companies. However, as in the analyses before, to set up an affiliate in country 2 for companies from country 3 would only be profitable at this distance cost if country 2 companies did not set up affiliates before. As in the chapters before, the internationalization process of country 2 companies would alter the trigger curves of home, host, and third-country companies.

It is interesting to see that, given no company has set up a foreign affiliate before, at $\tau_M=1.1$ the establishment of foreign affiliates in country 1 and country 3 would be more profitable for a country 2 company than exports to both countries. Production in the larger country 1 would be profitable for companies from a smaller country 2 before production in the smaller country 2 is profitable for the large country 1 companies. However, the establishment of affiliates in both foreign countries 1 and 3 is not the most profitable strategy for country 2 companies, since it involves cross-subsidization of losses from production in country 1 by profits in country 3 which could be avoided by exporting to country 1. Nevertheless, companies might follow this (feasible) strategy, because setting up an affiliate in country 1 changes the market structure and relaxes competition for the MNE based in country 2. Over time, losses of the affiliate in country 1 fall with falling distance costs.

The example shows how the distance of a country affects the international activities of the country's companies. The three-country case with different distances between country pairs allows for very different internationalization patterns. Real globalization patterns, however, are much more complex. Competition takes place between companies from various countries which are characterized by relative distances and size differences. But the fundamental pattern can be studied in this abstract three-country framework. In addition to country size, remoteness of a country is a distinctive characteristic for companies' international activities.

6.4   Conclusions

Globalization involves more than two countries. It is a complex multilateral process with various effects of bilateral economic relationships on third countries. In this chapter's analysis, a country's international activities (exports and production abroad) are analyzed with regard to their effect on a third country which seems a priori to be rather unaffected by the bilateral relationship. However, in a many-country world with competition of companies on various markets, there is no company which is unaffected. Market structure changes transmit the strategic decisions of other countries' companies. Certainly, due to the home bias which results from the separation of markets by distance costs, the effect of national competitors' actions is still strongest, but foreign competitors' decisions might also be felt in a change in the consumer price index. This change can also stimulate changes in the strategic decisions of home companies.

Differences in relative distances between country pairs strongly affect foreign activities. This is very clear in the model, since distance costs are the barrier which separates markets from each other. Distance is a strong impediment to trade and production abroad. A very complex internationalization pattern arises when there are companies in industries with different characteristics and in countries which differ in size and distance from different trading partners. This internationalization pattern is too complex to be modeled in this study. However, all effects are analyzed separately. The qualitative results of the theoretical analysis are very much in line with the empirical findings. Trade and production abroad are strongly affected by country size and distance and show very different characteristics in different industries.

7 Summary and Conclusions

The globalization of the world economy has changed international economic activity remarkably in the last two decades. Competition between companies from different countries takes place on many markets and through various channels. In addition to exports, which is the most important channel of foreign markets supply, companies use a wide range of international business activities. These include strategic alliances with foreign partners, joint ventures, licensing arrangements, and the setup of branches and affiliates in foreign countries on all levels of the value-added chain. Due to globalization, new opportunities in foreign countries have arisen. At the same time, competitive pressure in home markets has increased. Activities of foreign companies lead to new consumption choices for consumers and potentially to lower prices but also to costly adjustment processes of some companies in some industries.

This study offers a framework for the analysis of the increased economic integration of countries. The framework stands in the tradition of the proximity-concentration literature (Brainard 1993; Markusen and Venables 1998) to which the idea of "evolution" from the new economic geography (Fujita, Krugman, and Venables 1999) is added. A two-country general equilibrium model is introduced and solved under different conditions which mimic the globalization process, i.e., the degree of market segmentation is exogenously reduced. The model examines the adjustment of consumers and producers to these exogenous changes. Producers' choice of their internationalization strategy (exporting or producing abroad) is explicitly modeled. The resulting patterns of increased integration describe the observed internationalization patterns very well. It is shown that over the whole period welfare increases in economies which take part in globalization.

The study collects and discusses the stylized facts of the globalization process in order to derive a theoretical framework which is met as closely as possible by the empirical picture. Striking facts are the concentration of the bulk of international activities on developed countries and the strong sectoral concentration with high intraindustry coefficients in trade and production abroad. Within countries and sectors, a strong concentration on few dominant multinational companies is observed. In general, MNEs hold a strong position in the three channels of globalization analyzed in this study: in trade, in production abroad, and in the cross-border transfer of knowledge and technology. From this empirical picture it is concluded that a theoretical framework must explicitly account for (multinational) companies and their decisions. Moreover, it should above all reflect the conditions of international competition of companies from developed countries.

As the empirical patterns of trade and international production show, the proximity-concentration literature is a good starting point for developing a theoretical framework which meets these requirements. Proximity-concentration approaches explain trade and the emergence of MNEs in the absence of factor cost differentials and productivity differences by market imperfections, such as differentiated goods, an optimal technology which requires the use of fixed input factors, and the separation of markets by distance costs. Distance costs include costs of information, transport, communication, and doing business in a foreign environment. These costs are still surprisingly high among countries. Proximity-concentration models can explain intraindustry trade and intraindustry production abroad between two countries. MNEs in these general equilibrium models are a means to transfer knowledge rather than capital between countries.

In proximity-concentration models, companies have the choice between two strategies to serve the foreign market. They may export their goods or produce in the foreign country. Exports involve per unit distance costs whereas production abroad requires additional fixed costs for the second plant in the foreign country. MNEs emerge if this basic tradeoff between distance costs and additional fixed costs is solved in favor of a plant in the foreign country. That is, if the additional fixed costs are lower than the cost savings from the distance costs. Whether MNEs opt for exports or for production abroad depends on exogenous parameters. One line of the literature explores the effect of location advantages which stem from absolute and relative factor endowment differences of the two countries (Helpman 1984). Another line focuses more on developed countries by modeling symmetric countries (Krugman 1983; Markusen 1984). Technological parameters as fixed costs at plant and company level and demand characteristics as the degree of differentiation between two differentiated goods are important for companies' decision in the second line. In both lines, MNEs emerge with rising distance costs.

This study follows the second line of proximity-concentration approaches described above. It is augmented by the inclusion of intermediate goods in the framework because of the empirical findings. Furthermore, the theoretical framework proposed in the study accounts for the fact that globalization is a dynamic process by applying the "evolutionary approach" from the new economic geography to the proximity-concentration approach. Individuals and companies optimize as in a static optimization problem for only one period. The optimization result depends on some exogenous parameters. However, one of these parameters changes over time: distance costs fall. Falling distance costs are widely believed to be the driving force of globalization. Falling distance costs force companies and individuals to adjust to new conditions. A new equilibrium is reached when consumers cannot increase their utility by changing their consumption basket, when companies cannot increase their profits, when all factor and goods markets are cleared, and when trade is balanced. The optimization results of consumers and companies change in each period. With exogenously falling distance costs, economies "move" from equilibrium to equilibrium.

Exogenously changing distance costs affect also the two international activities of companies, i.e., export levels and foreign affiliates' production levels. The level of the international activity the company opted for increases with falling distance costs. The level of the other one is zero. The profitability of exports relative to production abroad and, therefore, the choice between the two strategies is also affected. Exporting is the more profitable strategy at high and low distance cost levels. At medium levels of distance cost, production abroad might be a profitable alternative. Whether or not production abroad is chosen at medium distance cost levels depends also on other exogenous parameters. For realistic parameter constellations, the model results predict an internationalization pattern with growing exports over time which precede production abroad in the supply of the foreign market. However, when distance costs fall below a certain threshold, companies internationalize production and start to supply the foreign market from their affiliate in the foreign country.

To derive this result, the existence of specific intermediate goods which cannot be substituted by the final-goods producer is a necessary assumption. Specific intermediate goods force foreign affiliates of MNEs to import the intermediate goods they need for production from the home country. Because of the assumed specificity of the intermediate goods, MNEs cannot source intermediate goods in the host country. However, they employ host country's labor. Because of the crucial role of the specific intermediate-goods assumption for the model, it is tested empirically. A testable equation for the relationship of imports of intermediate inputs and foreign activities of companies is derived from the model and tested against alternative hypotheses of increased trade in intermediate goods. Input-output data of six OECD countries for three different points in time are employed in cross-section estimations. Regression results support the hypothesis that, as assumed in the model proposed in this study, imports of intermediated goods increase with the size of networks of foreign affiliates in a country. A time-series analysis conducted with German data supports this result. Affiliates of foreign MNEs make above-average use of imported inputs from their home country.

The basic model describes the observed globalization patterns quite well. The advantage of the basic version is that the model can be solved analytically. However, relaxing many symmetry assumptions gives results which resemble the empirical picture even better. The drawback of allowing for asymmetries in country size and heterogeneity in industry and company characteristics is that results rely on numerical solutions. There is no closed-form solution anymore.

However, the advantage of the more realistic modeling of globalizing economies outweighs the drawback. Neither countries nor companies are symmetric in the real world. Some effects and problems, such as sectoral concentration, national and global internationalization waves, multiple internationalization strategies, or the coexistence of national companies and MNEs from one industry in equilibrium, can only be addressed in a framework which allows for heterogeneity.

Hotly debated issues such as the possible export of jobs caused by setting up foreign affiliates and supplying foreign demand by a plant in the foreign country are analyzed using this framework. It is shown that exports and production abroad are more likely to be complements than substitutes, because starting production abroad offers many new opportunities for exports of intermediate (and capital) goods, which overcompensate the loss of exports of the good which is now produced abroad. In line with empirical studies on this issue, the model predicts a complementary relationship for most realistic parameter values. Companies do not substitute exports of goods by exports of jobs. For the economy as a whole, there are no negative effects on jobs to observe which result from export reduction. The parallel increase in exports and production abroad in the last two decades supports this argument.

To account for the fact that globalization is a complex process which involves many countries, a slightly more complex three-country model is introduced. This extension allows the analysis of third-country effects. That is, the effects on a third country which seems, at first sight, to be unaffected by a country's activities in another country are studied. With falling separation between countries, third-country effects become stronger. Economies are more and more interrelated, because increasing competition of the same companies takes place in different markets at the same time. Such third-country effects might be the reason behind the internationalization waves of companies from different home countries into the United States, which merged into a global internationalization wave in the second half of the 1980s. Furthermore, the three-country model can be used to study the effect of differences in relative distances between countries on the international activities of country pairs. The large effect of distance costs found in the model is in line with empirical findings (Linneman 1966; Brainard 1997).

A highly integrated world requires more adjustment in the economies. Falling distance costs lower the separation of countries and therefore their opportunities to shield from competition by foreign companies. For consumers, this increase in competition yields more varieties and lower prices. Producers are forced to increase their efforts to hold their market share at home against foreign competitors. However, new profit opportunities in foreign countries arise, which might be exploited by exports or production abroad. In total, welfare gains can be realized for all countries. "Globalization is good for all of us" is the most important message of this study. Welfare gains arise here even without the huge dynamic gains of economic integration, which are existent in the real world but not modeled here.

To reap the full benefits of globalization, markets must be kept open and competitive. The theoretical analysis reveals that welfare levels are strongly affected by changes in the market structure. If, in the course of globalization, companies obtain a dominant position which results in a reduction of competition, negative welfare effects might occur. This might be one reason for the reserved attitude developing countries showed towards MNEs until the early 1990s. An active and powerful competition policy is, therefore, necessary to escort the globalization process. The recent merger wave, which is in wide parts a reflex to globalization, gives an impressive example for this need. To hinder companies to exploit market power and deter entry is necessary to ensure that the large welfare gains can be realized.

The study analyzes only international activities of companies from and in developed countries. This focus on developed countries allows to abstract from differences in relative factor endowments as a reason for international activities and concentrate fully on market imperfections and distance costs as causes of the observed internationalization pattern. Since the empirically observed pattern can be explained quite well by this approach, market imperfections and distance costs might be the most important variables affecting international activities between developed countries. However, for an analysis of increasing integration of developed with developing countries, a second factor of production must be introduced in the model, since differences in relative factor endowments play a much larger role in economic relationships between developed and developing countries. Furthermore, a framework for the analysis of integration of developed and developing countries should account for differences in productivity between these groups of countries. Although such an analysis is beyond the scope of this study, the framework can easily be augmented to explore the effects of stronger integration between developed and developing countries.

Globalization does not come without changes. But these changes bear much more chances than risks. People can choose from much more opportunities in consumption, at work, and in how to spend their spare time. A more efficient division of labor is a further source of welfare gains. These gains could, at least partly, be used to compensate the losers of this development. Protectionist pressures from special interest groups must be resisted to prevent countries from forgiving welfare and growth opportunities, as they have done several decades ago, when they stopped the last globalization period with the beginning of World War One. Globalization is not a destiny. It can be governed. And it can even be stopped to the harm of all countries. Economists who know about the merits of free trade and factor movements must contribute to make the process of globalization understood with all its risks and chances to fight the fears which stem from lack of understanding. Globalization is a chance not a destiny.

8 Appendix

8.1 Appendix A: Model Calculations

Demand for the Agricultural and the Aggregate Manufacturing Product

An individual's utility is given by

(1) $\quad U_j = Q_{A,j}{}^{1-\mu} Q_{M,j}{}^{\mu}, \quad \mu \in (0,1); \ j=H, F.$

The budget constraint is given by

(3) $\quad Y_j = P_{A,j} Q_{A,j} + P_{M,j} Q_{M,j}, \quad j=H, F,$

where $P_{A,j}$ is the price of the agricultural good and $P_{M,j}$ the price of the aggregate manufacturing good in country j. Individuals maximize their utility function subject to the buget constraint. The Lagrangian Λ is given by

(A1) $\quad \Lambda = Q_{A,j}{}^{1-\mu} Q_{M,j}{}^{\mu} + \psi [Y_j - (P_{A,j} Q_{A,j} + P_{M,j} Q_{M,j})],$

The first-order conditions are given by

(A2) $\quad \dfrac{\partial \Lambda}{\partial Q_{A,j}} = (1-\mu)(Q_{M,j}/Q_{A,j})^{\mu} - \psi P_{A,j} = 0,$

(A3) $\quad \dfrac{\partial \Lambda}{\partial Q_{M,j}} = \mu(Q_{A,j}/Q_{M,j})^{1-\mu} - \psi P_{M,j} = 0,$

(A4) $\quad \dfrac{\partial \Lambda}{\partial \psi} = Y_j - (P_{A,j} Q_{A,j} + P_{M,j} Q_{M,j}) = 0.$

Some transformations of (A2) and (A3) yield

(A5) $\quad (1-\mu)Q_{M,j}{}^{\mu} Q_{A,j}{}^{1-\mu} = \psi P_{A,j} Q_{A,j},$

(A6) $\quad \mu Q_{A,j}{}^{1-\mu} Q_{M,j}{}^{\mu} = \psi P_{M,j} Q_{M,j}.$

Summing (A5) and (A6) up and inserting (A4) yields

(A7) $\quad Q_{M,j}{}^{\mu} Q_{A,j}{}^{1-\mu} = \psi Y_j.$

Solving (A7) for ψ and inserting this term in (A5) and (A6) yields after some transformation the demand for the agricultural and the aggregate manufacturing good:

(4) $\quad Q_{A,j} = (1-\mu) Y_j / P_{A,j},$

(5) $\quad Q_{M,j} = \mu Y_j / P_{M,j}.$

The aggregate manufacturing good $Q_{M,j}$ is a bundle which consists of many differentiated goods according to (2):

(2) $\quad Q_{M,j} = \left[\sum_{i=1}^{\lambda} q_{i,j}{}^{\rho} \right]^{1/\rho}, \quad \rho \in (0,1); \; j=H, F.$

Demand for a Single Manufacturing Product

As seen above, μY_j is the expenditure consumers in country j spend on final manufacturing goods. The optimal quantity of any final-goods variety bought by the consumer is obtained through maximization under the budget constraints. The Lagrangian Λ is given by:

(A8) $\quad \Lambda = \left[\sum_{i=1}^{\lambda} q_{i,j}{}^{\rho} \right]^{-\frac{1}{\rho}} + \psi \left[\mu Y_j - \sum_{i=1}^{\lambda} p_{i,j} q_{i,j} \right],$

(A9) $\quad \dfrac{\partial \Lambda}{\partial q_{h,j}} = \dfrac{1}{\rho} \left[\sum_{i=1}^{\lambda} q_{i,j}{}^{\rho} \right]^{\frac{1-\rho}{\rho}} \rho q_{h,j}{}^{\rho-1} - \psi p_{h,j} = 0,$

(A10) $\quad \dfrac{\partial \Lambda}{\partial q_{k,j}} = \dfrac{1}{\rho} \left[\sum_{i=1}^{\lambda} q_{i,j}{}^{\rho} \right]^{\frac{1-\rho}{\rho}} \rho q_{k,j}{}^{\rho-1} - \psi p_{k,j} = 0,$

(A11) $\dfrac{\partial \Lambda}{\partial \psi} = \mu Y_j - \sum\limits_{i=1}^{\lambda} p_{i,j} q_{i,j} = 0.$

Transformation of (A9) and (A10) yields

(A12) $\left[\sum\limits_{i=1}^{\lambda} q_{i,j}{}^{\rho} \right]^{\frac{1}{\rho}} = \psi^{\frac{1-\rho}{\rho}} q_{h,j} p_{h,j}{}^{\frac{\rho}{1-\rho}} p_{h,j},$

(A13) $\left[\sum\limits_{i=1}^{\lambda} q_{i,j}{}^{\rho} \right]^{\frac{1}{\rho}} = \psi^{\frac{1-\rho}{\rho}} q_{k,j} p_{k,j}{}^{\frac{\rho}{1-\rho}} p_{k,j}.$

Taking the sum over all differentiated goods yields

(A14) $\left[\sum\limits_{i=1}^{\lambda} q_{i,j}{}^{\rho} \right]^{\frac{1}{\rho}} \sum\limits_{i=1}^{\lambda} p_{i,j}{}^{-\frac{\rho}{1-\rho}} = \psi^{\frac{1-\rho}{\rho}} \mu Y_j$ and solving for ψ

$\psi^{\frac{1-\rho}{\rho}} = \left[\sum\limits_{i=1}^{\lambda} q_{i,j}{}^{\rho} \right]^{\frac{1}{\rho}} \sum\limits_{i=1}^{\lambda} p_{i,j}{}^{-\frac{\rho}{1-\rho}} \Big/ \mu Y_j.$

Substituting $\psi^{1/(1-p)}$ in (A13) gives

$\left[\sum\limits_{i=1}^{\lambda} q_{i,j}{}^{\rho} \right]^{\frac{1}{\rho}} = \left[\sum\limits_{i=1}^{\lambda} q_{i,j}{}^{\rho} \right]^{\frac{1}{\rho}} \sum\limits_{i=1}^{\lambda} p_{i,j}{}^{-\frac{\rho}{1-\rho}} p_{k,j}{}^{\frac{\rho}{1-\rho}} p_{k,j} q_{k,j} \Big/ \mu Y_j$

and yields after some transformation the demand for one variety k of the differentiated good in market j:

(A15) $q_{k,j} = \dfrac{p_{k,j}{}^{-\frac{1}{1-\rho}}}{\sum\limits_{i=1}^{\lambda} p_{i,j}{}^{-\frac{\rho}{1-\rho}}} \mu Y_j.$

Equations (A9) and (A10) yield

$\psi = \left[\sum\limits_{i=1}^{\lambda} q_{i,j}{}^{\rho} \right]^{\frac{1-\rho}{\rho}} q_{h,j}{}^{\rho-1} \Big/ p_{h,j},$ or for one variety k

$$(A16) \quad \psi = \left[\sum_{i=1}^{\lambda} q_{i,j}{}^{\rho} \right]^{\frac{1-\rho}{\rho}} q_{k,j}{}^{\rho-1} \Big/ p_{k,j}, \quad \text{or} \quad \frac{p_{k,j}}{p_{h,j}} = \left(\frac{q_{k,j}}{q_{h,j}} \right)^{\rho-1}.$$

The relative demand of any two goods depends only on their relative prices.

$$p_{k,j} q_{k,j} = \left(\frac{q_{k,j}}{q_{h,j}} \right)^{\rho} p_{h,j} q_{h,j}, \quad k \neq h.$$

Taking the sum over all goods $h = 1, \dots, \lambda$ and substituting into (A10) leads to

$$\mu Y_j = \sum_{h=1}^{\lambda} \left(\frac{q_{h,j}}{q_{k,j}} \right)^{\rho} p_{k,j} q_{k,j} = \sum_{h=1}^{\lambda} q_{h,j}{}^{\rho} q_{k,j}{}^{1-\rho} p_{k,j} = Q_M{}^{\rho} q_{k,j}{}^{1-\rho} p_{k,j},$$

what can be solved for the expenditure for one variety:

$$p_{k,j} q_{k,j} = Q_M{}^{-\frac{\rho}{1-\rho}} p_{k,j}{}^{-\frac{\rho}{1-\rho}} \mu Y_j{}^{\frac{1}{1-\rho}}.$$

Taking the sum of the expenditures for all goods gives

$$\mu Y_j = \sum_{k=1}^{\lambda} p_{k,j}{}^{-\rho/(1-\rho)} Q_M{}^{-\rho/(1-\rho)} \mu Y_j{}^{-1/(1-\rho)}.$$

Solving for Q_M

$$Q_M = \left[\sum_{k=1}^{\lambda} p_{k,j}{}^{-\rho/(1-\rho)} \right]^{-\frac{1-\rho}{\rho}} \mu Y_j$$

and some transformation yields the price index $P_{M,j}$ in country j:

$$(25) \quad P_{M,j} = \frac{\mu Y_j}{Q_M} = \left[\sum_{k=1}^{\lambda} p_{k,j}{}^{-\rho/(1-\rho)} \right]^{-\frac{1-\rho}{\rho}}.$$

Plugging (25) into (A15) yields the demand for one variety of the differentiated goods:

(20) $q_{i,j} = \dfrac{p_{i,j}^{-(1+\gamma)}}{P_{M,j}^{-\gamma}} \mu Y_j,$ with $\gamma = \rho/(1-\rho)$.

The derivation of the demand for a single variety of the intermediate good is carried out accordingly.

Derivation of Labor Demand

Labor demand is derived by using Shepard's Lemma. The cost functions (7), (10), (16) through (18) are differentiated with respect to the factor price w. The labor demand for the goods smelted when exported which are given in the distance costs equations (31) and (32) is derived according to (A20) and (A21):

(A17) $L_{A,j} = \dfrac{\partial C_{A,j}}{\partial w_j} = Q_{A,j},$ with $j=H,F,$

(A18) $L_{Z,j} = \dfrac{\partial C_j^Z}{\partial w_j} = fz_j + z_j,$ with $j=H,F,$

(A19) $L_j^N = \dfrac{\partial C_j^N}{\partial w_j} = r_j + f_j + \left(\dfrac{Pz_j}{w_j}\right)^{1-\theta} \left(\dfrac{\theta}{1-\theta}\right)^{1-\theta} q_j^N,$ with $j=H,F,$

(A20) $L_{j,j}^M = \dfrac{\partial C_{j,j}^M}{\partial w_j} = r_j + f_j + \left(\dfrac{Pz_j}{w_j}\right)^{1-\theta} \left(\dfrac{\theta}{1-\theta}\right)^{1-\theta} q_{j,j}^M,$ with $j=H,F,$

(A21) $L_{j,h}^M = \dfrac{\partial C_{j,h}^M}{\partial w_h} = f_h + \left(\dfrac{Pz_j^M}{w_h}\right)^{1-\theta} \left(\dfrac{\theta}{1-\theta}\right)^{1-\theta} q_{j,h}^M,$ with $j,h=H,F;\ j\neq h,$

(A22) $L_{t,j} = \left(\dfrac{Pz_j}{w_j}\right)^{1-\theta} \left(\dfrac{\theta}{1-\theta}\right)^{1-\theta} t_j,$ with $j=H,F,$

(A23) $L_{tz,j} = tz_j,$ with $j=H,F.$

Calculation of Profits

Profits of affiliate production net of fixed costs are given by

$$
(A24) \quad \phi_M = \frac{1-\rho}{\rho} c^M \frac{\left(\dfrac{c^M}{\rho}\right)^{-\frac{1}{1-\rho}}}{\Gamma} \mu Y = (1-\rho) \frac{\left(\dfrac{c^M}{\rho}\right)^{-\frac{\rho}{1-\rho}}}{\Gamma} \mu Y .
$$

Equation (A25) gives the first derivative of the profits with respect to distance costs:

$$
(A25) \quad \frac{\partial \phi_M}{\partial \tau_M} = \frac{(1-\rho)\left(-\dfrac{\rho}{1-\rho}\right)\left(\dfrac{c^M}{\rho}\right)^{-\frac{1}{1-\rho}} \dfrac{1}{\rho}\dfrac{\partial c^M}{\partial \tau_M}\Gamma}{\Gamma^2} \mu Y
$$

$$
- \frac{\left(\dfrac{1-\rho}{\rho}\right) c^M \left(\dfrac{c^M}{\rho}\right)^{-\frac{1}{1-\rho}} \dfrac{\partial \Gamma}{\partial \tau_M}}{\Gamma^2} \mu Y
$$

$$
= \frac{-\left(\dfrac{c^M}{\rho}\right)^{-\frac{1}{1-\rho}} \dfrac{\partial c^M}{\partial \tau_M}\Gamma - \left(\dfrac{1-\rho}{\rho}\right) c^M \left(\dfrac{c^M}{\rho}\right)^{-\frac{1}{1-\rho}} \dfrac{\partial \Gamma}{\partial \tau_M}}{\Gamma^2} \mu Y .
$$

The derivatives of affiliate's costs and of the price index with respect to distance costs are given in (A26) and (A27):

$$
(A26) \quad \frac{\partial c^M}{\partial \tau_M} = \frac{\partial \left[\left(\dfrac{w_n}{\theta}\right)^{\theta} \left(\dfrac{Pz_j^M}{1-\theta}\right)^{1-\theta} \right]}{\partial \tau_M}
$$

$$
= \left(\frac{w_n}{\theta}\right)^{\theta} (1-\theta)\left(\frac{Pz_j^M}{1-\theta}\right)^{-\theta} \frac{1}{1-\theta}\left(-\frac{1}{\phi}\right)\left[s_j\left(pz_j e^{\tau M}\right)^{-\phi}\right]^{\frac{1}{\phi}-1}
$$

$$
\times (-\phi) s_j \left(pz_j e^{\tau M}\right)^{-(\phi+1)} pz_j e^{\tau M}
$$

$$
= \left(\frac{w_n}{\theta}\right)^{\theta}\left(\frac{Pz_j^M}{1-\theta}\right)^{-\theta} Pz_j^M
$$

$$
= (1-\theta) c^M ,
$$

(A27) $\quad \dfrac{\partial \Gamma}{\partial \tau_M} = -\dfrac{\rho}{1-\rho} n \left(\dfrac{c^N e^{\tau_M}}{\rho} \right)^{-\frac{\rho}{1-\rho}} = -\dfrac{\rho}{1-\rho} n \left(\dfrac{c^N}{\rho} \right)^{-\frac{\rho}{1-\rho}} e^{\tau_n \left(-\frac{\rho}{1-\rho} \right)}.$

Plugging (A26) and (A27) into (A25) yields

(A28) $\quad \dfrac{\partial \phi_M}{\partial \tau_M} = \dfrac{-\left(\dfrac{c^M}{\rho} \right)^{-\frac{1}{1-\rho}} (1-\theta) c^M n \left(\dfrac{c^N}{\rho} \right)^{-\frac{\rho}{1-\rho}} \left(1 + e^{\tau_M \left(-\frac{\rho}{1-\rho} \right)} \right)}{\Gamma^2} \mu Y$

$\qquad - \dfrac{\dfrac{1-\rho}{\rho} c^M \left(\dfrac{c^M}{\rho} \right)^{-\frac{1}{1-\rho}} \left(-\dfrac{\rho}{1-\rho} \right) n \left(\dfrac{c^N}{\rho} \right)^{-\frac{\rho}{1-\rho}} e^{\tau_M \left(-\frac{\rho}{1-\rho} \right)}}{\Gamma^2} \mu Y$

$\qquad = \dfrac{c^M \left(\dfrac{c^M}{\rho} \right)^{-\frac{1}{1-\rho}} n \left(\dfrac{c^N}{\rho} \right)^{-\frac{\rho}{1-\rho}} \left[e^{\tau_M \left(-\frac{\rho}{1-\rho} \right)} - (1-\theta) \left(1 + e^{\tau_M \left(-\frac{\rho}{1-\rho} \right)} \right) \right]}{\Gamma^2} \mu Y.$

Profits of exports are given by

(A29) $\quad \Phi_N = \dfrac{1-\rho}{\rho} c^N \dfrac{\left(\dfrac{c^N}{\rho} e^{\tau_M} \right)^{-\frac{1}{1-\rho}}}{\Gamma} \mu Y.$

The first derivative of export profits, with respect to distance costs τ_M, is

(A30) $\quad \dfrac{\partial \Phi_N}{\partial \tau_M} = \dfrac{\dfrac{1-\rho}{\rho} c^N \left(-\dfrac{1}{1-\rho} \right) \left(\dfrac{c^N}{\rho} e^{\tau_M} \right)^{-\frac{1}{1-\rho}} n \left(\dfrac{c^N}{\rho} \right)^{-\frac{\rho}{1-\rho}} \left[1 + e^{\tau_M \left(-\frac{\rho}{1-\rho} \right)} \right]}{\Gamma^2} \mu Y$

$\qquad - \dfrac{\dfrac{1-\rho}{\rho} c^N \left(\dfrac{c^N}{\rho} e^{\tau_M} \right)^{-\frac{1}{1-\rho}} n \left(\dfrac{c^N}{\rho} \right)^{-\frac{\rho}{1-\rho}} \left(-\dfrac{\rho}{1-\rho} \right) e^{\tau_M \left(-\frac{\rho}{1-\rho} \right)}}{\Gamma^2} \mu Y$

$$c^N \left(\frac{c^N}{\rho} e^{\tau_M} \right)^{-\frac{1}{1-\rho}} n \left(\frac{c^N}{\rho} \right)^{-\frac{\rho}{1-\rho}} \left[e^{\tau_M \left(-\frac{\rho}{1-\rho} \right)} - \frac{1}{\rho} \left(1 + e^{\tau_M \left(-\frac{\rho}{1-\rho} \right)} \right) \right]}{\Gamma^2} \mu Y.$$

The second derivative is:

$$(A31) \quad \frac{\partial \phi_M'}{\partial \tau_M} = \frac{-\frac{\rho}{1-\rho} \left(\frac{c^M}{\rho} \right)^{-\frac{1}{1-\rho}} (1-\theta) c^M n \left(\frac{c^N}{\rho} \right)^{-\frac{\rho}{1-\rho}} \left[e^{\tau_M \left(-\frac{\rho}{1-\rho} \right)} - (1-\theta) \left(1 + e^{\tau_M \left(-\frac{\rho}{1-\rho} \right)} \right) \right] \Gamma^2}{\Gamma^4} \mu Y$$

$$+ \frac{\left(\frac{c^M}{\rho} \right)^{-\frac{1}{1-\rho}} c^M n \left(\frac{c^N}{\rho} \right)^{-\frac{\rho}{1-\rho}} \left[-\frac{\rho}{1-\rho} e^{\tau_M \left(-\frac{\rho}{1-\rho} \right)} - (1-\theta) \left(-\frac{\rho}{1-\rho} \right) e^{\tau_M \left(-\frac{\rho}{1-\rho} \right)} \right]}{\Gamma^4} \mu Y$$

$$- \frac{\left(\frac{c^M}{\rho} \right)^{-\frac{1}{1-\rho}} c^M n \left(\frac{c^N}{\rho} \right)^{-\frac{\rho}{1-\rho}} \left[e^{\tau_M \left(-\frac{\rho}{1-\rho} \right)} - (1-\theta) \left(1 + e^{\tau_M \left(-\frac{\rho}{1-\rho} \right)} \right) \right] 2\Gamma}{\Gamma^4} \mu Y,$$

and after some transformation:

$$(A32) \quad \frac{\partial \phi_M'}{\partial \tau_M} = - \frac{\frac{\rho}{1-\rho} \left(\frac{c^M}{\rho} \right)^{-\frac{1}{1-\rho}} c^M n \left(\frac{c^N}{\rho} \right)^{-\frac{\rho}{1-\rho}} \left[e^{\tau_M \left(-\frac{\rho}{1-\rho} \right)} - (1-\theta)^2 \left(1 + e^{\tau_M \left(-\frac{\rho}{1-\rho} \right)} \right) \right] \Gamma^2}{\Gamma^4} \mu Y$$

$$- \frac{\left(\frac{c^M}{\rho} \right)^{-\frac{1}{1-\rho}} c^M n \left(\frac{c^N}{\rho} \right)^{-\frac{\rho}{1-\rho}} \left[\theta e^{\tau_M \left(-\frac{\rho}{1-\rho} \right)} - (1-\theta) \right] 2\Gamma}{\Gamma^4} \mu Y.$$

The second derivative is negative for low τ_M and positive for high τ_M. Both terms are negative at low distance costs τ_M. The second term changes sign to positive at τ_M lower than in the first term as can be seen by a comparison of (A33) and (A34). "High" and "low" depend on the share of intermediate goods $(1-\theta)$ and on the price index Γ. The profits of foreign production increase at falling rates up to a certain point and decrease thereafter first at an increasing then at an decreasing rate with distance costs τ_M. This implies that the function must change sign from positive to negative at lower distance costs, then its slope changes sign from negative to positive. From (A28) the point at which $\partial \Phi_M / \partial \tau_M = 0$ can be calculated. This is at

(A33) $\quad e^{\tau_M\left(-\frac{\rho}{1-\rho}\right)} = (1-\theta)\left(1 + e^{\tau_M\left(-\frac{\rho}{1-\rho}\right)}\right) \Leftrightarrow (1-\theta) = \theta e^{\tau_M\left(-\frac{\rho}{1-\rho}\right)}.$

At this point the second derivate is negative, what can be seen using (A32). The second term is zero at this point. Hence, the sign of the first is decisive. The first term equals zero at

(A34) $\quad e^{\tau_M\left(-\frac{\rho}{1-\rho}\right)} = (1-\theta)^2\left(1 + e^{\tau_M\left(-\frac{\rho}{1-\rho}\right)}\right) \Leftrightarrow (1-\theta)^2 = (2\theta - \theta^2)e^{\tau_M\left(-\frac{\rho}{1-\rho}\right)},$

which requires higher distance costs τ_M. At lower distance costs the term in brackets is positive, the whole term negative. Since the slope of Φ_M changes signs at lower distance costs, at the point where the first derivative is zero, the second is negative. The function changes from being concave to being convex at

$$\frac{-\dfrac{\rho}{1-\rho}\left(\dfrac{c^M}{\rho}\right)^{-\frac{1}{1-\rho}} c^M n\left(\dfrac{c^N}{\rho}\right)^{-\frac{\rho}{1-\rho}}\left[e^{\tau_M\left(-\frac{\rho}{1-\rho}\right)} - (1-\theta)^2\left(1 + e^{\tau_M\left(-\frac{\rho}{1-\rho}\right)}\right)\right]\Gamma^2}{\Gamma^4} - \mu Y$$

$$= \frac{\left(\dfrac{c^M}{\rho}\right)^{-\frac{1}{1-\rho}} c^M n\left(\dfrac{c^N}{\rho}\right)^{-\frac{\rho}{1-\rho}}\left[\theta e^{\tau_M\left(-\frac{\rho}{1-\rho}\right)} - (1-\theta)\right]2\Gamma}{\Gamma^4} - \mu Y$$

$\Leftrightarrow$

$$-\frac{\rho}{1-\rho}\left(\frac{c^N}{\rho}\right)^{-\frac{\rho}{1-\rho}}\left(1 + e^{\tau_M\left(-\frac{\rho}{1-\rho}\right)}\right)\left[(1-\theta)^2 - (2\theta - \theta^2)e^{\tau_M\left(-\frac{\rho}{1-\rho}\right)}\right]$$

$$= 2\left[\theta e^{\tau_M\left(-\frac{\rho}{1-\rho}\right)} - (1-\theta)\right].$$

The two differences in brackets must have different signs. (A33) and (A34) show that the term on the right-hand side turns positive first. Hence, the turning point lies in the interval with borders described by (A33) and (A34). Let τ_M^* denote the distance costs which equalize the condition above. At τ_M^* the function Φ_M changes from being concave to being convex.

(A35) gives the second derivative of export profits with respect to distance costs τ_M:

$$\frac{\partial \Phi_N'}{\partial \tau_m} = \frac{-\frac{1}{1-\rho}c^N\left(\frac{c^N}{\rho}e^{\tau_M}\right)^{-\frac{1}{1-\rho}}n\left(\frac{c^N}{\rho}\right)^{-\frac{\rho}{1-\rho}}\left[e^{\tau_M\left(-\frac{\rho}{1-\rho}\right)}-\frac{1}{\rho}\left(1+e^{\tau_M\left(-\frac{\rho}{1-\rho}\right)}\right)\right]\Gamma^2}{\Gamma^4}\mu Y$$

$$+ \frac{c^N\left(\frac{c^N}{\rho}e^{\tau_M}\right)^{-\frac{1}{1-\rho}}n\left(\frac{c^N}{\rho}\right)^{-\frac{\rho}{1-\rho}}\left[\left(-\frac{\rho}{1-\rho}\right)e^{\tau_M\left(-\frac{\rho}{1-\rho}\right)}-\frac{1}{\rho}\left(-\frac{\rho}{1-\rho}\right)e^{\tau_M\left(-\frac{\rho}{1-\rho}\right)}\right]\Gamma^2}{\Gamma^2}\mu Y$$

$$- \frac{c^N\left(\frac{c^N}{\rho}e^{\tau_M}\right)^{-\frac{1}{1-\rho}}n\left(\frac{c^N}{\rho}\right)^{-\frac{\rho}{1-\rho}}\left[e^{\tau_M\left(-\frac{\rho}{1-\rho}\right)}-\frac{1}{\rho}\left(1+e^{\tau_M\left(-\frac{\rho}{1-\rho}\right)}\right)\right]2\Gamma}{\Gamma^4}\mu Y,$$

or after some transformation:

$$(A35) \quad \frac{\partial \Phi_N'}{\partial \tau_m} = \frac{-\frac{1}{1-\rho}c^N\left(\frac{c^N}{\rho}e^{\tau_M}\right)^{-\frac{1}{1-\rho}}n\left(\frac{c^N}{\rho}\right)^{-\frac{\rho}{1-\rho}}\left[e^{\tau_M\left(-\frac{\rho}{1-\rho}\right)}\left(\rho-\frac{1}{\rho}\right)-\frac{1}{\rho}\right]\Gamma^2}{\Gamma^4}\mu Y$$

$$- \frac{c^N\left(\frac{c^N}{\rho}e^{\tau_M}\right)^{-\frac{1}{1-\rho}}n\left(\frac{c^N}{\rho}\right)^{-\frac{\rho}{1-\rho}}\left[-\frac{1-\rho}{\rho}e^{\tau_M\left(-\frac{\rho}{1-\rho}\right)}-\frac{1}{\rho}\right]2\Gamma}{\Gamma^4}\mu Y.$$

The second derivative of export profits with respect to distance costs τ_M is always positive. The negative slope of export profits becomes less and less steep.

Welfare analysis

Changes in distance costs affect sales at home and abroad. Prices change as well as quantities and the number of companies and therefore the number of goods. Hence, consumer utility changes. Sales of a national company are given by

$$p_i^N q_i^N = \left(\frac{c^N}{\rho}\right)\frac{\left(\frac{c^N}{\rho}\right)^{-\frac{1}{1-\rho}}}{\Gamma}\mu Y_H + \left(\frac{c^N e^{\tau_M}}{\rho}\right)\frac{\left(\frac{c^N}{\rho}e^{\tau_M}\right)^{-\frac{1}{1-\rho}}}{\Gamma}\mu Y_F,$$

where $\Gamma = \Gamma(\tau_M) = n\left(\frac{c^N}{\rho}\right)^{-\frac{\rho}{1-\rho}}\left(1+e^{\tau_M\left(-\frac{\rho}{1-\rho}\right)}\right).$

The first derivative with respect to distance costs yields

$$\frac{\partial\left(p_i^N q_i^N\right)}{\partial \tau_M} = -\frac{\left(\dfrac{c^N}{\rho}\right)^{-\frac{\rho}{1-\rho}} n\left(\dfrac{c^N}{\rho}\right)^{-\frac{\rho}{1-\rho}}\left(-\dfrac{\rho}{1-\rho}\right)e^{\tau_M\left(-\frac{\rho}{1-\rho}\right)}}{\Gamma^2} \mu Y_H$$

$$+\left(-\frac{\rho}{1-\rho}\right)\frac{\left(\dfrac{c^N}{\rho}e^{\tau_M}\right)^{-\frac{\rho}{1-\rho}} n\left(\dfrac{c^N}{\rho}\right)^{-\frac{\rho}{1-\rho}}\left(1+e^{\tau_M\left(-\frac{\rho}{1-\rho}\right)}\right)}{\Gamma^2}\mu Y_F$$

$$-\left(-\frac{\rho}{1-\rho}\right)\frac{n\left(\dfrac{c^N}{\rho}\right)^{-\frac{\rho}{1-\rho}}e^{\tau_M\left(-\frac{\rho}{1-\rho}\right)}\left(\dfrac{c^N}{\rho}\right)^{-\frac{\rho}{1-\rho}}e^{\tau_M\left(-\frac{\rho}{1-\rho}\right)}}{\Gamma^2}\mu Y_F$$

$$=\frac{\rho}{1-\rho}n\left(\frac{c^N}{\rho}\right)^{-\frac{2\rho}{1-\rho}}\mu Y/\Gamma^2\left[e^{\tau_M\left(-\frac{\rho}{1-\rho}\right)}-e^{\tau_M\left(-\frac{\rho}{1-\rho}\right)}\right]=0.$$

Total sales do not change with falling distance costs. Sales gains in the export markets are equalized by losses at home. However, profits are asymmetrically affected, since foreign sales are c.i.f. sales (including distances costs), but only f.o.b. sales are profit-relevant. Variable profits π_i of a national company are given by

$$\pi_i^N = (1-\rho)\left(\frac{c^N}{\rho}\right)\frac{\left(\dfrac{c^N}{\rho}\right)^{-\frac{1}{1-\rho}}}{\Gamma}\mu Y_H + (1-\rho)\left(\frac{c^N}{\rho}\right)\frac{\left(\dfrac{c^N}{\rho}e^{\tau_M}\right)^{-\frac{1}{1-\rho}}}{\Gamma}\mu Y_F.$$

Variable profits change with distance costs as can be seen by the first derivative:

$$\frac{\partial \pi_i^N}{\partial \tau_M} = n\left(\frac{c^N}{\rho}\right)^{-\frac{2\rho}{1-\rho}}\mu Y/\Gamma^2\left[\rho e^{\tau_M\left(-\frac{\rho}{1-\rho}\right)}\left(1-\frac{1-\rho}{\rho}e^{\tau_M\left(-\frac{\rho}{1-\rho}\right)}\right)-\frac{1}{\rho}e^{-\tau_M}\right].$$

Distance cost changes affect profits of national companies positively, as long as the distance cost level is not too small. With falling distance costs, companies' profits decrease. Some companies exit. For very small distance costs $(1<(1-\rho)/\rho*e^{\wedge}(-\tau*\rho/(1-\rho))-1/\rho*e^{\wedge}-\tau)$, profit changes are negatively affected by distance cost changes. With further falling distance costs, profits of companies increase. Some new companies might enter.

For MNEs in a pure MNE equilibrium, the first derivatives of sales and profits with respect to distance costs are given by

$$\frac{\partial\left(p_i^M q_i^M\right)}{\partial \tau_M} = (1-\theta)\frac{\rho}{1-\rho} m\left(\frac{c^N}{\rho}\right)^{-\frac{2\rho}{1-\rho}} \mu Y / \Gamma^2 \left[e^{\tau_M (1-\theta)\left(-\frac{\rho}{1-\rho}\right)} - e^{\tau_M (1-\theta)\left(-\frac{\rho}{1-\rho}\right)} \right] = 0,$$

where $\Gamma = \Gamma(\tau_M) = m\left(\frac{c^N}{\rho}\right)^{-\frac{\rho}{1-\rho}}\left(1 + e^{\tau_M (1-\theta)\left(-\frac{\rho}{1-\rho}\right)}\right)$ and

$$\frac{\partial \pi_i^M}{\partial \tau_M} = \rho(1-\theta)m\left(\frac{c^N}{\rho}\right)^{-\frac{2\rho}{1-\rho}} \mu Y / \Gamma^2$$

$$\times \left[e^{\tau_M (1-\theta)\left(-\frac{\rho}{1-\rho}\right)} - \left(e^{\tau_M (1-\theta)\left(-\frac{\rho}{1-\rho}\right)}\left(1 + e^{\tau_M (1-\theta)\left(-\frac{\rho}{1-\rho}\right)}\right) - e^{\tau_M (1-\theta)\left(-\frac{2\rho}{1-\rho}\right)}\right) \right]$$

$$= 0.$$

Costs of MNEs are given as functions of national companies' costs in their home country to make the effects of distance cost changes on MNE comparable to those of national companies. Distance costs do not affect profits. There is no difference in consumer and producer prices in affiliates goods. The number of companies does therefore not fall with distance costs in a MNE equilibrium.

8.2   Appendix B: Description of the Parameters

To describe the general equilibrium, 17 exogenous parameters are needed. These are: (i) the total endowment with only one factor of production, labor, in each country; (ii) five parameters which describe the technology used in each country, i.e., fixed costs at plant and company level of the final-goods producer, fixed costs of the intermediate-goods producer, the share of intermediates in the production of the final good, and the degree of differentiation of the intermediate goods, (iii) two demand parameters in each country, i.e., the share consumers spend on manufacturing goods and the degree of differentiated goods of these goods, and (iv) the level of distance costs. For some model specifications, some parameters are split further.

(i)   The endowment level is chosen to generate a tractable number of companies. It is a scaling parameter. Multiplying endowment in both economies by some value only changes the number of companies in the economies but leaves all other variables unaffected. However, the relative size of both endowment parameters has an effect on the equilibrium as discussed in Chapter 4.

(ii) Technology parameters:
   - Fixed costs at the company level of the final-goods producer are chosen (in most cases to be larger than fixed costs at the plant level) at about 15–25 percent of the variable costs of a final-goods producer.
   - Fixed costs at the plant level of a final-goods producer are smaller than those at company level; about 10–15 percent of the variable costs per plant.
   - Fixed costs of the intermediate-goods producer stand at about 10–20 percent of his variable costs.
   - The input share of intermediate goods in the production of the final goods is set to 20–30 percent in the various regression runs.
   - The degree of differentiation between different varieties of intermediate goods is set fairly close to one. The underlying elasticity of substitution is at about 10.

(iii) Demand parameters:
   - The share of monopolistically competitive industries is set to 60 percent. It is therefore slightly larger than the share of the perfectly competitive sector. This variable is a scaling variable, too; changing it only changes the number of companies in equilibrium.
   - The degree of differentiation between the final goods is a bit higher (the coefficient ρ is lower) than for intermediate goods. The elasticity of substitution is between 4 and 5.

(iv) Distance cost levels:
   - Distance costs, which are more comparable to border effects in their effects, change from almost prohibitive (i.e., the borders reduces trade to 0.5 percent of domestic trade) to zero.

8.3   Appendix C: Empirical Analysis

The Data

Intermediate goods can be derived from input-output tables, which characterize the interrelations among sectors. The tables show how much oil, chemicals, or steel are used in machinery, for instance. The value of inputs used in every sector is reported. The OECD (1997) published input-output tables for ten countries for several years between the late 1960s and 1990. The economy is divided into 35 sectors, of which 24 are goods-producing industries, 22 of these industries are manufacturing. These input-output tables include an imported-transactions matrix, which reports the imported inputs of every sector from every other sector. However, the sectoral disaggregated data is aggregated over all countries. For instance, the imported inputs of machinery by the French chemical industry combine all machinery imports from all countries which export to France. There are no bilateral data. The total use of intermediate goods and gross production of every industry was derived from these statistics. Although the most recent input-output matrix dates back to 1990, the OECD tables provide a very impressive data set over a time span of 20 years (except for Italy with only 1985 data).

Data on sectoral disaggregated inward and outward FDI stocks of the same quality is not available. Again, the OECD offers the best data. *The International Direct Investment Statistics Yearbook* (OECD 1993), based on national statistics, reports data on FDI for 23 OECD countries, including all ten countries for which input-output data are available. The quality of the data differs depending on the national raw data the OECD receives. Especially information on FDI stocks is quite rare. The United States and Germany report a sectoral breakdown of FDI stocks equal to the one in OECD input-output tables back to the late 1970s, Australia's figures date back to the early 1980s. Japanese statistics collect only FDI flows, which are then aggregated to stock figures. France started to conduct company surveys of outward and inward FDI stocks only in the late 1980s and early 1990s. Statistical data on FDI stocks for the United Kingdom are available from the mid-1980s for agriculture and eight manufacturing sectors. Although Italian FDI stock data are available, Italy is excluded from the econometric analysis because input-output data for 1990 are missing. Canada, the Netherlands, and Denmark report no FDI stock data or only for a very small number of sectors. Therefore, they are excluded, too.

Test for Stationarity of the Variables

I(0) variables follow stationary stochastic processes. They have a finite and constant mean and a finite and constant variance-covariance matrix. A variable is called integrated of order 1, I(1), if it has to be discretely differenced once to form a stationary process. Whereas stationary variables return to their pre-shock level after a shock, integrated variables do not. They change to a new level.

Table A1 gives test for non-stationarity for the imported intermediate inputs (I), the stock of German outward FDI ($FDI_{outward}$) and inward FDI (FDI_{inward}).

Table A1:
Phillips–Perron Tests[a] for Unit Roots

$\ln(I)$	$\Delta \ln(I)$	$\ln(FDI_{Outward})$	$\Delta \ln(FDI_{Outward})$	$\ln(FDI_{Inward})$	$\Delta \ln(FDI_{Inward})$
-1.5559	-4.395^{***}	-0.0475	-3.6375^{**}	2.0329	-2.9969^{**}
I(1)	I(0)	I(1)	I(0)	I(1)	I(0)

[a]Phillips and Perron (1988). The test is carried out with two lags included, which ensures freedom of autocorrelation.— **, *** denote rejection of the hypothesis of an unit root at the 5 and 1 percent level, respectively.

Johansen Cointegration Tests for a System Including Imported Inputs, the Demand Variable, and the Inward FDI Stock

The asymptotic distribution of the LR test statistic for the Johansen cointegration test depends on assumptions made with respect to deterministic trends. Johansen (1995) provides tests for five possibilities. As in Table 23 the results for two are presented in Table A2: (i) constant, no trend in the cointegration equation, and no deterministic trend in the data and, (ii) constant and trend in the cointegration equation, test allows for linear deterministic trend in the data.

The hypothesis of two cointegration equations could not be rejected for either of the two specifications.

Table A2:
Johansen Cointegration Test

	Cointegration rank	Trace statistic	5 percent critical value
Model (i)	r=0	43.7978	34.91
$\ln(I) \ln(VA)$	r=1	23.6451	19.96
$\ln(FDI_{Inward})$	r=2	8.9298	9.24
Model (ii)	r=0	34.43	29.68
$\ln(I) \ln(VA)$	r=1	15.8137	15.41
$\ln(FDI_{Inward})$	r=2	1.7823	3.76

References

Agarwal, J.P. (1980). Determinants of Foreign Direct Investment: A Survey. *Weltwirtschaftliches Archiv* 116 (4): 739–773.

Akamatsu, K. (1961). A Theory of Unbalanced Growth in the World Economy. *Weltwirtschaftliches Archiv* 86 (2): 196–217.

Anderson, M.A., and S.L.S. Smith (1999). Canadian Provinces in World Trade: Engagement and Detachment. *Canadian Journal of Economics* 32 (1): 23–38.

Anderson, S.P., A. de Palma, and J.-F. Thisse (1992). *Discrete Choice Theory of Product Differentiation*. Cambridge, Mass.: MIT Press.

Andersson, T., and T. Fredriksson (2000). Distinction Between Intermediate and Finished Products in Intra-Firm Trade. *International Journal of Industrial Organization* 18 (5): 773–792.

Antràs, P. (2003). Firms, Contracts, and Trade Structure. *Quarterly Journal of Economics* 118 (4): 1375–1418.

Baldwin, R.E., and P. Martin (1999). Two Waves of Globalization: Superficial Similarities, Fundamental Differences. In H. Siebert (ed.), *Globalization and Labor*. Tübingen: Mohr Siebeck.

Baldwin, R.E., and G.I.P. Ottaviano (1998). Multiproduct Multinationals and Reciprocal FDI Dumping. NBER Working Paper 6483. Cambridge, Mass.

Banerjee, A., J.J. Dolado, and R. Mestre (1998). Error-Correction Mechanism Tests for Cointegration in a Single Equation Framework. *Journal of Time Series Analysis* 19 (3): 267–283.

Barrell, R., and D.W. te Velde (1999). Manufactures Import Demand: Structural Differences in the European Union. Discussion Paper 146. National Institute of Economic and Social Research, London.

Blomström, M., R.E. Lipsey, and K.M. Kulchycky (1988). U.S. and Swedish Direct Investment and Exports. Research Paper 6342. Ekonomiska Forskningsinstitutet, Handelshoegskolan i Stockholm, Stockholm.

Blomström, M., A. Kokko, and M. Zejan (2000). *Foreign Direct Investment: Firm and Host Country Strategies*. London: Macmillan.

Blonigen, B.A. (2001). In Search of Substitution between Foreign Production and Exports. *Journal of International Economics* 53 (1): 81–104.

Blonigen, B.A., R.B. Davis, and K. Head (2002). Estimating the Knowledge-Capital Model of the Multinational Enterprise: Comment. NBER Working Paper 8929. Cambridge, Mass.

Brainard, S.L. (1993). A Simple Theory of Multinational Corporations and Trade with a Trade-off between Proximity and Concentration. NBER Working Paper 4269. Cambridge, Mass.

Brainard, S.L. (1997). An Empirical Assessment of the Proximity-Concentration Trade-Off between Multinational Sales and Trade. *American Economic Review* 87 (4): 520–544.

Brainard, S.L., and D.A. Riker (1997). Are U.S. Multinationals Exporting U.S. Jobs? NBER Working Paper 5958. Cambridge, Mass.

Brander, J.A., and P.R. Krugman (1983). A 'Reciprocal Dumping' Model of International Trade. *Journal of International Economics* 15 (3/4): 313–321.

Bruelhart, M., and F. Trionfetti (2000). Home-Biased Demand and International Specialization: A Test of Trade Theories. Research Papers 2000.2. Centre for Research on Globalisation and Labour Markets, Nottingham.

Buch, C. (2003). Information or Regulation: What Is Driving the International Activities of Commercial Banks? *Journal of Money, Credit, and Banking* 35 (6): 851–869.

Buckley, P.J., and M.C. Casson (1976). *The Future of the Multinational Enterprise*. London: Macmillan.

Buckley, P.J., and M.C. Casson (1985). *The Economic Theory of Multinational Enterprise*. London: Macmillan.

Cairncross, F. (1997). *The Death of Distance: How the Communications Revolution Will Change Our Lives*. Boston, Mass: Harvard Business School Publ.

Campa, J., and L.S. Goldberg (1997). Evolving External Orientation of Manufacturing Industries: Evidence from Four Countries. NBER Working Paper 5919. Cambridge, Mass.

Cantwell, J.A., and F. Sanna Randaccio (1992). Intra-Industry Direct Investment in the European Community: Oligopolistic Rivalry and Technological Competition. Discussion Papers in International Investment and Business Studies, Series B 160. University of Reading, Department of Economics, Reading.

Carr, D.L., J.R. Markusen, and K.E. Maskus (2001). Estimating the Knowledge Capital Model of the Multinational Enterprise. *American Economic Review* 91 (3): 693–708.

Casson, M.C. (ed.) (1986). *Multinationals and World Trade*. London: Allen & Unwin.

Chamberlin, E. (1933). *The Theory of Monopolistic Competition*. Cambridge, Mass.: Harvard University Press.

Co, C.Y. (2001). Trade, Foreign Direct Investment and Industry Performance. *International Journal of Industrial Organization* 19 (1/2): 163–183.

Coase, R.H. (1937). The Nature of the Firm. *Economica* 4: 386–405.

Deutsche Bundesbank (1999). *50 Jahre Deutsche Mark*. Frankfurt am Main.

Deutsche Bundesbank (2000). *Technologische Dienstleistungen in der Zahlungsbilanz*. Frankfurt am Main.

Deutsche Bundesbank (2001). *Kapitalverflechtung mit dem Ausland.* Frankfurt am Main.

Deutsche Bundesbank (various issues). *Balance of Payments Statistics.* Frankfurt am Main.

Dixit, A.K., and J.E. Stiglitz (1977). Monopolistic Competition and Optimum Product Diversity. *American Economic Review* 67 (3): 297–308.

Dunlevy, J.A., and W.K. Hutchinson (1999). The Impact of Immigration on American Import Trade in the Late Nineteenth and Early Twentieth Centuries. *The Journal of Economic History* 59 (4): 1043–1062.

Dunning, J.H. (1973). The Determinants of International Production. *Oxford Economic Papers* 25 (3): 289–336.

Dunning, J.H. (1977). Trade, Location of Economic Activity and the MNE: A Search for an Eclectic Approach. In B. Ohlin, P. O. Hesselborn, and P. M. Wijkman (eds.), *The International Allocation of Economic Activity.* London: Macmillan.

Dunning, J.H. (1980). Toward an Eclectic Theory of International Production: Some Empirical Tests. *Journal of International Business Studies* 11 (1): 9–31.

Dunning, J.H., and R.D. Pearce (1985). *The World's Largest Enterprises 1962–1983.* Aldershot: Gower.

Eaton, J., and A. Tamura (1994). Bilateralism and Regionalism in Japanese and U.S. Trade and Direct Foreign Investment Patterns. *Journal of the Japanese and International Economies* 8 (4): 478–510.

Eckel, C. (2000a). Fragmentation, Efficiency-Seeking FDI, and Employment. Passauer Diskussionspapiere V-19-00. Universität Passau, Passau.

Eckel, C. (2000b). *Verteilungswirkungen der Globalisierung: Folgen für den Arbeitsmarkt.* Wiesbaden: Deutscher Universitäts-Verlag.

Ethier, W.J. (1986). The Multinational Firm. *The Quarterly Journal of Economics* 101 (4): 805–833.

Ethier, W.J., and J.R. Markusen (1996). Multinational Firms, Technology Diffusion and Trade. *Journal of International Economics* 41 (1/2): 1–28.

Feenstra, R.C. (1998). Integration of Trade and Disintegration of Production in the Global Economy. *The Journal of Economic Perspectives* 12 (4): 31–50.

Feenstra, R.C., and G.H. Hanson (1995). Foreign Investment, Outsourcing and Relative Wages. NBER Working Paper 5121. Cambridge, Mass.

Feenstra, R.C., and G.H. Hanson (1996). Globalization, Outsourcing and Wage Inequality. *American Economic Review, Papers and Proceedings* 86 (2): 240–245.

Flowers, E.B. (1976). Oligopolistic Reaction in European and Canadian Direct Investment in the United States. *Journal of International Business Studies* (2): 43–55.

Frankel, J.A. (1997). *Regional Trading Blocs in the World Economic System.* Washington, D.C.: Institute for International Economics.

Frankel, J.A. (2000). Globalization of the Economy. NBER Working Paper 7858. Cambridge, Mass.

Freeman, R.B. (1995). Are Your Wages Set in Beijing? *Journal of Economic Perspectives* 9 (3): 15–32.

Fujita, M., and T. Mori (1997). Structural Stability and Evolution of Urban Systems. *Regional Science & Urban Economics* 27 (4/5): 399–442.

Fujita, M., P.R. Krugman, and T. Mori (1999). On the Evolution of Hierarchical Urban Systems. *European Economic Review* 43 (2): 209–251.

Fujita, M., P.R. Krugman, and A.J. Venables (1999). *The Spatial Economy*. Cambridge, Mass.: MIT Press.

Gould, D.M. (1994). Immigrant Links and the Home Country: Empirical Implications for U.S. Bilateral Trade Flows. *Review of Economics and Statistics* 76 (2): 302–316.

Graham, E.M. (1978). Transatlantic Investment by Multinational Firms: A Rivalistic Phenomenon. *Journal of Post Keynesian Economics* 1 (1): 82–99.

Graham, E.M. (1996). The (not Wholly Satisfactory) State of the Theory of Foreign Direct Investment and the Multinational Enterprise. *Economic Systems* 20 (2/3): 183–206.

Greenaway, D., and J. Torstensson (1997). Back to the Future: Taking Stock on Intra-Industry Trade. *Weltwirtschaftliches Archiv* 133 (2): 249–269.

Grossman, G.M., and E. Helpman (2002). Outsourcing versus FDI in Industry Equilibrium. *Quarterly Journal of Economics* 117 (1): 85–120.

Grubel, H.G., and P.G. Lloyd (1971). The Empirical Measurement of Intra-Industry Trade. *The Economic Record* 47 (December): 494–517.

Harris, R.I.D. (1995). *Using Cointegration Analysis in Econometric Modelling*. London: Prentice Hall.

Head, K., and J. Ries (2001). Overseas Investment and Firm Exports. *Review of International Economics* 9 (1): 108–122.

Heitger, B., K. Schrader, and J. Stehn (1999). *Handel, Technologie und Beschäftigung*. Tübingen: Mohr Siebeck.

Helliwell, J.F. (1997). National Borders, Trade and Migration. *Pacific Economic Review* 2 (3): 165–85.

Helpman, E. (1984). A Simple Theory of International Trade with Multinational Corporations. *Journal of Political Economy* 92 (3): 451–471.

Helpman, E. (1985). Multinational Corporations and Trade Structure. *Review of Economic Studies* 52 (3): 443–457.

Helpman, E., and P.R. Krugman (1985). *Market Structure and Foreign Trade*. Cambridge, Mass.: MIT Press.

Hillebrand, R., and P.J. Welfens (1998). Globalisierung der Wirtschaft. In D. Cassel (ed.), *50 Jahre Soziale Marktwirtschaft*. Stuttgart: Lucius und Lucius.

Horst, T.O. (1972). Firm and Industry Determinants of the Decision to Invest Abroad: An Empirical Study. *Review of Economics and Statisics* 54 (3): 258–266.

Horstmann, I.J., and J.R. Markusen (1987). Licensing versus Direct Investment: A Model of Internalization by the Multinational Enterprise. *Canadian Journal of Economics* 20 (3): 464–481.

Horstmann, I.J., and J.R. Markusen (1992). Endogenous Market Structures in International Trade (Natura Facit Saltum). *Journal of International Economics* 32 (1/2): 109–129.

Hufbauer, G.C. (1975). The Multinational Corporation and Direct Investment. In P. B. Kenen (ed.), *International Trade and Finance*. Cambridge, Mass.: Cambridge University Press.

Hummels, D., and P.J. Klenow (2002). The Variety and Quality of a Nation's Trade. NBER Working Paper 8712. Cambridge, Mass.

Hummels, D.L., D. Rapoport, and K.-M. Yi (1998). Vertical Specialization and the Changing Nature of World Trade. *Economic Policy Review* 4 (2): 79–99.

Hymer, S.H. (1960). *The International Operations of National Firms: A Study of Direct Foreign Investment*. Cambridge, Mass.: MIT Press.

IMF (International Monetary Fund) (2000). *International Financial Statistics*. Washington, D.C.

IMF (International Monetary Fund) (2002). *Balance of Payments Statistics*. CD-ROM. Washington, D.C.

IMF (International Monetary Fund) (various issues). *Balance of Payments Statistics Yearbook*. Washington, D.C.

Johansen, S. (1991). Estimation and Hypothesis Testing of Cointegration Vectors in Gaussian Vector Autoregressive Models. *Econometrica* 59 (6): 1551–1580.

Johansen, S. (1995). *Likelihood-Based Inference in Cointegrated Vector Autoregressive Models*. Oxford: Oxford University Press.

Jones, R.W., and H. Kierzkowski (2000). A Framework for Fragmentation. Discussion Paper 56/2. Tinbergen Institute, Amsterdam.

Katseli, L.T. (1992). Foreign Direct Investment and Trade Interlinkages in the 1990s: Experience and Prospects of Developing Countries. CEPR Discussion Paper 687. Centre for Economic Policy Research, London.

Keller, W. (2002). Geographic Localization of International Technology Diffusion. *American Economic Review* 92 (1): 120–142.

Kleinert, J. (1999). Bestimmungsgründe für die Auslandsaktivitäten deutscher Unternehmen. *Die Weltwirtschaft* (4): 463–478.

Kleinert, J. (2001). The Time Pattern of the Internationalization of Production. *German Economic Review* 2 (1): 79–98.

Kleinert, J. (2003). Growing Trade in Intermediate Goods: Outsourcing, Global Sourcing or Increasing Importance of MNE Networks? *Review of International Economics* 11 (3): 464–482.

Klodt, H. (1999). International Direct Investment: Export of Headquarter Services or Export of Jobs? In W. Filc and C. Köhler (eds.), *Macroeconomic Causes of Unemployment: Diagnosis and Policy Recommendations*. Berlin: Dunker&Humblot.

Knickerbocker, F.T. (1973). *Oligopolistic Reaction and Multinational Enterprise*. Boston: Harvard University.

Kojima, K. (1973). A Macroeconomic Approach to Foreign Direct Investment. *Hitotsubashi Journal of Economics* 14 (1): 1–21.

Koop, M.J. (1997). Trade, Foreign Direct Investment, and Multinational Enterprises in a General Equilibrium Model. Kiel Working Paper 833. Kiel Institute for World Economics, Kiel.

Krugman, P.R. (1979). Increasing Returns, Monopolistic Competition, and International Trade. *Journal of International Economics* 9 (4): 469–479.

Krugman, P.R. (1980). Scale Economies, Product Differentiation, and the Pattern of Trade. *American Economic Review* 70 (5): 950–959.

Krugman, P.R. (1983). The New Theories of International Trade and the Multinational Enterprise. In D. Audretsch and C. Kindleberger (eds.), *The Multinational Corporation in the 1980s*. Cambridge, Mass.: MIT Press.

Krugman, P.R. (1991). Increasing Returns and Economic Geography. *Journal of Political Economy* 99 (3): 483–499.

Krugman, P.R. (1995a). Growing World Trade: Causes and Consequences. *Brookings Papers on Economic Activity* (1): 327–377.

Krugman, P.R. (1995b). Increasing Returns, Imperfect Competition and the Positive Theory of International Trade. In G. M. Grossman and K. Rogoff (eds.), *Handbook of International Economics*. Volume 3. Amsterdam: Elsevier.

Krugman, P.R., and A.J. Venables (1995). Globalization and the Inequality of Nations. *The Quarterly Journal of Economics* 110 (4): 857–880.

Leamer, E.E., and J.A. Levinsohn (1995). International Trade Theory: The Evidence. In G. M. Gossman and K. Rogoff (eds.), *Handbook of International Economics*. Volume 3. Amsterdam: Elsevier.

Linneman, H. (1966). *An Economic Study of International Trade Flows*. Amsterdam: North-Holland.

Lipsey, R.E., and M.Y. Weiss (1981). Foreign Production and Exports in Manufacturing Industries. *Review of Economics and Statistics* 63 (4): 488–494.

Markusen, J.R. (1984). Multinationals, Multi-plant Economies, and the Gains from Trade. *Journal of International Economics* 16 (1): 205–226.

Markusen, J.R. (1997). Trade versus Investment Liberalization. NBER Working Paper 6231. Cambridge, Mass.

Markusen, J.R. (1999). Global Investment Liberalization: Effects on Labor and the Location/Agglomeration of High-Tech Activities and Production. In H. Siebert (ed.), *Globalization and Labor*. Tübingen: Mohr Siebeck.

Markusen, J.R. (2002). *Multinational Firms and the Theory of International Trade*. Cambridge, Mass.: The MIT Press.

Markusen, J.R., and K.E. Maskus (1999). Discriminating among Alternative Theories of the Multinational Enterprise. NBER Working Paper 7164. Cambride, Mass.

Markusen, J.R., and K.E. Maskus (2002). General-Equilibrium Approaches to the Multinational Firm: A Review of Theory and Evidence. In J. Harrigan (ed.), *Handbook of International Trade*. London: Basil Blackwell.

Markusen, J.R., and A.J. Venables (1998). Multinational Firms and the New Trade Theory. *Journal of International Economics* 46 (2): 183–203.

Markusen, J.R., A.J. Venables, D.E. Konan, and K.H. Zhang (1996). A Unified Treatment of Horizontal Direct Investment, Vertical Direct Investment, and the Pattern of Trade in Goods and Services. NBER Working Paper 5696. Cambridge, Mass.

Maurer, R. (1998). *Economic Growth and International Trade with Capital Goods: Theory and Empirical Evidence*. Tübingen: Mohr Siebeck.

McCallum, J. (1995). National Borders Matter: Canada-US Regional Trade Patterns. *The American Economic Review* 85 (3): 615–623.

METI (Ministry of Economics, Trade and Industry) (2001). White Paper on International Trade 2001. Via Internet <http://www.meti.go.jp/english/report/data/gWP2001cpe.html> accessed on November 9, 2001.

MITI (Ministry of International Trade and Industry) (1998). *The 27th Survey of Overseas Business Activities of Japanese Companies*. Tokyo.

MITI (Ministry of International Trade and Industry) (2000). *1999 Survey of Overseas Business Activities*. Tokyo.

Mundell, R.A. (1957). International Trade and Factor Mobility. *American Economic Review* 47 (3): 321–335.

Nitsch, V. (2000). National Borders and International Trade: Evidence From the European Union. *Canadian Journal of Economics* 33 (4): 1091–1105.

OECD (Organization for Economic Cooperation and Development) (1993). *International Direct Investment Statistics Yearbook*. Paris.

OECD (Organization for Economic Cooperation and Development) (1997). *The OECD Input-Output Database*. Paris.

OECD (Organization for Economic Cooperation and Development) (2000). *Basic Science and Technology Statistics*. Paris.

Ohmae, K. (1990). *The Borderless World: Power and Strategy in the Interlinked Economy*. New York: Harper Business.

Panić, M. (1997). The End of the Nation State? *Structural Change and Economic Dynamics* 8 (1): 29–44.

Pavitt, K., and P. Patel (1999). Global Corporations and National Systems of Innovation: Who Dominates Whom? In D. Archibugi, J. Howells, and J. Michie (eds.), *Innovation Policy in a Global Economy*. Cambridge: University Press.

Pfaffermayr, M. (1996). Ownership Advantages, Home Production, Foreign Production and Exports of Direct Investing Firms: Some Evidence from Austrian Firms. *Empirica* 23 (3): 317–328.

Phillips, P., and P. Perron (1988). Testing for a Unit Root in Time Series Regression. *Biometrica* 75 (2): 335–346.

Rauch, J.E. (1999). Networks versus Markets in International Trade. *Journal of International Economics* 48 (1): 7–35.

Rodrik, D. (1998). Symposium on Globalization in Perspective: An Introduction. *Journal of Economic Perspectives* 12 (4): 3–8.

Saggi, K. (1999). Foreign Direct Investment, Licensing, and Incentive for Innovation. *Review of International Economics* 7 (4): 699–714.

Schmitt, N., and Z. Yu (2002). Horizontal Intra-Industry Trade and the Growth of International Trade. In P. Lloyd and H.-H. Lee (eds.), *Frontiers of Research on Intra-Industry Trade*. Basingstoke, Hampshire: Palgrave.

Siebert, H. (1997). Die Weltwirtschaft im Umbruch: Müssen die Realeinkommen der Arbeitnehmer sinken? *Aussenwirtschaft* 52 (3): 349–368.

Siebert, H. (2002). *The World Economy*. London: Routledge.

Siebert, H., and H. Klodt (1999). Towards Global Competition: Catalyst and Constraints. In OECD (ed.), *The Future of the Global Economy: Towards a Long Boom?* Paris.

Slaughter, M.J. (2000). Production Transfer within Multinational Enterprises and American Wages. *Journal of International Economics* 50 (2): 449–472.

Spence, M. (1976). Product Selection, Fixed Costs, and Monopolistic Competition. *Review of Economic Studies* 43 (2): 217–235.

Stehn, J. (1992). *Ausländische Direktinvestitionen in Industrieländern: Theoretische Erklärungen und Empirische Evidenz*. Tübingen: Mohr Siebeck.

Swedenborg, B. (1979). *The Multinational Operations of Swedish Firms. An Analysis of Determinants and Effects*. Stockholm: Almqvist & Wiksell International.

U.S. Department of Commerce (1998). *U.S. Direct Investment Abroad: 1994 Benchmark Survey, Final Results*. Washington, D.C.

U.S. Department of Commerce (1999). *Survey of Current Business*. September. Washington, D.C.

U.S. Department of Commerce (2000a). *Foreign Direct Investment in the United States*. September. Washington, D.C.

U.S. Department of Commerce (2000b). *U.S. Direct Investment Abroad*. September. Washington, D.C.

U.S. Department of Commerce (2001a). *Survey of Current Business*. September. Washington, D.C.

U.S. Department of Commerce (2001b). *U.S. Affiliates of Foreign Companies: Operations in 1999*. August. Washington, D.C.

U.S. Department of Commerce (various issues). *Survey of Current Business*. Washington, D.C.

UNCTAD (United Nations Conference on Trade and Development) (1997). *World Investment Report 1997*. New York.

UNCTAD (United Nations Conference on Trade and Development) (1998). *World Investment Report 1998*. New York.

UNCTAD (United Nations Conference on Trade and Development) (1999). *World Investment Report 1999*. New York.

UNCTAD (United Nations Conference on Trade and Development) (2000). *World Investment Report 2000*. New York.

UNCTAD (United Nations Conference on Trade and Development) (2001). *World Investment Report 2001*. New York.

Venables, A.J. (1999). Fragmentation and Multinational Production. *European Economic Review* 43 (4/6): 935–945.

Vernon, R. (1966). International Investment and International Trade in the Product Cycle. *Quarterly Journal of Economics* 80 (2): 190–207.

White, H. (1980). A Heteroskedasticity-Consistent Covariance Matrix and a Direct Test for Heteroskedasticity. *Econometrica* 50 (1): 1–26.

Williamson, O.E. (1973). Markets and Hierarchies: Some Elementary Considerations. *American Economic Review, Papers and Proceedings* 63 (2): 316–325.

World Bank (2002). *Globalization, Growth, and Poverty: Building an Inclusive World Economy*. New York: Oxford University Press.

WTO (World Trade Organization) (various issues). *Annual Report*. Geneva.

Yu, C.J., and K. Ito (1988). Oligopolistic Reaction and Foreign Direct Investment: The Case of the US Tire and Textiles Industries. *Journal of International Business Studies* 19 (3): 449–460.

Index

Kiel Institute for World Economics

Symposia and Conference Proceedings
Horst Siebert, Editor

Quo Vadis Europe?
Tübingen 1997. 343 pages. Hardcover.

Structural Change and Labor Market Flexibility
Experience in Selected OECD Economies
Tübingen 1997. 292 pages. Hardcover.

Redesigning Social Security
Tübingen 1998. 387 pages. Hardcover.

Globalization and Labor
Tübingen 1999. 320 pages. Hardcover.

The Economics of International Environmental Problems
Tübingen 2000. 274 pages. Hardcover.

**The World's New Financial Landscape: Challenges for
Economic Policy**
Berlin · Heidelberg 2001. 324 pages. Hardcover.

Economic Policy for Aging Societies
Berlin · Heidelberg 2002. 305 pages. Hardcover.

Economic Policy Issues of the New Economy
Berlin · Heidelberg 2002. 251 pages. Hardcover.

Global Governance: An Architecture for the World Economy
Berlin · Heidelberg 2003. 276 pages. Hardcover.

**Berlin · Heidelberg: Springer-Verlag (springeronline.com)
Tübingen: Mohr Siebeck (http://www.mohr.de)**

Kiel Institute for World Economics

Global Governance:
An Architecture for the World Economy

Edited by Horst Siebert

Berlin · Heidelberg 2003. 285 pp. Hardcover. ISBN 3–540–00439–4

I. Fears and Benefits of Globalization

On the Fears of the International Division of Labor: Eight Points in the Debate with Anti-Globalizationers. Horst Siebert

Coping with Anti-Globalization. Jagdish Bhagwati. – Discussant: Kevin Watkins

International Economic Integration and the Poor. Pranab Bardhan. – Discussant: Rainer Klump

Do National Governments Lose Their Maneuvering Space in the Era of Locational Competition and What Can They Do? Oliver Lorz. – Discussant: Horst Raff

II. Designing Global Governance

From Protest to Participation: The Role of Civil Society in Global Governance. Ann Florini. – Discussant: Thilo Bode

What Are the Necessary Ingredients for the World Trading Order? Sylvia Ostry. – Discussant: Meinhard Hilf

Predicting and Preventing Financial Crises: Where Do We Stand? What Have We Learned? Barry Eichengreen. – Discussant: Lukas Menkhoff

Globalization & Climate Protection: Some Microeconomic Foundations for Integration. Jason F. Shogren, Stephan Kroll. – Discussant: Timothy Swanson

Biodiversity and Globalization. Geoffrey Heal. – Discussant: R. David Simpson

Looking 30 Years Ahead in Global Governance. Gary C. Hufbauer. – Discussant: Robert Z. Lawrence

Berlin · Heidelberg: Springer-Verlag (springeronline.com)

KIELER STUDIEN · KIEL STUDIES

Kiel Institute for World Economics

Editor: *Horst Siebert* · Managing Editor: *Harmen Lehment*

*More information on publications by the Kiel Institute at http://www.ifw-kiel.de/pub/
pub.htm, more information on the Kiel Institute at http://www.ifw-kiel.de*

Berlin · Heidelberg: Springer-Verlag (springeronline.com)